J. M. Whittemore

TRIFLETON PAPERS.

BY

TRIFLE AND THE EDITOR.

BOSTON:
WHITTEMORE, NILES, AND HALL.
MILWAUKIE: A. WHITTEMORE & CO.
MDCCCLVI.

TO

GEORGE STILLMAN HILLARD,

WHO HAS PROVED THAT THE PURSUITS OF LITERATURE ARE NOT INCONSISTENT WITH THE DUTIES OF A PRACTICAL AND PROFESSIONAL LIFE,

THIS VOLUME IS CORDIALLY INSCRIBED BY THE

AUTHORS.

PREFATORY.

One bright day in the summer of '55, when the sun glared fiercely upon the bricks and slates of the hard-baked city, and the fashionable world had fled to Saratoga, or Newport, or the sea-shore, the writers of the following papers turned aside from the hot and dusty streets to the green sward of the Common; and under the shadow of the old elms reclined for a season, to indulge in fresher airs and in friendly discourse. Trifle had recently migrated from the town, and pitched his tent in the country, where he could look upon wooded hills and hear the music of the sea. The relief from the oppression of city life, and the genial influences of the country, expanded his generous heart, and with a kindly impulse he proposed to write a letter from his new domicile for the Editor's paper. The offer was gladly accepted, together with the condition that a reply should follow in the same columns.

It was thus that the Trifleton Papers were commenced, and there it was supposed they would end, nothing farther being contemplated. But, once begun, the letters promised to become a pleasant pastime, and were continued from week to week — suspended by no sorrow or misfortune — recording thoughts, impressions, emotions, and fancies, and, more than all, ripening a friendship begun years before, and opening new sources of enjoyment.

And the letters found generous readers. "Who is Trifle?" "Who writes the Trifleton Papers?" were not infrequent inquiries. Then there were friends, perhaps too partial critics, who expressed a warm interest in the successive papers, and commended them as worthy of more numerous readers, and a more enduring form. Finally, there were those whose literary taste and judgment may not be questioned, who warmly urged the collection of the papers and their publication within the covers of a book.

Therefore it is that the authors of the Trifleton Papers have come to find their literary pastime shaped into a volume under the auspices of Messrs. WHITTEMORE, NILES, and HALL, with the understanding that every copy is to amuse, cheer, or — disappoint somebody.

THE ARM CHAIR,
In the Spring of '56.

TRIFLETON PAPERS.

I.

TRIFLETON HOUSE,
In July, A. D. '55.

MR. EDITOR: — We have done the deed. We have left the town behind us. We have said "good-bye" to the proud world. We have gone home, to —— ourselves, in a certain sense, — to our interior nature, to our God, it is to be hoped. At least, we are where we are surrounded by the evidences of His greatness and goodness and love. We are sandwiched betwixt the ocean and the hills. We are or shall become amphibious, as I told my wife on the day we first examined Trifleton House.

"Why! look out of this window (our chamber window), Trifle," said she. "D'ye call this a house in the country?" There rolled, at our feet, God's great, moaning, toiling sea.

"Why, look out of this window, Pat." (short for *Patience*), said I, pulling her away to another, on the opposite side of the room, and there, heaving away in the distance, were God's eternal hills.

We came, we saw, we conquered our prejudices in favor of the town, where we, at least, had daily contact with certain cultured and selectest spirits, such as your own, my Achates, and we became the owners of Trifleton House. For no mere summer residence, mark you, but "for better, for worse;" "for richer, for poorer," — for "all the year round," to use a most elegant and felicitous expression. Yes, *sir*, we are fixed; — we are become incorporated. Henceforth, our chief distinguishing trait is that we occupy and own Trifleton House. Do you hear that, sir? — *own*. I have not wrangled "in business" so long for nothing. I don't rush to town with a diurnal rashness and fierceness, which is intensely American, or Yankeeish, if you please, without *making* something. I've actually "*laid up*," in the last ten years, quite a surprising number of dollars, which, with Pat.'s dowry, you remember, makes a considerable sum. But we havn't paid a *very* great deal. All I know is, we have paid, — actually paid "something handsome" *on account* of Trifleton House. The rest of the purchase-money, which is only some five or six thousand dollars, Pat.'s father kindly advanced for us, and we gave him a mortgage, as the lawyers call it, which makes it all right, you know.

I don't think I ought to write so much about our property to an editor, for it might make you envious or avaricious. If you want to be a man of property, you must "study economy;" yes, sir, "study economy." Those words I've heard my father utter for years. They are his. They belong to him. He's told me to "study economy," from my earliest childhood, and I've done it. But he never told me to "practice economy," — not he, and I've never done it. I hold to obeying one's parents. We are too self-reliant, not to say self-sufficient, — we of this generation. We are too apt to think those who are more ancient than ourselves "old fogies." But it won't do. They know some things as well as we. Hence, let us acknowledge their wisdom, and obey their admonitions. But, I digress, — I wander. I always do, when I think of owning Trifleton House.

I don't observe that it has affected Pat. much yet, but then, you know, she's so simple.

"Trifle," said she, a few evenings since, "do you feel proud, — proud as you expected to, — now that we own Trifleton House?"

"No, Pat.," said I, — "not as I expected to, — but — I expect I shall."

"Well, Trifle," said she, "now that Pa has repaired it for us, I think it's a house good enough for anybody to live in. I'm sure it's a nicer house than Serene Complacency's house in Boston, or Betty Dasherton's house in Roxbury. If their fathers are rich, they didn't either of them marry so well,— such an active, business, money-making man, as I did, Trifle. Still, they have very good houses, — very good, indeed, and —— tolerable husbands. One would think, to hear them talk, that they were all in the world; but in my opinion, we, — though I'm by no means proud about it, or "stuck up," as Stubs says, — we —— "

"Own Trifleton House, my dear!"

I wound my arms about her neck and saluted her with a kiss, and lighting a cigar, I proceeded into the garden to examine my beets, and Pat.'s tomatoe plants. We have both. We've got a *bed* of the latter, and an indefinite extra quantity scattered, one at a time, in all sorts of by-places in the garden. Pat. says she wants tomatoes enough to last into the fall. If we get any, I shall regard it as a prodigious triumph, for, to tell you the truth, *I* have been raising them. *I'm* the individual, "*adsum qui feci*," and I don't believe I'm "death" on gardening. I do it all my own way, you see. I do it for amusement and exercise and profit. Doubtless, though, it's the mission of men to dig and grub and grovel since that shabby trick of Adam, and that shabbier one of Eve. I never knew a woman who did not like sour green apples. It's a trait they inherit from Eve.

I hardly calculate much on the profit from my garden this year, because, at the very outset, I had to bribe a gardener to dig me, and plant me, and set me starting, and he has imposed upon me, I verily believe. Else, why do my potatoes grow so impetuously? They've already beat the corn. They're up to your chin. Zounds! man, I've been laughed at on account of 'em. My lazy brother-in-law says I've cultivated them too much. But there's as much sense in his opinion as there was in that of a friend of mine, who advocated in my hearing the other day, the stupendous absurdity, that we educated our people too much here in New England. Sons of the Pilgrims, hear you that? Are education and cultivation despicable, in God's name? No! No! forever and forever, No! Produce and cultivate! but —— out with the weeds! Don't lop 'em off, but dig them out, out by the roots — away with 'em! — the weeds — and leave the rest to Providence! Certain others of my friends are of opinion that their rankness, as they call it, will result in — "all vines and no potatoes." But this is pure envy and the most malevolent scandal. I'll have potatoes, — I'm determined on it, — of my own raising, and they won't cost me more than six times as much as I could buy them for, neither.

But the radishes, Mr. Editor. I claim them as a personal triumph. "Don't plant 'em," said my Nestor. "They won't grow," exclaimed my Ulysses. "They'll be all wormy," vouchsafed my Solomon. I planted 'em indignantly; and — haven't they succeeded? Havn't we "*had 'em*," I'd like to know? Soft, delicate, touchey, impressible, facile, yielding as the cheek of Pink. (We have a neighbor, and her name is Pink, just as we have a neighbor whose name is Stubs.) There are no worms or fibres about 'em; but they are radishes indeed. They are a compensation. They are a satisfaction. They make amends for the potatoes. (Isn't there a potatoe rot about?) They redeem, they sustain, they establish Trifleton House. Oh, crisp, brittle, delectable radish — forever and forever, hail!

But, calmest and most placid of editors, it's time I'd bequeathed my farewell. You are, even in your dual or plural number, (notwithstanding your "you," or your "ye," or your "we,") — you are too inconsequential and inconsiderable to occupy more of "our" attention. Hence "farewell!" We give you a "*vale*," — and, not only a "vale," but a "longum vale!"

"*Macte virtute!*" Be wise and just and generous, as men are, some of them, (who ever saw a generous woman, except in a scene or hour of distress?) and you will accomplish your mission! Keats failed, and

Byron capitally failed (weak and irreligious fool); but, with a sweet and delicious childlike trust, you can succeed. Consider that you are travelling *home!* You are walking this dusty earth but for a season. If you are not ripe, it is to be hoped you will be soon. Take care that you do not fall green! Good bye — dear Editor (to be affectionate, *dearest* Editor), good bye! appreciate and be grateful for this letter from Trifle — and — farewell!

Alas! Did I forget the boy? the new, the last, the incipient boy. Suffice it to say, "he has come!" He has adventured into this world. He has come to tempt its joys and essay its sorrows. But, chiefly, thus far, he has — screamed. He's a "stunner;" he's a — in a word — he's "a perfect screamer." Prig evidently likes him, and apologizes for him. Prig, you remember, is approximating four years. Hence, is he important.

"What makes your little brother cry?" say I.

"He's a little fellow. He don't know any better," says Prig.

Ah! Presently Prig himself is screaming outrageously.

"Why does Prig scream?" I say to him.

"'Cause," is his reply.

What a facile, ready word is "'cause." We condemn, we excuse the faults of others, it may be, but when we are asked why we do so and so, we answer, "'cause!" Will it do, Mr. Editor — will it do in the great hereafter? Can we sin along in this world, and plead "'cause" in the next? Ask yourself! Where many are called and but few chosen, can we plead successfully — "'cause?" Think, think, oh think!

But I will leave you thinking, and meantime remember me sweetly and affectionately to *Mrs.* Editor. Say to her that Trifle salutes her; that Trifle says this to her — exactly this — no more, no less. Trifle says, "Mrs. Editor — Hail! and Farewell!"

II.

The Arm Chair,
Summer Time.

The *sang froid* with which you presume to address an editor through his own columns, O ingenuous Trifle, is deserving of notice truly, and we, the editor and the arm chair — regard our dual mightiness more reverently henceforth — will even condescend or aspire, just as you please, to send you greeting in a similar manner, not forgetting to thank you for having your wondrous chirography metamorphosed into plain print.

We congratulate you that you have at last chosen the better part, and left the city, with its eternal deafening din, its brick and mortar, its toil and traffic, its folly and fashion, its poverty and penury, its vice and crime, all behind you, and have gone "into the country." The half-smothered aspirations of your soul have at length found expression, and have been developed into deeds — rather should we say into the *deed* which conveyed to you the broad domain of Trifleton House. Broad domain, we say, most guileless friend, for we measure not by Gunter's chain, and though your estate of Trifleton comprises only a few rods, evidently you are rich in the bounteous supply of satisfaction which it yields, more to be husbanded and garnered and valued than all your potatoes or radishes, beets or tomatoes. Rich you are, Trifle, even in that delightful disregard of mortgage deeds which makes Trifleton House so emphatically yours. Rich and in the country, — what more can we desire for you, O fortunate Trifle, when we remember that with these blessings you have Pat. and sundry little trifles to add to your happiness?

But absolutely refreshing is it to hear you talk, or rather to read your talk on rural matters. You have gone to live in the country; — pray, have you read, and has Mrs. Trifle read, the experiences of Mr. and Mrs. Sparrowgrass? *They* lived in the country — thorough-bred city folk, they wished to prove by experience the delights of rural life; and so they did. You are doing likewise — you and Mrs. Trifle — and is it with like success? In the course of your life in your daily walks to and fro in the stony streets of the city — (what potent influence in those stones petrifies the hearts and souls of those who day after day tramp over them to toil?) — doubtless in these daily walks you have seen a tree, and in your occasional excursions, during your brief vacation from the ledger, you have found something in your soul expand as you looked upon mountains, woods, and the never-ending, varied beauty of nature. We admit, most genial friend, that you have a soul, and that, with proper advantages, you might be a lover of nature, yea, a poet; but the fates have spared us that, while the lurking sentiment about you has almost spoiled a respectable clerk, and quite ruined your prospects as a successful merchant; — for all which we congratulate you, since now you may become a *man*.

But what do you know practically about things rural and agricultural? Can you tell the difference between a turnip and a cabbage, when growing? between a pear tree and an elm? between an aster and a dahlia? *We* can speak *ex cathedra.* When we were a boy, we used to roll in clover, climb apple trees for birds' nests, rest upon a pumpkin in a corn-field, or sleep on the new-mown hay. Vegetables and fruit were known to *us*, not when transformed into something else by some city *cuisine*, but in their natural state; for didn't we study agriculture practically and experimentally by digging up seed to see if it had sprouted, or by exploring into the mystery of potatoe hills? — and flowers were not mere leafless bunches of fading blossoms, yclept bouquets, but robes of living beauty, which clothed the garden.

We looked out upon hill and vale, dark woods and waving fields; we played and sported under the tall old trees, and lay down on the soft green turf scented with blossoms, to dream those golden dreams that come to childhood and youth alone. Never, save for a brief space, have brick walls hemmed *us* in, or the fiery pavement scorched *our* feet. And though the mighty humbug "improvement" comes gradually robbing us of the rural delights of old, we are still a lover of nature's beauty and of rural pursuits, with an affection which is the growth of our life-time, not the half-conscious desire of a soul ignorant of what it desires; and we still enjoy the *rus in urbe* with more than the olden delight. Remember, therefore, most confiding of correspondents, that we *know* something about potatoes and radishes, — not that we admire the latter as you, with your simple and uncultivated taste, profess to do,—and we advise you to expect only very "small potatoes, and few in a hill," or to make up your mind that there *is* a *rot* quite prevalent among these esculents.

But while potatoes are our theme, let us tell you that our neighbor, Shrimp, has a small patch of potatoes that would unceremoniously overshadow yours. They were planted at the foot of a pear tree, but they have completely overtopped it now, and Shrimp, who is as simple as you are in all things rural and agricultural — *his* forte is *fishing* — has procured some poles for them to grow on, he having heard that beans are poled, and not fully appreciating the difference in the plants. And then your *bed* of tomatoes — but you will learn in time, and your ignorance is a misfortune for which, doubtless, your plants weep each night; pray do you not find them in tears each morning?

But to pick up those radishes which we just now dropped so unceremoniously, — those radishes over which you fall into ecstasies, and go off into such wild exclamations, calling them "soft, delicate, touchey, impressible, facile, yielding as the cheek of Pink." *De gustibus*, etc. — you may have heard the quotation. But to call a radish *soft*, *impressible*, *yielding!* Can ignorance excuse that, or infatuation farther go? Is it not a *crisp*, *curt*, *biting* thing, like some tempers? Manifestly were you thinking of Pink's cheek, rather than of this plant, whose growth is downward into the earth, not upward towards heaven.

How is it that you are so prone to root-crops,— potatoes, beets, radishes, earthy things entirely? You do not talk of trees and their delicious fruits, nor even of peas, or beans, or vines, much less of flowers. Is it because your theory of cultivation applies only to such crops? You will find (we have hopes of your learning much now you are in the proper school) that to "root out the weeds and leave the rest to Providence," is not what Providence expects, either in the material or the moral field. There are plants, beautiful and productive, to which you must give sustenance, moisture to sustain them against the scorching heat of the sun; soil, lest on the stony ground they wither for want of root; you must train and nurse and support their delicate branches, till they are strong and vigorous to bear their blossoms and their fruits; ay, you must even prune and lop off their limbs, that they may not, by too great luxuriance, overshadow or interfere with other no less valuable plants. All this and more must you do; Providence is not to be your gardener.

One of the most lamentable exemplifications of your want of rural culture, O townbred Trifle, is your most ungenerous and unsupported assertion that all women inherit from Eve a propensity to eat "sour green apples." Pshaw! man, you haven't lived in the country long enough to know that it is *ripe* fruit only that tempts the accustomed eye, — doubtless all your apples will be eaten before they are half ripe. But were not Adam and Eve placed in Paradise at the outset? — in that delightful garden where were

> "Groves whose rich trees wept odorous gums and balm;
> Others whose fruit burnished with golden rind,
> Hung amiable, Hesperian fables true,
> If true, here only, and of delicious taste."

And could *they* be tempted by "sour green apples?" Besides, the forbidden fruit was one

> ——"which to behold
> Might tempt alone;"

and it had a "smell so savoury," that you may be quite sure that it was not "sour green apples." Eve was not to be tempted by such "sour green apples" as grow about Trifleton House, nor that mean, sleek, deceitful, insinuating serpent either; not they, — so you can as well retract your shabby assertion, and no more, like a great shirk, try to put the burden of *your* digging on Father Adam's back.

Akin to this shabby "sour green apple charge," is another parenthetical inquiry. Such a parenthesis is a most uncourteous intruder, — doubtless a town-bred fellow. "Whoever saw a generous woman, except in a scene or hour of distress?" A pregnant exception truly, by which we may acknowledge the presence of angels when manifested by transcendent goodness and mercy. Do you realize, most condescending of men, what heavenly qualities you allow to women even in those half churlish words? Yet how much do you deny them; else, if your implied proposition be true, then is man's whole life a scene of distress. True, women don't go to State street or Wall street to lend money at twelve per cent., and go home and endow colleges, or do other charitable deeds which are duly chronicled in the journals; these walks are fully occupied by generous man. But look at yourself, O honest preacher, and out of your own experience evolve a general and a generous truth. Can you look in your wife's face and utter that same parenthesis without a blush? Is she not hourly doing or contriving something for your pleasure, or comfort, or good, even while you sit writing such disloyal words? Does she not pray for you each night, and each morning shower blessings on you? Where is her dowry but in Trifleton House for *your* benefit? and has she not signed that mortgage deed just to gratify *you*? For the rest, ask Prig; ask the incipient boy. They shall teach you lessons,—they and the benign influences of rural life.

But we must pause; time is not to be wasted always. Your suggestive letter, most genial Trifle, has led us further than we intended. We find in it touches on which we should stop to think, and so we will lay aside the pen, without imparting that instruction which we might vouchsafe to a neophyte in things rural. Not, however, till we request—(ought not "we" to command?) that you send us another token—yea, repeated tokens of your remembrance. The delectable Pink is unknown to us, save by that superlatively inapt simile; let us have a more pleasing glimpse. In short, write us *another letter*, Trifle,—write us *letters;* we'll give them all to—"the devil." Commend us and our household to the household of Trifleton, and so good-bye.

III.

TRIFLETON HOUSE,
In the incipient Dog Days, '55.

THE style in which you, a City Editor, press your claims to be considered peculiarly "rural," rustic, or green (to comprehend all in a word), is extremely engaging. Who ever disputed them? The following sentence in your letter, however, troubles me exceedingly:

"In short, write us *another letter*, Trifleton, — write us *letters;* we'll give them all to — *the devil.*"

I can't decide which is the more admirable, — its profanity or its assurance. In a state of phrenzied excitement, I rushed out among the corn, and stretching forth my hand towards the cucumbers (in which my interest has been so constantly growing of late that I felt I could confide in them), I addressed them "substantially as follows," as the newspapers said that reported my first harangue in public.

"Is the man beside himself, that he expects me to throw off these brilliant things at his bidding? — Am I to *frequently* furnish his readers with letters such as Charles Lamb never would, — never could (exclaimed I, waxing warmer) have written?" The cucumbers, at this stage, maintained the most respectful silence and attention, but when I said, —

"And, moreover, (here I ground my teeth and curled my lip with the most withering scorn and indignation,) it is to be supposed, for a single moment, — nay, nay for a single —— (here I broke down slightly, till I happened to think of the word "instant") — if I might be permitted to use such an expression — *instant* (with forcible, feeble emphasis), is it to be expected that I am not only to send him letters, but that he is to give them all — 'to the devil?' What say you, my friends, for a single moment, — *or* instant, — I pray to know?" When I uttered this, the agitation of the corn was apparent, and the cucumbers visibly crept and crawled all over.

The meeting dissolved, however, — (mercury above 90) — without arriving at any fixed conclusion, it being determined that the question was too momentous to be settled without serious consideration.

Upon conferring with Pat., she recommended me to sleep upon it. I accordingly tucked "The Editor's" paper under my pillow (which seemed very soft that night, doubtless because I was so tired), and awoke with the firm conviction that I would better write again in order to provoke a reply from you, for Pat. read with the serenest complacency what you indited upon the "heavenly qualities" of women. She says you accurately understand and have evidently studied the sex, and when I remarked upon the "masculine vigor" of one of your periods, she hotly resented it, and said it was more distinguished for its refinement and delicacy of sentiment and all such feminine traits, — which was probably true, for — whoever yet knew a woman to be mistaken?

I shall write, then, my Pythias, with a sedulous zeal; but take care how you throw open your columns to me, for I do not always write with a gold pen. I shall have at you with a corroded steel one at times, or with a blunt pointed quill. I shall often trouble your small imps to decipher out my words, and, possibly, I shall trouble and annoy your readers still more.

"What does this Trifle, with his Pat. and his Prig and his Pink and his Stubs, amount to?" I hear one of your "*smart*" subscribers say. "What does he prove? What is there practical or useful about him? Why should he write?"

Sure enough, my crisp commentator! Your interrogatories are apt, and so is your sagacity. You are evidently too many guns for me, and so I will quietly step out of your sunshine, and you may go to the ———.

No! I wasn't going to say *that*. It's not surprising that you thought I was, because it's the language you hear on the 'change, and which you are quite used to in your wranglings in State street and Wall street, but it is not the language of Trifleton House.

There is, sir, no good, valid and substantial reason why I should write (to answer as curtly as you ask), except — except — "for the fun of it." Do you understand what that means, my fellow pilgrim? (Come, now, let us meet in a common humanity, and show each other our hearts!) You knew what it meant once, when you were a boy; — when your nature was fresher, and you were not quite so "cultured" as you are now, did you not? What! have got no heart to show me?

Why! "how you talk!" as Pat. would say.

You wouldn't have me understand that this splendid career you are running is blunting and warping your affections, certainly? In accomplishing your mission you don't find your heart is growing hard, do you? This "*business*" in which you are so merged and absorbed, don't spoil you for everything else, does it? Don't you ever talk and laugh with your wife and play with your babies, and thus try to exorcise the devils of care and anxiety that consume you day and night? If not, make a beginning now, and after some sharp bargain you may have consummated in the "shrewdest" and "smartest" and most "practical" style, sit down and amuse yourself with the harmless platitudes and innocuous nonsense of Trifle of Trifleton House. Compare yourself with him, and when he says a flat thing here and there, chuckle over it! See how much better your teeth have been cut than his; — in a word, see his weakness and your own strength, — if you choose, that is! If not, you can pass on. I am touching my hat as I say it. (Such are the polite manners at Trifleton House.) But, my Christian friend, consider how and whither you are travelling! You look dusty and toil-worn! You are already passed beyond the noon of life, and, if I am a judge, you are by no means happy. There's a great aching void in your heart. You see I know you have a heart, after all, however you try to conceal it from the world. Rumor says you are rich; — I'm afraid you are! You look like a rich man, and — I — pity you! "It is easier for a camel," &c., and, if I am correct in my reading, "a certain rich man" wasn't so well off in the end as poor hungry and despised Lazarus, who begged at his gate, as he swept by him daily, in his "purple and fine linen."

I trust we shall meet again. You will, doubtless, continue to toil on for "a little more" money, and will become more weary and overburdened than you are now, if you do not change. But I trust we shall meet again. What you need is rest and retirement. You don't wan't any more ships or houses. Take one of your houses and *live* in it. Understand and appreciate the great mystery of life. Study and ponder upon your mission.

Humanize and educate yourself, and your household, and, once more I will say it, I trust we shall meet again; *there*, walking in the light of "the glory of God;" *there*, reclining and *resting* on the banks of the "rivers of water clear as crystal," with our burdens ended, our anxieties past, and our victory over the world and ourselves accomplished.

And you, most fair and most exuberant Miss of nineteen summers, who have sedulously rushed to "the Rehearsals," and periodically exhausted your appetite and your wit at Vinton's, who have gone into raptures over that exquisite love of a singer, Mario, (when he is in humor enough with his audience to vouchsafe to sing, that is,) but have failed to see his palpable inferiority to Salvi, Perelli even, and perhaps Vietti (the best Edgardo, all things considered, that we have had), nor have seen anything in Grisi but "a mere actress," (whose prototype, however, could have been nothing short of a Siddons,) — you, glibbest of talkers, with your bright eyes and your buoyant nature (a less polite person than Trifle would say giddy), who have been to Saratoga, and are going to Newport — not to listen to the sad voices of the sea, but to the — Germanians, — you, most impulsive creature, who have shed no tears, as yet, except for the young man with the feeble and almost hopeless moustache — by moonlight, — will you read the history of Trifleton? Possibly not; but Pink is a handsomer and far more brilliant woman than you will ever be, and no such man as Stubs will ever regard you, till you shall have been disciplined, with any stronger feeling than that of curiosity and, shall I venture the assertion? — compassion. The world is real, my child, and life is earnest, as you will discover, if God spares your life.

But *revenons à nos moutons!* For you, at least, I will write, my placid Editor, and for you alone, if need be, with such of your readers as can be entertained by simple and unsophisticated folk like those who frequent Trifleton House.

The tomatoes are doing wonders, and the cucumbers and squashes making the most steady headway; but the most important announcement (you say I do not talk of beans) I have to make (and this, as you will perceive, is, from its nature, most strictly confidential), is that, somehow, the beans where the poles are, refuse to run; and the poles — a whole regiment of them — stand stiff and stark and disconsolate; whereas the beans, where the poles are not, are stretching their fond arms about for something to embrace and lean upon, in the most sweetly affectionate style. The manner in which they evidently yearn for a support is extremely touching. But I encourage them all I can with such admonitions as —

"Creep along, creep along! You are young yet, and can't expect to walk very bravely! But do your best, without assistance! Support yourselves, by hook or by crook. Acquire, by degrees, a sure and steady self-reliance, and you will in the end surpass beans that started with you, petted and supported by all the appliances of extraneous aid and comfort. Climb, in a word, without poles, and indicate to the world that, by the sheer force of your own worth and dignity of character, you can and will conquer! Climb alone, if need be! Friends and sympathy are desirable, but not indispensable. At all events, climb! Even if you should fall, you would be no worse off than if you were lying, impotent, upon the ground, longing and waiting and weeping for poles. Climb! — steadily, calmly, surely! It seems impossible, I am aware, but it is not. Climb, climb, oh beans despondent, climb! Try! and despair not, and you will be surprised to find how undoubtedly you will mature and ripen. Be less impatient, but, keeping steadily at work, be content to bide your time, and, my word for it, you will never disgrace Trifleton House."

By such simple, and, it may be, child-like talk, do I encourage them. Doubtless it is very silly, but I have observed, that just this sort of talk works wonders, oftentimes, with the faint hearted.

Stubs is perfectly great at it. Why, an old woman told me, not long since, "A kind, good man is Mr. Stubs, sir. Folks call him proud, and so he is, like, but he never forgets me in my poverty; and, when I was sick last winter, he was always coming to see me to comfort me and encourage me. He's as good as a minister, sir, and, then, how well he talks! I'm sorry Miss Pink is so hard upon him. She says he is too stiff and — uncompromising, or some such thing. But she don't know everything, and besides, if she is so beautiful, and her father is so rich, and her name was in the newspapers about the grand ball, at Newport, I believe they call it, she is not so kind-hearted as she might be. Why, she never walked into my house in her life. She sometimes stops and says a word or two as she goes by my door. But *she's* grand, and I hope it's a mistake — what they say — that she is to marry Mr. Stubs. He's too good for her, *I* think, and I'll stick to it."

I shall have to look into this thing a little, Mr. Editor. I can't say how true it is, but I know that Stubs and Pink have long been intimate, and strangely enough, too, for their natures are inharmonious. His mission is, evidently, to suffer; hers (don't mention it, for she is very lovely and has many fine points), just as evidently to make others suffer. She is too thoughtless and, possibly, heartless. We shall see.

But I must have done and — fare you well! Meantime, in these dog days, the sea, and the stars and the sunsets are my companions, — the sea chiefly. What its voices utter, what the music of the stars reveals to my soul, I cannot quite tell you as yet. Their language is vague and indistinct, but none the less appreciable. I seem to be oppressed, almost, with a sense of beauty which would intoxicate if it did not subdue; exhilarating but chastening. Prig is evidently conscious of it, and undertook, an evening or two since, to tell me what the sea *said*. He has gotten to be a fluent talker, and is beginning to exhibit traits.

The sight of a flower or a star will hush him to peace, when he is most boisterous;—which is a good sign. I asked him, some time since, who made a flower he held in his hand. "Papa," was his reply. "Who?" said I somewhat solemnly. "God," was his answer,—and, with those large, inquiring eyes of his, he gazed into mine in a most interrogative and searching manner, by which he meant "will you please to explain?" doubtless. Explain! When can I? When he is older and wiser? Oh, my friend, as he grows older, and I plod on, will he grow wiser from teachings such as mine, or will a still small voice, in a moment, "in the twinkling of an eye," teach him the mystery lifetimes of knowledge getting, money getting, fame getting, and Progress, as we call it, cannot comprehend; "because He has hid these things from the wise and prudent, and revealed them unto babes." But, how I preach!

Your comments upon the radishes as compared with Pink's cheek, were excessively shabby. Why not "soft, impressible, yielding?" Take a young, tender radish, and what can be more appropriate than to apply all of these epithets to it—with *some few grains of salt*?

You allege that a cheek is "soft" and a radish "hard"; but don't we say "a *stiff* upper lip," "*marble* forehead," "beautifully *carved* features, "*chiselled* features," "a well *cut* nose," "a *hard* faced man or woman," "an *iron* look," "a *stony* expression," and all such illegitimate and hard things, which are all correct enough, and so why not "a soft, impressible radish," with the "grains of salt," that is?

Ask your "smart" subscriber if you are not cornered? And bid him hail! notwithstanding my serene and excessively polite good-bye to him. He has his good points after all, and when there is anything argumentative or "practical" going on, we need him to settle the question.

As to a woman's cheek being "yielding, soft and impressible," or her nature, either, I have not much to say to such a handsome man as you. Women, *O puer carissime*, are curious creatures. Beauty, like yours, will not conquer them — always.

> "O formose puer, nimium ne crede colori."

They are captivated by "a verie smooth and pleasant wit," like that of Trifle. You can procure them to like you, if you try, but it's such an effort to try. You may say "oh vainest of Trifles," but what I say is true, notwithstanding it be also true that the love of a woman, excepting always that of Pat., is the vainest of trifles. *Pro ex*, what said the Dane?

> "But two months dead! Nay, not so much, not two;"

and then again,

> "Thrift, thrift, Horatio; the funeral baked meats did coldly furnish forth the marriage tables."

I think so, Hamlet, most decidedly! You had a right to be most stupendously indignant about it. "What's to be done?" "what's to be done?" you asked very naturally, but I never could make out that you did much. The fact is, Hamlet, you were a great talker, and that's about all. You've made a good many tragedians, though, in our day, but a little of your advice wouldn't hurt 'em. "Great American Tragedians" they are, most of 'em.

But, Mr. Editor, this letter is inconceivably long. I bequeath to you the spirit and influence of Trifleton House! And, if you were a woman, I would kiss your hands.

Item. I sat last evening reading the newspaper, and throwing it down, said, "Let us thank God for the crops and the harvest."

"Amen," said Stubs, solemnly.

"Let us thank God for Robert Burns, 'Lake George,' 'Saratoga,' and 'Newport,'" ejaculated Pink.

"It is well," said I, platitudinizing in reply, "to be thankful for the sources of our amusement, but we ought first to be grateful for our health, food, raiment, and reason, however limited they be."

"So I think," said Stubs.

"You — do?" inquired Pink, apparently somewhat pointedly.

"Yes! and I not only think so, but I feel so."

"Feel! What preaching! What do I know of feeling?" (A cloud passed over his face; — passed, I say.)

"Or care," said I.

Her eye flashed, kindled rather, and she turned its full blaze upon me.

"He means," exclaimed Pat., instantly, "that you know nothing of care, because you've never had any."

Perhaps I did. She "chucked" my elegant edition of Burns, which cost me eight dollars and a half, down upon the sofa, in a most sprawling condition, and rushing up to Pat., hugged her and kissed her (they are old friends — intimate before we owned Trifleton House) in the most ridiculous and passionate manner, and screaming out "Good-bye" — "Come," was off in a moment.

Stubs followed, looking very foolish, as I thought.

Said I, "Pat., if I had the training of her, I'd——"

"You'd what?"

"I'd curb her and conquer her, or ——"

"Get conquered yourself! I've no doubt of it. Pink is much spoiled, but I by no means despair of her."

The man with the morose moustache, and the corn-colored gloves has not yet arrived, but is expected. Pink met him last summer at Catskill, and, as I am told, he brings letters to her father. His income is "ten thousand a year."

IV.

THE ARM CHAIR,
Sirius Ascendant.

WE suppose we are in duty bound to acknowledge the receipt of your — favor, we were about to say — but we mean your obedience to our commands in writing us another letter, most docile Trifle. After the manner of Trifleton House we thank you, and take off our hat to you — that is, we should do the latter thing, but our arm chair tolerates no "tile" in its presence, — not even our broad-brim straw, under the shadow of which we watch the changes of nature, and sometimes muse on what you would term the "glories" of Trifleton House, but what to us seems to be its mirth-provoking ridiculousness, to wit, its garden and its gardener. We thank you, notwithstanding the supreme conceit which almost forbade your compliance with our command, thou "vainest of Trifles," truly.

But thank ye for what? For two and a half mortal columns of—— ? (We won't say the word that comes *pat* in that place.) Let us see what you have done, what you say. First an address to the cucumbers! There's an audience for you! Prone to admire and communicate with grovelling, procumbent, creeping things, still, are you, Trifle? After such an address to such an audience, it is very delightful to hear you admonish the beans. It seems you can aspire to the top of a bean-pole — but alas! for the practical results of your aspirations in the garden of Trifleton House. Verily, you are a reformer, Trifle; not quite so fiercely philanthropic as some of your class, since you do not yet take the world for your field, but confine yourself to your — you call it "a garden," don't you? Pray, why didn't you fix your poles for those creeping and crawling cucumbers to climb upon? Or better, why have you not chopped them up into kindling wood? You are not yet so ethereal, though you have lived six weeks in the country, as not to need a fire under the pot; — pray put the poles to some use, and let them not stand forever like so many weird and giant fingers pointing at your disgraceful ignorance. Having burnt your poles, apply yourself to reform. The task you assume is not half so herculean as those which some of your co-reformers attempt. *Talk* to your beans, — bid them climb; they — or we — shall delight in your eloquence, at least. By-and-by, when Stubs tells you of his detectable "Limas," run you out to see the fruits of your preaching, — you will look in vain for the fruits of your "despondent beans."

Another year, if your life is spared, possibly you may remember that mere admonitions are not very good bean-poles. There are plants, as there are human souls, which will surely climb heavenward, if you give them a steady staff. They must grow; their tender shoots, their yearning tendrils will reach out and clutch at weeds, if nothing better offer, — frail and transient supports which must be prostrated by the first storm. Shall they be left thus to be cast down, fruitless, lost forever? Not thus has the good Gardener left us, O fellow-mortal. Firm, steady, heaven-high staves has he placed all about us; and if we will stretch out our hands, and wind about those unfailing supports with never-untwining tendrils, we shall grow upward into the pure air and the glorious sunlight.

We have some hopes of you, most fickle Trifle, in another way. Rural life is evidently exerting a humanizing influence on you, and you have arrived at that stage when you can at times, by fits and starts, acknowledge some good in woman, — only in such cases you can't look beyond the amiable Pat. She didn't have any such narrow notions. Evidently her generous nature is a compensation (don't you believe in compensations?) for Trifle's conceit. We have a higher regard for her opinion than for yours; for didn't she approve of what we said? But you are not altogether hopeless and crusted over with impervious self-conceit, since you can *now* ask "who ever yet knew a woman to be mistaken?" There you are on the other extreme, — the golden mean seems impossible with you. Doubtless you were thinking, all the while, of Pat., and how many times she had proved *you* to be mistaken; and you forgot all about that one great mistake of her life, her choice of a husband.

But see how you spoil even that tribute to woman by the sorry commonplace of all vain preachers like yourself, that "the love of a woman is the vainest of trifles." To be sure a sort of instinctive dread of consequences led you to except Pat.; otherwise the slander is general. And you quote that crazy fellow, Hamlet, in support of your lunatic conceit. What did he know about it? He was indeed a great talker, as you say, but he didn't therefore *know* much about it. The great question with him was

"To be or not to be."

A very serious question, truly; but if he had been a sane, practical man, he need not have made such a fuss about it, exclaiming

"What should such fellows as I do crawling between earth and heaven!"

He might have settled it all "with a bare bodkin." Moreover, he behaved very shabbily towards Ophelia, who also went mad, for love of him, and showing more "pluck" than he could muster with all his "stale, flat and unprofitable" talk, went and drowned herself. Was her love "the vainest of trifles?" How was it, too, with Imogen and Juliet, Portia and Rosalind? — not to go any farther in the records of that true reader of human life.

Turning again to your letter, we know not which most to admire, the audacity with which you presume to lecture our "smart subscriber" and the "exuberant Miss of nineteen summers," or the verdancy with which you seem to suppose that they will read what you say. Possibly we may have *such* a "smart subscriber" as you assume, but the genial influences of our journal preclude the possibility of there being such an individual among our *readers.* If there were, think you he would read your lucubrations? *He* must read the price of stocks, look over the arrivals, study the importations, run through the advertisements, to find out where and how money can be made. For amusement he will look at the reports of the crops, read the details of the last defalcation, or glance at the accounts of carnage before Sebastopol, all which may directly or indirectly affect the figures on his ledger. He read *your* unpractical, thriftless, useless stuff! Not he, — least of all when you talk to him, and at him, and all about him, individually. You think you find a "great aching void" in his heart, but when you tell him so he covers it all over with the hard crust of money-making worldliness, so that there is no crack or crevice through which your soft words, your goodly counsels or your sharp admonitions can penetrate into the mysterious chambers which he so sedulously closes and locks up, as he is wont to lock up his gold or his bills receivable. And so you waste your long paragraphs on him, until he shall seek that rest and retirement which you prescribe for him, — and that will be, when no more money is to be made, when bowed down with disease, or the weight of his money bags, he totters down to the grave. So plod on the class of which he is the type; let us hope for some at least an earlier and a better rest.

And the "exuberant Miss," will *she* read your platitudes? She looks at the catalogue of marriages — still sighing for that morose moustache which totters about on spindle shanks, — or she reads perhaps a gossiping letter about the "hops" at Nahant, or the prospective fancy ball at Newport, or the brilliant company at Saratoga. Possibly her eye might be caught by some of the words in that long paragraph addressed to her, but fairly into it, she'll toss her pretty head one way and your letter the other,—Trifleton may sink, and Stubs be hanged, for all she cares,—she has more congenial pursuits. But as you say, Trifle, she will in time discover the reality of life; love, care, sorrow, shall teach her better lessons than you can.

But do not despair, O simple and verdant friend, for there are those who will read even what you and we may say, in our simple way, about very simple things. They are few, perhaps,—the more unfortunate the world, therefore,—but pleasant, intelligent, genial men and women do exist somewhere, and it is, of course, your mission to find them out.

How excessively full of conceit is this last letter of yours! We thought we had disposed of it all, but lo, here you ask if we are not "cornered" on that *radish* business. Appeal not to our "smart subscriber;" ask rather the brilliant Pink, if a cold, crisp, watery radish is the type of her warm, soft, impressible cheek, and the flash of her eye will doubtless render your comparison odious, even to yourself—which, we believe, is already the case, since you are so anxious to have it taken *cum grano.* And then again you boast of that "verie smooth and pleasant wit," with which you can captivate women! Your assurance must be really charming to Pat. and Pink, and all the other feminine friends who know you so well. This leads you quite naturally to woman's love, which we have already noted. And so let us end our comments.

Did you note with a white mark on the Calendar, Friday the 3d of August, in this blessed year of '55, that bright, effulgent day, the crowning glory of these summer months? Did not Trifleton assume a new beauty in that clear air and golden sunlight? Did not the foliage wave with a brighter green, and the corn, the squashes, the cucumbers even, give visible tokens of delight? Had your boyhood been passed amid rural beauties instead of in the hard, dry, stony town, you would have found much in such a day to recall the far off joys of those careless and unweary days. You might have sprawled your manly length upon the grass, and gazed up into those measureless depths of blue, anon driving the fleecy clouds like chariots over the trackless way, or closing your eye to listen to the mysterious music which the winds and the leaves sing together, — dreaming dreams of wild ambition, yet full of the *dolce far niente* spirit (or want of spirit), so congenial to your feelings, — all as you would have done when a boy, on some such resplendent day, had you then been a rustic. But, poor unfortunate, all this is lost to you, as well as the deeper, sweeter joys of maturer thought with such antecedents. Ay, you are lost, yourself, in the mysteries of many-voiced nature; — bewildered with her beauty and her music, you wander about almost unhappy under the oppression of vague, indistinct, unappreciated ideas. Is it not so, O Trifle? — or have you crossed the threshold into the calm, holy light of a close communion with nature?

It was on the eve of that superlative day that we watched from the hill-side the brilliant sunset, gorgeous with crimson and golden clouds, and saw the purple twilight steal over the landscape as if to bathe it in beauty more complete, while the little stream winding far below in the valley, awhile so bright under the shining clouds, gradually disappeared beneath the mist which (mysteriously) gathered over it. From the dark sea the shadow of the horizon stole slowly up the Eastern sky, as shadows at the close of life steal over the scenes and memories of youth. Ah! what a time and scene for impressions and thoughts; and we were launching out upon the limitless ocean, when Madame Hard and her son came by.

Madame Hard is a widow, wealthy, cold, practical and commonplace; her son is — a mystery to most people. Once — and now at times — ardent, enthusiastic, poetical, he becomes more and more cold, gloomy, misanthropic even. Some three or four years out of college, talented, rich and good-looking, (all but his moody expression,) why should such a fellow get into such state? We shall try and fathom it, by-and-by, Trifle, if you and Mrs. Trifle would like to hear the gossip.

"A fine sunset," said Madame Hard.

We expatiated on the beauties of the scene — earth, sea and air.

"Very red clouds," remarked Madame, in reply; "we shall probably have rain again to-morrow, and we *must* go to Newport."

Our words had all passed for nothing; beauty, glory, splendor, loveliness, peace, serene, holy, — the whole vocabulary had been wasted, and we should probably have rain again to-morrow! That is the way to look upon clouds and sunsets. None of your poetry, none of your artist-talk; — what is that to the weather? or to Mrs. Hard?

Young Hard — his name is Abel, after his father — was all the while absorbed in the beauties of the evening, but said nothing. At the sound of "Newport," he incontinently started, and passed on with a half-haughty bow, saying to his mother, "It is very damp," which was all-sufficient to hurry her home. Damp? ay, it *is* damp, and Mrs. Hard gathers her shawl about her; but there seems to be a greater dampness about the heart of Abel; and so they leave the twilight to us.

But more of this anon. Setting a proper example to correspondents, it becomes us to cut short our letters. And so, with all blessings to Trifleton House, *vale*.

P. S. Shrimp's premium potatoes are prostrated by the wind and rain (he glories in the tops, you know, not the tubers), while he is absent, studying ichthyology.

V.

TRIFLETON HOUSE,
Still in the Dog Days.

A CALAMITY has befallen us; — sharp, sudden and severe. It touches Prig more nearly than the rest of us, but still we are all in tears.

Little Buff-y is dead! Do you hear? — dead! He was quite unwell yesterday. His vivacity seemed to be gone, and he drooped palpably. He leaned his head against my hand, when I went to bid him good morning, in a manner that impressed and touched me; for what being, human or brute, ever indicated any interest in me, — ever yearned for my sympathy, and appealed to my affection, without a response? I sympathized with him, and gave him some water and clover and catnip. But he drank and ate but little. He seemed grateful, however, and repeatedly kissed my hand, (which you remember Pat. says is a good looking one.) Prig was much concerned about him, but I consoled him with, "He'll be better to-morrow."

So this morning, after breakfast, which consisted of the richest coffee you ever tasted, with cream, — fried potatoes, — cucumbers (sliced in pieces of ice) of my own raising, — rough, unbolted wheat bread, with Vermont butter, — corn bread (Pat.'s weakness from the

South — the only "*chivalric*" notion I have n't talked her out of since she crossed Mason and Dixon's line, for Yankee land and a life with me), and various other small trifles, too numerous to mention, I rushed into the garden, and looking into his pen, or cage, or what not, I saw Buff-y lying down, his eyes wide open and his head resting upon the floor! and looking very weary and very sick. I sallied instantly towards the cellar for some dry straw. It was from a basket of silver tops that I obtained it. Returning with it, and putting my hand gently, and oh! how tenderly, into the cage, past White-y upon Buff-y, a little, to raise him, in order to put the nice, clean straw under him, — a cold chill ran over me. He was stark! With the tears streaming from my eyes, I ran up to Prig, who was not yet out of his new trundle bed, but was waiting for his "Mary."

"Prig," said I, "poor little Buff-y is dead!!!!"

Prig was dumb. He was stupefied. He was like Lot's wife.

I will not wring your heart, by recounting the details of our mourning. It is enough that we are miserable.

An early hour was appointed for his burial. I will strive — of course vainly — to describe it to you. The place was under the great apple tree, in the northwest corner of the garden; the time, towards eleven o'clock, which, for once, caused me to take an excessively light glass of claret and water, as a tonic, — as a medicine, you will understand, to my grief.

The great staring sun looked down upon the procession with a sort of knowing look, which seemed to say, I've seen a good many things in my day, and I've been looking pretty sharply for a few thousand years, but by Jupiter and Saturn, and several signs of the zodiac, I never did see anything quite so dire and awful as this. There's Prig! he's chief mourner, probably, for he heads the ranks, and his tears are genuine. I'll not dry them up. I'll go into a cloud as he passes, for a child's grief is a sacred thing in its way, and is to be respected. Let his tears flow! Next comes Trifle. He indicates that he has suffered, but he looks better and wiser and happier for it. I'll shine on him, for he needs sunshine and warmth. All bright things please and encourage him. His nature is already too melancholy. Hence his tears would better not flow. (I stopped crying at this point.) Last comes Pat., the most faithful and constant of all. For, even as the wife of the lamented Rogers, she comes "with one at the breast," following hard upon the footsteps of Trifle, like a dutiful and affectionate wife. So walk through life together, united by a common tie of love; close together, in joy and in grief, in despondency and hope. Father, mother, child! O family relationship, sympathy, love! In all I have seen these thousands of years, I have gazed upon nothing more beautiful. It is pure and unselfish, and likest that which subsists in Heaven.

We came to the grave, we — (it's too painful) we — buried Buff-y. I pronounced a succinct eulogy. I did as the tombstones do, and the orators when a great man dies — I paraded his virtues most skilfully and artfully concealed his faults. I did it in the most adroit manner. I made everybody think he was a perfect pink of a rabbit. Not a word said I of his shabby thieving in my beet bed, — not I. Oh, it was most cunningly done!

But, no doubt, you are bursting to hear whether the man with the corn-colored gloves has come. I judge so from the fact that you said nothing about him in your letter, for I have always observed that in the imperfect life we illustrate in this slight world, that people say the least in regard to what they think of most. Humanity is secretive, and candor is a rare trait.

> "When will man learn to bear
> His heart nailed on his breast?"

Sure enough, most lamented, most tender, plaintive Motherwell! As Pink says, the world should be grateful for thy life, though it was indeed a life of suffering. Except for it, we should never have had "Jeanie Morrison."

It is undoubtedly true, however, that "he has come." The last three words you perceive are in quotation marks. I seek to indicate, thereby, that they are not original, but are borrowed. They belong to Pink. She uttered them in a most bewildered and excited manner to Pat., and the latter reiterated them to me several times, so that they are, in fact, become rather old, and deserve the quotation marks. I trust you will receive them calmly, and with a becoming degree of moderation.

The distinguished individual went on a sailing excursion with us, for you must know that, of late, we have been much addicted to the ocean in one way or another. We bathe, and sail, and even fish in the most human fashion.

Upon the occasion I have referred to, the day came in with a glory unsurpassable. Astounding as the fact may seem, I saw the sun rise. A dark, purple line marked the eastern horizon, above which I saw him slowly rising, and looking stealthily around. He was so cautious, on the start, that I thought he lacked pluck. But as he gazed over the water, and looked upwards upon the mountains of frowning maroon clouds, piled like Ossa upon Pelion over his head, as if to break him down, a ray of peculiar satisfaction, as it seemed to me, which gradually developed into a look of proud defiance, almost, indicated that he was ready for the conflict. He came out of it triumphantly. For he made the sea leap and sparkle before him ; — and he dissipated the frowns of the angry clouds, and converted them into smiles. Blessed be the sunshine forever, and all warm and sunny natures in a world like this! They make our pulses leap and our hearts beat; they kindle our courage, and dry our tears. We can struggle with obstacles; we can possibly conquer difficulties, and fight against all dark and gloomy things valiantly. But gentle, warm, affectionate natures subdue us, and soften and harmonize us all. God knows, however, that they are rare.

The day, I said, was beautiful and bright; and so was Pink. Pat., in her simplicity, of course admired everything. None but "cultivated" people find fault.

I cannot quite say I was as much bedazzled by

"*him*" as I expected to be. Coming from New York city, you perceive, with the prestige of having been pronounced "a great match," — having summered at Newport and wintered at Paris so long, I was prepared for great things; but, between you and me, he was of the same race we have seen so many of. He talked a great deal, but really said nothing, Stubs evidently thought. Repeatedly, a few quiet and polite words from Stubs exposed the shallowness of many of his opinions, which he vouchsafed in a decidedly "travelled" style. The clever wit of Pink, however, made him shine by a reflected light occasionally. He was her father's guest, and she probably felt bound to pick him up when he stumbled. He had never read "Evangeline," and (incredible as it may seem) was perfectly innocent of Motherwell. He could n't see the force of the "Potiphar Papers," any more than he could see the peculiar expression in Pink's eye, or on Stubs' face. — One thing I must tell you. He said he thought it extremely funny that I, myself, worked in my own garden, and asked if it were true; at which Stubs very groutily remarked, in *my* behalf entirely, — for he would not have been so impolite himself, —

"The true occupation of man is to till the soil, doubtless. Nothing can be more gratifying than to see before our eyes that which has been produced from the earth by the labor of our own hands, with the accession of the rain and the sunshine, which are God's gifts. It is an occupation which is dignified and purifying, and one calculated to draw out and develope the resources, generally, of our country.

look forward to the day when we shall be known and distinguished as an agricultural people, almost exclusively."

He relapsed into silence, and Pink's eye kindled. She thought him too real, too good, too open, perhaps. But this may be merely my fancy. I have observed often enough, however, that the thoughts of a true man, feelingly expressed, are quite wasted, or, at least, are inopportune, in the society of what are called "young people" of our day — particularly of the feminine gender. Indeed, feeling, away from home, is rather a practical absurdity than otherwise. In any sense, it's a commodity of somewhat questionable value.

We left our vessel about noon, and landed on an island beautifully situated in mid ocean. I wandered away from our party, and stretched myself at full length upon the grass. I shall never forget the sensations of that hour. On every side around me was the broad Atlantic; above me the cloudless sky; and stealing over me, the delicious summer air, — bewildering my senses, and addressing the better part of my nature. I mused, and then I slept. I dreamed I was in a sort of fairy land. Paradise was unfolded before me. There were pure sunlights, without clouds; gorgeous birds; singing fountains; peaceful and serene hill-sides and valleys; — all that was beautiful, nothing that was sad. I said to my soul, "Is *this* heaven?" My soul answered palpably (as I dreamed) and somewhat reproachfully, "Heaven is *of the spirit*, and addresses not the senses. Heaven is *home*; — is with Christ who has suffered and conquered; — is a cessation of yearning and longing; is — *rest!*"

Presently the cry that the chowder was ready brought me back to this practical and bread and butter eating world. I was rallied upon being a sleepy head. Perhaps I was. I said nothing, but quietly laughed in my sleeve. I felt purified and refreshed by my thoughts and my dreams, but I ate chowder, and said nothing. One of the objects in life is to eat chowder, doubtless.

I have to record this *item*. Most of the time, Pink was generous, sincere, and extremely clever, — as why should she not be with her talents? She behaved, mostly, extremely well. Stubs was openly and palpably proud of her, for he reflected, as I rather think, that she had often told him that she loved him, but, as we landed from our boat, the same wagon, with the yellow-colored wheels, which we thought so ridiculous at Newport, you remember, (we didn't know it was "*his*" then,) appeared at the landing, and to my utter astonishment and disgust, (to say nothing of Stubs,) Pink, with a real look of gratification, entered it with him and rode home, tossing a kiss from her glove to Stubs. It was not so much the incident as the manner of it that startled me. I saw a cloud come over his face. He was evidently hurt; — extremely hurt. He never seemed so near to me as then. I could have hugged him to my heart, — have clasped him to my soul. A noble nature, wounded by the thoughtlessness or caprice of a woman, always provokes my sympathy. However, I should never thought of daring to sympathize, unasked, with Stubs. He is too proud for such a familiarity. But enough of *this*.

Let me see. It is thus you write to me:

"Did you note with a white mark on the Calendar, Friday, the 3d of August, in this blessed year of '55, that bright, effulgent day?"

Of course I did; — for upon that day, as my mother says, I was — (yes, you are right,) —— years old. To consider that I have lived so long, and accomplished so little, is anything but flattering to myself. And yet, serenest of editors, I have no desire to go back. I'm not a day or an hour too old, nor should I be if I were ninety. I cannot quite appreciate this common dread of growing old. While we are growing on, are we not ripening, — I would like to know, — maturing, culminating? Else, are we in the wrong path! Won't you please to inform me why we should live here, — the object of it, that is, unless it be to become pure, and raise beans and cucumbers, and potatoes and corn, as we do at Trifleton House? Except to do this sort of thing, and educate ourselves, life is quite a farce.

If so be we can only reach heaven, and wear white robes, and walk those streets with harps in our hands, what matter how old we grow. Growing old is coming to the test; — is — not flinching from the judgment; is tempting eternity; is looking (or ought to be) to the time when we shall be burdened by no sorrows, perplexed by no anxieties, worried by no hunger for bread, and wealth, and power; and distressed by no thirst for human love — for fame — for victory over ourselves. It is a loooking forward to a true social ism, where the small frettings we are subjected to, in what we call society, shall be forever done away.

Hail! hail to such a Thule! No, serenest and most dear friend, as well as editor, not a Thule! It is near; — but a few years of toil away at best. Let us thank God, take courage, and hasten on! Let us cheerfully, and trustfully, and with a good degree of humility, grow old.

Most kindred and genial of friends, and placidest of all editors, unless you wish to be preached to, don't stir up my birth-day again. Let us hear more of Hard. Pat. is curious on his account, which is remarkable, as you know women are seldom curious.

Trifle's continuous remembrance to Mrs. Editor, and the incipients.

VI.

THE ARM CHAIR,
As the Summer Wanes.

TRULY, O fickle Trifle, in spite of your idiosyncracy, you are like the rest of the world. You are loud in your lamentation over a deceased rabbit, but even in the midst of your grief, lo! that vanity, which extends even to the tip of your fingers, must find a parenthetical expression. Your sorrow is minutely described, and so is your breakfast. The last sickness of Buff-y is affecting to your wonderfully tender heart, but you don't forget the silver-tops in your cellar; and as you go out to perform the last rites, you cannot omit the indulgence of that "eleven o'clock" habit which you acquired in your city life.

And behold how quickly your grief is forgotten in that all-important announcement that "he has come," he, the wearer of the "corn-colored gloves," and the owner of the wagon with "yellow wheels." Thus are old friends forgotten in the novelties of the world. But we had hoped better things of you under the influence of rural life. In the busy din of the city, where things come and go, and are forgotten ere they are fairly gone; where men die and their places are so quickly occupied that they are not missed; where change comes so closely following change that man knows not the past; the heart may become a mere kaleidoscope, or at best a camera, reflecting the present only. But in the country, amid the everlasting hills, or by the ocean's ceaseless roar; where nature passes through her changes only to return us each in its immutable succession; where the oak attains its growth in a century, and generations repose under its shade; where man's works are *accessory* only to the works of God; where the benign sun shines ever the same on foliage, blossom and fruit, and the same mysterious voices are whispering ever; the heart may, should, *must* become more steady and unchanging, — faithful still to the memories of the lost, which are not chased away by hasty and inane successors. Live on, and nature shall in time conquer you, and adopt you as her child.

But to return to that breakfast table, — you can have no objection to that, since it is a pleasure to you even to enumerate the edibles. Behold what a breakfast for a countryman! "The richest coffee you ever tasted, with cream." How know you that? Haven't we indulged in the fragrant Mocha? Not often, to be sure, for it is one of the luxuries that come not to the frugal table, but then we have "dined out." As for the cream, you seem to think that a novelty, and doubtless it is to city folk like you. But why do you drink coffee? Is there no crystal spring, no well, at Trifleton? The pure element which God has given you, — why do you not drink that, the clear, refreshing, invigorating beverage of nature? Will you not cast away your Mocha and your Java, your silver-tops and your claret, and follow the example of the hermit of Walden Pond?

"Fried potatoes." Well, that *sounds* rural, but you get your idea of fried potatoes at Young's or Parker's; they are not country fried potatoes. "Cucumbers (sliced in pieces of ice) of my own raising." That seems a little like living in the country, eating the fruit of your own (cucumber) vine. But then *such* fruit,— bah! couldn't you put the ice to better use? "Rough, unbolted wheat bread, with Vermont butter." The bread is good for you, and we approve your taste there, but do you go to Vermont for butter? Are there no Ayreshire or Devonshire kine in your vicinity, who fill the foaming pail and eke the churn? Are there no rosy-faced dairymaids whose plump hands can form those tempting lumps of sweet, fresh butter, stamped with roses?

"Corn bread." *That* you would like to dispense with, and you would fain persuade the sensible Pat. to give up her taste for yours, selfish fellow! (By the way, have you any green corn — soft, tender, delicious sweet corn in your garden?) But she is right. Corn bread — beautiful in its golden color, light, sweet, nutritious — that is a dish to grace a rural breakfast table, to satisfy a rural appetite and please a rural palate. A *chivalric* notion, indeed! A chivalric regard for your Pat.'s most excellent taste would not be amiss at Trifleton House. In addition to these things, you had "various small trifles too numerous to mention!" Ah, miserable *gourmand!* is it thus that you enjoy the country? And all the while you were discussing those things, Prig was abed, and Buff-y was dying. Don't attribute our strictures on that breakfast to envy; for you ought to know we don't stoop to that kind — but between us (tell it not in Trifleton) we should like to *see* one of those breakfasts.

And so, for once in the course of your — can it be so long! — pilgrimage, you have seen the sun rise. Evidently it has made an impression on you as it ought; for what more glorious sight can meet the unaccustomed vision? But you have not yet learned to see all the glories and beauties of the time and the scene. You saw in the sun a Titan, who would climb over the mountain clouds up to high heaven, with proud, satisfied, defiant look. The sparkling splendor of the ocean did not escape you, for it glared into your eyes with blinding power. But far away on the purple hills that smiled a welcome to the jocund day, or where the valleys sleeping still in misty shadows lay; where the light of violet and gold over the heavens spread, and glistening gleams of beauty into the dew drops shed, on white webs spotting every field; where matin chorals rung, as the bright winged worshippers on leafy branches swung, — thitherward your eye turned not, and your soul saw not the serene and quiet beauty of the morn. But not everything is to be seen at a glance, nor all the glory and beauty and goodness manifested in God's works to be appreciated by the soul just awaking from the stupor of worldliness. Up from the drowsy pillow, arise early, each morning, expanding Trifle, and you shall behold and enjoy splendor and loveliness hitherto hidden from your imperfect vision.

At Trifleton you even "fish in the most human fashion." Did you ever reflect on that picture of a line with a hook at one end and a fool at the other?

That was Dr. Johnson's idea of a disciple of old Izaak Walton, was it not? Shrimp doesn't look on piscatory sport in such a light, not he. Even when he went a mile or two on a dark and gusty night — so dark that one could scarcely feel distinctly, and so gusty that there was danger of being blown away into the darkness — such an idea didn't cross his mind. He carried a lantern, which he hung over the dark and chafing waters that the fish might see to bite, but he never thought of Dr. Johnson's description. He didn't get a bite — not a nibble; yet the wise saw of the old bear never occurred to him. Nor was he discouraged — late, cold, fishless, his gear in a snarl, he was just as ready as ever to go the next day with no better prospects. Can you boast of such a steadfast purpose in realizing the saying of the old lexicographer? — or in doing anything else? Such zeal and earnestness we commend to you in other things, such as cultivation of the garden at Trifleton House, the affections, the virtues, and all else that shall yield *good* fruits.

We are glad to hear more of Pink and Stubs and "him;" only we should not care how you dropped the latter subject in mid ocean. Is it possible that even on the top of all his money bags he can be tall enough to overtop Stubs? If so, Pink shall be the delectable Pink no longer, and we will not quarrel with your radish comparison.

To satisfy Pat.'s curiosity — intercede with her for "a thousand pardons" to our familiarity! — we would gladly say a word of Hard; but he is out of our sight now, gone to Newport — and misery. Only your allusion to the "plaintive Motherwell," recalls a scene which may throw a gleam of light on the shadow which surrounds him. He was in our library, where the cherry tree shadows the northern window, and sat there long, reading and dreaming, — dreaming and reading Motherwell. We let him have his way, for we were engaged in the delightful occupation of "paragraphs." At length he threw down the book, and in a tone as plaintive as Motherwell's he said, — not to us, for when he talks thus he speaks to the winds, the trees, the stars, anything that is not human, —

> "Oh! Dream of Life's early day, farewell forever."

We looked up in wonder to hear a *youth* talk thus. Yet was he in earnest, — it was all real to him. Silently, with a look, we inquired his meaning, and for a moment the ice was thawed, — that ice that had gathered about his warm, sensitive heart, under the chilling influence of circumstances, and cold, worldly natures about him. These latter were with him still when he made a European tour, chilling him even in sunny Italy and amid the warm airs of southern France. Florence he had seen and felt a sunbeam ; he had met

> ——" one of those forms that pass us by
> In the world's crowd, too lovely to remain, —
> Creatures of light we never see again."

So he expressed it. If you knew Hard — and you have seen his counterpart, doubtless — you might imagine how the ray that shot through the icy crust lighted a fire within. Since that time the crust has been growing colder and harder and thicker, and the fire is more compressed and concentrated. And so he lives, without aims or hopes; without occupation, for his family are above it — they think; without display and fashionable folly, for he is too sensible for that.

Gently we dropped a few wise words for his benefit — words such as he might feel the worth of, if he chose, — to plant a little seed of purpose in his soul. Most likely it fell not on good ground — but let us hope. Nature has wondrous balms for such wounds as his; and good works, deeds of charity, a little self-sacrifice, shall be an occupation in spite of the foolish pride of others. Yes — we have some hopes of him.

Shall this be enough for you, this time? — for it is *you* who would fain ask questions and ascribe your curiosity to the innocent Pat.

Let us not be forgotten in the circle of Trifleton House, — and so — till we meet at that breakfast table, or hear from you, good bye.

VII.

TRIFLETON HOUSE,
While the Crickets sing.

I TURN, calm friend, from the crickets to you; for by the crack *cricket club* of the class of '44, I shall run mad at this rate.

Oh! *crackey!* — crickey! — my sweet little crickey, do stop a little while, for don't you perceive the Editor must be written to, and how do you suppose Trifle can think with your ubiquitous and eternal "wh-re-w," — "her-rh," — "her-h?"

Ah, thank you! you are becoming polite. I should know you frequented Trifleton House. Your tones are softer, more polished, and natural than before. You will be quite a Trifleton cricket, soon!

But sir! — sir Editor! — what you mean by "the indulgence of that 'eleven o'clock' habit which you acquired in your city life," is beyond us all. Pat. says she knows nothing of any habits of mine — except your remark be intended as a poor fling at the thread-bare coat in which I used to march to my seat at that hour, when you and I were in the great and General Court together.

It is quite true I had that identical coat on at Buff-y's grave. It is also true that I "acquired" it in Boston, and have, of necessity, "indulged" it, because

Trifle must treat his clothes tenderly;—otherwise, Pat. and Prig would be restricted in bread and butter, and corn cake.

I told Pat. that I didn't think you meant any such thing as she suggested ; for, although you were guilty sometimes of a feeble joke, I had never convicted you of anything so jejune and barren as *that*. You must refer to some habit you city men are familiar with, but which is as a sealed book to such as we are. — No doubt.

"Fried potatoes" at "Young's," too, or "Parker's!" — Stubs thinks that these men must *sell* fried potatoes. How extremely comical! Said I, "Do they sell 'nothin' else?" He replied, "I don't know!" After a little reflection, however, we called to mind that this Parker might, perhaps, be the same man who used to furnish us "woodcock," &c., in a sepulchral cellar, some years ago, when we were boys at Harvard. He had fried potatoes, then ; but we saw the folly of this supposition, because that clement Parker, and also another continent man, named Taft, used to give us certain kindly drinks with our "woodcock," and "fried potatoes," and it has been ascertained in our Courts of Justice, of late, that nothing of the kind is furnished in Boston now, and that none but Temperance men of many years standing (fourteen years say, for instance) frequent those places where they sell liq—— "fried potatoes," I would say.

So, who these individuals are, — this Parker and this Young, — is still a pleasant mystery to us. Let it be conceded, however, that their occupation (if it be such) of selling fried potatoes is an honorable one, and goes far towards sustaining and conserving their community. I have heard aldermen say so, and aldermen are as oracular, often, and impress me as forcibly as do "intellectual," and "polished," and "strong-minded" women. Both are indispensable conditions of our serene system of society, doubtless, and I try to be adequately grateful when an alderman vouchsafes to speak to me, or a "brilliant" woman condescends an opinion in my presence. A great many such women have imparted to me the benefit of their opinions on matters of taste, manners, habits, &c., and an alderman had the assurance once, I mean did me the honor, unasked, to take my arm in the street.

But, it having been resolved, by juries of their peers, that those mythical individuals, like Parker and Young, (*et id omne genus*) attract young men no longer to their "woodcock," and "fried potatoes," by the vivacious and exhilarating persuasiveness of Schreider, and Heidsieck, and sparkling Hock, how extremely grateful we ought to be all! — Oh, beneficent results of the Maine Law! Except for such a God-send, who knows but college boys would still be drinking Champagne, and anxious Governors, or those anxious to be Governors, be resolving, from policy, to commit themselves openly to abstemious and carefully guarded habits, forever. Let us be sufficiently grateful that nobody sells "intoxicating drink" in Boston. Could we have foreseen that such would have been the effect of the Maine Law, should we have voted against it, as we did when we were legislators? Alas, no! Incontestably, no! It is clear we shall never become statesmen. We have no prophetic glance, my Editor. We can forsee nothing.

I consider, therefore, that you are bound to own up to the world, as I do now, and hereby, as the lawyers say, that you approve of the Maine Law, and regard Neal Dow as a projector whose results and consequences are not to be murdered (to borrow a word) by so indifferent a nobody as Trifle. Let us hear from you upon this subject.

But enough of "woodcock" and "champagne," and — no! not of "fried potatoes." They are harmless, to a degree; but I wish you would persuade "Mary" not to cut and fry the pork in such thick slices. She is absolutely incorrigible upon this point. When you come to "see" that breakfast, don't, please, fall in love with her, pretty as she is; for "Robert" has undoubtedly worked upon her sensibilities. Do you consider, delectablest of editors, that cooks are human and have hearts like as we have, and are capable of affection? I know it to be a fact; and even you could stand no chance against "Robert." Please apprise Mrs. Editor of *that.*

Yes, *sir!* It is quite time we were done with the small frivolities of "woodcock" eating (and oysters —Prince's Bay's — fried in crumbs), and the drinking of slender drinks. If we must ever drink, let it be only "occasionally" of such things as intoxicate some, or give the headache to all; but let us rather drink deeply of those things that give the headache to none, and intoxicate all with a most delicious sense. Deeply, O deeply let us drink at the fountains of purity, virtue and love; at the springs of hope and the wells of faith. When we are worn by the toil of life — are desponding, and well nigh discouraged —

are become faint and sick in our pilgrimage — are breaking up, and yearning for the grave, let us drink, into our very souls, the beauty and harmony of God's works, — the serenity of the stars, the eloquence of the sea, the eternal silence of the hills, and, chiefest of all, the unutterable tenderness of His mercy and His love.

We thirst for power, position, wealth, fame, — which is very well. Let us also thirst for an educated nature, a purified life, a victory over ourselves which shall be the earnest of a mightier and more glorious victory in the coming eternity.

You were extremely felicitous, fastidious Editor, in rapping my knuckles for attempting to describe a sunrise. However, I thought, and still think, it was tolerably well done for a man who has only seen this phenomenon twice, — once at Trifleton and once at Catskill. Since I wrote you, however, I have seen him set. One evening, in particular, I watched his decline. He went with a march down behind some thunder-clouds that were full of rain; clouds that lacked *expression*, in a word, till he came along. He made a golden diamond of every rain-drop, and fitted it, for a moment, to show me the force of beauty heightened by power. He then proceeded to burn his diamonds all up; and, shedding the lustre of his parting smiles upon the bewildered clouds, which by this time were making off somewhat hastily, down he went — first marking out, however, a sharp and well-defined line of crimson upon the edge of the southern and western horizon, far as the eye could reach, which lingered, until — calm, twilight over the hills came stealing, and the moon rose up from the sea, and group after group of stars, revealing God's power, love, mystery, shone forth; while over the waves came pealing the musical sound of bells, addressing my innermost soul of feeling, and opening memory's cells.

I saw, O how clearly! the past before me. I trembled, I shuddered with fears; my life, from the time my mother bore me, I looked on through burning tears. I cried with all the passion that tore me, "O life, to unfaithfulness given!" — when, hark! the sweet stars that were shining o'er me, out-whispered, "Hence live for heaven!"

A glorious figure, with wings, and bearing a scroll in his hand, flew by; in letters of fire I read, in my daring: "Thy life, as recorded on high!" Yes, there stood the story; — my sins were all glaring; — I read, while my courage died fast, O God! to the *end!* — these golden words bearing: "Accepted through Jesus at last."

And the bells, once again, in their music hushing the murmuring voice of the sea, pealed forth, with an almost passionate gushing, in their exquisite harmony; and the moon, with a flood of brilliancy flushing, hill, sea and plain, saw the thoughts that came, all tranquilly rushing, thrice purified, through my brain.

Have we "any green corn, soft, tender, delicious sweet corn" in our garden? Well, I should suppose we had. I should rather think we had, — I'm pretty confident we have; for I have some faint recollections of having had to pluck it for dinner for about three weeks past every day. But we are about done with it. We consider that to be corned for three weeks is quite as much as we can reasonably stagger under. However, I agree with Stubs, that your inquiry, after all I have said upon the subject of my farming, is a very queer one. It seems to convey a doubt, or at least a suspicion, that Trifleton farming is not *much*. Come and see, sir! I say it, and I say it boldly; for Pat. and I have concluded upon the most critical examination of this remark of yours — "we should like to *see* one of those breakfasts," that you've rather caught us, and that we can't very well "dodge" saying "Come!" But I trust you will consider what it is you've invited yourself to, sir! You've read of Charles Lamb's suppers, I suppose, and Rogers' breakfasts. Possibly you might have got along with either by slily keeping dumb while others talked — looking very wise, as Lamb's alderman did; but, at Trifleton House, you can't do any such thing. We have a way of drawing people out, and if you are not sufficiently brilliant, you won't shine in Pat.'s eyes, for the fact is, my dear friend, I've rather set you up to Pat. I've said this sort of thing — "He is very much of a scholar. He is ornate and cultured; has correct tastes, is appreciative, genial, natural, &c. I told her you could "cut me all out," so that if you wish to maintain your reputation with her, I rather think you would better not come. Not that I think you would laugh at my garden — not that I'm afraid you could talk me down. But you see how it is.

"I'd like to have him come," said Pat. "If he

can talk better than you I'd like to have him do it, that's all."

I really want you to come; but, but—if, by any possibility, or mere accident, you know, you should happen—just for one morning, to appear "smarter" than Trifle, why see how Pat. would feel. You perceive I don't think of myself at all; I'm only a little anxious on your account and Pat.'s. But if you choose to come and "see" my breakfasts, and criticize my garden and my cigars, and my—(I tell you plainly there are only three or four bottles left,)—if you choose to do it, why, do it! Yes, sir, I say as Pat. says: I'd like to see you do it—I dare you to do it; and, what's more, I'll call in Stubs, though he's rather abstracted of late. Pink is at Newport, and "*he*" is in her party and has been much devoted to her. Stubs concluded not to go; I don't know why. We are talking a little of Niagara. Pat. stands somewhat in her own light about it; but we will manage it, and Stubs will go with us; as where wouldn't he go with me?

We have been engaged lately in reading "Maud, and other Poems." If you have read "Maud" but once, my advice is, read it again; study it, in fact, and you may then see something worthy of Tennyson in it, though Tennyson, in my judgment, is by no means an admirable poet. He is extremely infertile in incident, and all that he creates is vague, impalpable and indistinct. He deals in shadows pertinaciously, and is never real except when he is unreal. He was evidently off his guard when he wrote the *May Queen*, and he has amply atoned for the sweet naturalness of that delicious little poem, by the strained bitterness and acidulated sourness, — not to say affectation, cant and occasional nonsense of "Maud."

Won't you please to inform me why the Poet Laureate of England should write, much less print, such stuff as *this* ?

> "I keep but a man and a maid, ever ready to slander and steal,"

Is that any reason for him to hate everybody, and "smile a hard set smile," when it is notorious that "*help*," honest withal, can be hired for a reasonable compensation ? And again:

> "We whisper, and hint, and *chuckle*, and grin at a brother's shame."

Do we, in point of fact ? and, if we do, my Christian friend, where's the need of prating it all over creation, to disgust men with themselves and each other ? They will never become better by being told such things, and the poet's mission is, or should be, to make men better. And again :

> "I have not made the world, and He that made it will guide."

This would be a noble utterance, and sound philosophy, if it were warmed by, and were a consequence of, or even accompanied by — *Faith ;* but it is not, but is, in the connection, equivalent to saying — among these "long neck'd geese of the world," and this "clamor of liars," and this cloud of "poisonous flies" — "I'm not responsible for the world ; I didn't make it. Let him that did, take care of it."

What a fine sentiment *this* is, to be sure !

"Thanks, for the fiend best knows whether woman or man be
the worse.
I will bury myself in my books, and the devil may pipe to his
own."

Again:

"Ah, what shall I be at fifty
Should *Nature* keep me alive,
If I find the world so bitter,
When I am but twenty-five?"

Whom does *Nature* keep alive, and where is that Heavenly *Father*, in whose sight the hairs of our heads are numbered?

Again:

"Till a morbid hate and horror have grown
Of a world in which I have hardly mixt."

It is to be conceded that it is not Mr. Alfred Tennyson who speaks, but a very foolish, weak, jealous, crazy young man, whose occupation seems to have been to manufacture all the misery he could for himself.

Nor was it Lord Byron, but *Childe Harold* who spoke, when he retailed off, with much noble poetry, an indefinite mass of misery, made to order, with which to provoke the tears of sentimental misses and impracticable men, till doomsday. I have no sympathy with any such nonsense. If a man has griefs, let him go and expose them to his God, and ask for submission under them.

But when it is considered what the cause of this extremely interesting young man's grief or madness was, it is really quite ludicrous. Love it was, to start with, of course; next, it was covetousness of his neighbor's good fortune. It went against his grain that his neighbor was rich, and he himself was poor. The father of the one broke in a speculation and killed himself, and the father of the other "made money," as near as I can make out, for the *story* part isn't told in very English English. It is so very poetical that it is hard to understand. What though the one family was "gorged" and the other "flaccid and drained?" What then? Isn't it so everywhere; in the same families even? Should a brother hate his brother for his successes in trade, and a sister a sister because she has married a wealthy man?

Our interesting hero was "nameless and poor"— the old whine, you see. Then why not make himself a name and wealth? That's what *men* do, to a reasonable extent, everywhere. As the story proceeds, the *interest* increases by his meeting Maud and her brother "abroad." He cut the one, and the other cut him.

If *this* be not thrilling, what is?

"I met her abroad with her brother, but not to her brother I bowed."

This is a flatter line, though, than can be found elsewhere in the poem. In fact, if there were more commonplace in it, there would be more light and shade, which it lacks. After a while, very much to the reader's relief, they "make up."

A lord comes in as a suitor, but our hero engages the affection of Maud and becomes happy, and, like a sensible man, kisses her with a "long lover's kiss," gets into a quarrel with her brother, kills him in a duel, becomes crazy, suffers real grief and agony, and after some very fine talk, as nearly as can be ascertained, goes out to the Crimea to take a part in the taking of Sebastopol. When that interesting event occurs, we shall, doubtless, hear from him again.

To be serious, I like not this poem, though it contains many exquisite passages, and some though not many very natural ones. How fine is *this :*

> "Ah, Christ, that it were possible
> For one short hour to see
> The souls we loved, that they might tell us
> What and where they be."

And *this :*

> "And a million horrible bellowing echoes broke
> From the red-ribbed hollow behind the wood,
> And thundered up into Heaven the Christless code,
> That must have life for a blow."

And *this :*

> "Not die ; but live a life of truest breath,
> And teach true life to fight with mortal wrongs." —

How natural is *this :*

> "Who shall call me ungentle, unfair,
> I longed so earnestly then and there
> To give the grasp of fellowship."

The vigor and force of *this* is terrific :

> "Gorgonized me from head to foot
> With a *stony British stare.*"

How eloquent and grand is *this* — the noblest and most pregnant passage in the poem :

> "Ah, God, for a man with heart, head, hand,
> Like some of the simple great ones gone

Forever and ever by,
One still strong man in a blatant land,
Whatever they call him, what care I,
Aristocrat, democrat, autocrat — one
Who can rule and dare not lie."

There spoke a man! —

And how beautiful is *this:*

"And she touched my hand with a smile so sweet,
She made me divine amends
For a courtesy not returned."

How exquisitely beautiful and natural is *this*, after a solitary and passionate denunciation of her brother:

"Peace, angry spirit, and let him be!
Has not his sister smiled on me?"

It half redeems such nonsense as

——"the scream of a *maddened beach*,"

And

— "the heart of the citizen *hissing* in war on his own hearth-
stone;"

And many other things quite as far fetched and unnatural.

There is no lack of force, or iron compactness in this poem. It is strong enough, but it has no breadth. It is inharmonious in its details, and though it be compact, as I have said, it is not from the result of elements blending and flowing, and being naturally cemented together; but it is gold and brass, and iron and steel, and lead and dross (not to speak of old nails, without heads) all fused together by a terrific and quasi infernal heat. There is nothing for you to stand upon, and if it make you feel, at all, it will make you shudder and weep. It will not fill your eyes with sweet, tender, and purifying tears, as will "In Memoriam," — and make you happier; but, if it start your tears, they will burn and scald you. It is no advance upon "Locksley Hall," in power of thought, and is far inferior to it in true, real, earnest manhood. It will never address the universal human heart, which is the test of genuine poetry, and will make few happier and none wiser. There is nothing spontaneous and gushing about it, and hereafter, when I feel inclined towards Tennyson, I shall read his "In Memoriam," and skip his "Maud."

The piece entitled "The Letters," is quite natural and beautiful; and the "Ode on the Death of Wellington," is noble beyond account. The spirit of Nelson being agitated by the advent of Wellington's spirit, is a fine fancy, and indicates the genius of a real poet. But what Trifle thinks of Tennyson is of small consequence, you will say, no doubt. However, farewell, and forgive the infliction! You, and all of you, are held in continual remembrance.

VIII.

The Arm Chair,
In Autumn.

Autumn — do you mark that, mellowing Trifle ? — golden Autumn, with its yellow sheaves and its luscious fruits, has come, and the year is travelling onward to its close ; — onward through the gorgeous forests to the bleak, crisp fields beyond, where in the wail of the wintry wind it shall expire. Ah, friend, in its soft springtine and its leafy summer how have we grown ? What flowers and fruits have we borne ? what precious harvests have we garnered, that in the dark and wintry days we may sit us down and rejoice ? What store have *ye* gathered, ye plodders in the dusty streets of trade — what besides your gold, hoarded to rust beneath the sweat of your anxiety, or thriftlessly lavished in that cold display which crushes into the dust the hearts of the poor and unfortunate ? Or *ye* who have yawned out your *ennui* in the interregnum of " the seasons,' sighing for those weeks of social mockery, that came at last, at the watering places — what have ye reaped for your exhausted bodies and collapsing minds, except weariness and bitter regrets ? Priceless fruits in inexhaustible fields are all about us — but alas ! for the dearth of reapers. The summer of life, too, is passing, senescent Trifle, and its autumn steals on — steals on so gently that we heed it not, till the sere leaf shall be already upon us. God grant that those soft, golden days may be ours, — those days when the splendor of ripened leaves and fruits glows in the rich, hazy sunlight of an Indian Summer, and all is peace and beauty.

"Behold a wonder!" we exclaimed, most miraculous Trifle, as we finished your last plethoric epistle. Often have we marvelled how the little seed cast into the ground should become a spreading plant, a blooming shrub, a lofty, fruit-bearing tree, and how the substance and fluids of this solid earth should be so transformed into beauty. But we are *amazed* now, finding you, the city-bred drudge among figures and the hard facts of trade, when set down in the garden of Trifleton House, where you can smell the fresh earth, feel the warm sunlight and inspire the pure air, suddenly transformed into a humorist, poet, and critic! Verily, that garden has produced something — not under your cultivation, presumptuous husbandman, but under the genial influences of nature — better than down-growing radishes or procumbent vines.

We should not have believed it. It is quite true that from time to time, you have dropped some sayings — unpremeditated, of course — which seemed quite smart, — palpable hits, funny resemblances of wit; but then they were manifestly to be set down as the accidents of verdancy. Else were they the unconscious buds of this new product of Trifleton, which has so suddenly blossomed. Beware lest the frost, which Wolsey says comes "the third day," shall nip its root.

But, look you, oblivious Trifle! if in the transmutations which you have undergone, Young and Parker are as myths to you, it becomes us to recall the past, that among your other unpardonable sins you may not count ingratitude, — ingratitude to those who (for a consideration) have so often fed you and made your heart glad with delectable — purified Cochituate. Do you not remember that it was *you* who led us thither, to resorts until then unknown to us? Let one memorable instance recount a score. With what familiar steps you ascended the stairs and proceeded to a quiet room, where we found a table spread for four! With what a conscious air you played the host, in anticipation of Trifleton House! And then the courses, — from oysters and soup to dessert, were they not after your own taste, with all the accompaniments, *fried potatoes* and all? Was not your tongue fluent (not with words) while we were liquidating the affairs of Schreider and Johannisberger? And did that last fragrant weed — genuine Cuban — render you so oblivious that you remember not the pleasant-faced man, whom governors and other great men familiarly call "George," when he came to receive the *quid pro fried potatoes*? Was it so Lethean as to last to this day? What a pity that Orestes had not discovered it, — not Brownson, for though he has sighed for "rest" often enough, he is probably sufficiently oblivious of his antecedents.

And after this you want us to "own up" that we approve of the Maine Law. Possibly we might, but then it is rather awkward to follow Dogberry's command in public. Still, its beneficent results are not to be overlooked, and we cannot but "smile," when we think how the simple writing of that, "perfection of human reason," has brought it about that no "spirituous and intoxicating liquors" are sold in Boston. Are not these liquors the "fruitful source" of all the crime, vice and misery in the world? Lo, then, this Boston, which you so incontinently deserted, has become a serpentless Eden, calling you back to its unpolluted streets, — its peaceful, unpolluted streets, where only virtue dwells and poverty is not. Then pæans to the Maine Law! the law that "executes" itself, and never is violated. Henceforth "cobblers" shall stick to the last, and if Hamlet lived now and here, he would have no occasion to complain of

"The *slings* and arrows of outrageous fortune."

Ay, then, sing *Io Bacche!* — tut, tut! we should say, pæans to the Maine Law!

Sunsets are glorious sights. But of all the beautiful, inspiring sunsets that one "in particular" must have been superlative which made a new poet at Trifleton House. A poet, but no verse maker. Know you not where your lines begin, O wondrously stupid poet? Perceive you not the jingle of your rhymes, that you should thus write on as if in plain prose, stupefying the printer and putting your reader at fault? Yet it is evident you do not count out your lines upon your fingers, and so you give promise that the world is not to be afflicted with your effusions. As we read this part of your letter, however, we began to fear that we were in haste when we said, formerly, that the fates had spared us the infliction of your playing the poet. Happily the symptoms are favorable, as above noted; and the matter you have given us, — ah! that is the utterance of the soul, deep-toned and sweet, — the utterance of a soul wherein faith dwelleth. We shall show this to Hard; he is appreciative and it may do him good.

And now, sir — most courteous Trifle, your statement that you can't very well *dodge* saying "Come," is somewhat of the coolest. We invite ourself to Trifleton House! — that is marvellous. And all because we expressed our wonder at your breakfast — and *such* a breakfast — in the homely way that we should like to see one such. Well, we should like to *see* the sea-serpent, but it don't follow that we expect that retiring individual to invite us to such a sight. But you say "Come" in an exceedingly shabby manner, and then you try to buy us off, lest, in our light, Pat. should be able to see those deficiencies which you flatter yourself are now hidden from her. But we are not to be begged off, nor frightened by any bug-bears. If we come to one of these breakfasts, what is it to us if it surpass those of Rogers in the cultivation or genius of the company? We shall not come to *shine* — we shall come to *eat*; and we warn you that, living in the country, (don't call us a city man again!) we are blessed with a good appetite; and fried potatoes and corn-cake, unbolted-wheat bread and the et ceteras — we abominate cucumbers, though — will disappear before us like Sweaborg before the allies.

Nor shall we condescend to meddle with your culinary department, or show the "incorrigible Mary" how to slice pork. When we go out to breakfast we expect other folks to cook it — and to fall in love with their cooks, too, if they choose, for *we* shan't; we come to — *eat.* With this warning — that you may provide accordingly — we accept your challenge to come. Yet, after what you say about being "sufficiently brilliant" and saying smart things, we have some misgivings lest your delectable breakfast may consist of talk, of poetry, of moonshine and other "unsubstantial phantoms" — which we set down as pretty pòor eating. Eating is a good thing — a necessary work, a pleasant process. It is a work to be frequently done, well done, and done gratefully, — especially is it to be done gratefully, that "good digestion" may "wait on appetite." Yes, sir — we'll come, with doubts, but with gratitude — even though the last "three or four bottles" be already gone.

"But what Trifle thinks of Tennyson is of small consequence." A wonderful conclusion to arrive at, truly, after a column of criticism. Had you any misgivings that your "slashing" criticism was not quite sound, most pungent critic? *We* have. Notwithstanding we might agree with some of your notions a little smoothed about the jagged corners, we don't subscribe to all your crudities, and have no idea of being your accomplice in despatching the Poet Laureate with blunt knives and bludgeons.

And in the first place we don't think it necessary to *study* "Maud" in order to see something worthy of Tennyson in it. We found out almost numberless beauties in it at the first running (or riding) perusal. Hardly is there a page in it but contains lines of beauty or thoughts worthy of the poet. Such things meet our eye first, and unlike you, O carping Trifle, we find the defects when we study, as you recommend. We don't propose to point out these fine things, even to your defective vision, lest our paragraphs might emulate yours in number. You have, indeed, found something to approve; and possibly by a little more study, you might discern more to admire.

But the one grand error of your estimate of "Maud" is, that you find in it a "strained bitterness," an "acidulated sourness," (what is that?) and all that sort of thing, which you opine should be avoided by the poet. But are not all the expressions which call forth these strictures the natural utterance of one situated as the hero of "Maud"? And is not this a legitimate way for the poet to utter his earnest cry against the sins and follies and corruptions of society? He tells hard truths — must he wink them out of sight? Must the poet sing ever, in melodious numbers, of beings and things always good and beautiful, just as they are *not* in this world? Must he leave it always for the prosy essay or the stupid novel to deal blows at social wrongs and decay? Trifle thinks so, but Tennyson does not, and so he (the poet, not the critic) writes in the spirit of earnest sadness, not "strained bitterness," painting things as they are, and calling them by their right names, that the world may know them and abhor them. Is it not so?

As for the story which you consider so shadowy and not "very English English," that is simply a thread on which to string his pearls. It is suggested rather than told, just as a poet ought to convey his story to the reader's mind, if he has got anything else to say. And if you will study "Maud" a little more, you may see with what consummate art the story is suggested; not merely the incident, but the soul-life of the hero, the rise, the flow, the swell of the passionate current in his heart, and the dark tide of horror and despair which flooded it after the ringing of that

——— "passionate cry,
A cry for a brother's blood."

But let us talk no more of Tennyson, now, except to commend your inclination for "In Memoriam." Happily you may yet think better of "Maud," or we think less than we now appear to. In either case the Laureate's fame will scarcely suffer.

May joys cluster about Trifleton House.

IX.

TRIFLETON HOUSE,
In time of the fading leaf.

YES! the leaf is fading. The days are become shortened. The sun goes earlier to his rest. The flowers have quite passed. The golden summer of '55, like the Paradise of Adam, has gotten to be but a reminder. For better or worse, it is over; and,—farewell to it. It will never return; but—who cares for that? The lapse of time is nothing to a soul that is buoyed by—*Faith.* Time, like opportunity, is but a means. Ends have nothing to do with it. Their dealing is with Eternity. Confessedly, though, it is somewhat sad at Trifleton House.

Our friends have come—and gone. It is well. What has been uttered and thought and felt, (for, possibly, among the many who have been at Trifleton House there has been some genuine feeling,) is recorded and can never be altered. It is fixed and irrevocable. It is past. Our friends have come and gone, and our best wishes and prayers are with them. Will they forget Trifleton House? We shall see, and we shall also see who are our friends. Real affection is demonstrative and sincere attachment cannot but be evidenced.

We have had friends of both sexes, and some very near and dear ones. But they are gone. Will they ever return? or will they change? Better never return than change. Absence is comparatively nothing. Death even is of small consequence, for we look to a meeting with all who are worthy and lovely in the great hereafter; but change is in some sense formidable and terrible because it goes to prove — what we claim not to believe at Trifleton House — that human nature is rotten and selfish; that feeling is a valueless commodity, and that what is called, in these latter days, *society*, blights and warps and poisons all that is simple and natural; for show me a change of genuine affection that cannot be traced directly or indirectly to the thousand and one conventionalisms of the day, and I will show you a miracle.

We kiss our hands, then, to those who shall change.' We bid them good bye in advance. If they prefer to pass, they can. We can quite afford to do without them. We are simple and unsophisticated folk, and have no feeling to *waste*. We have lived long enough to have had experience with all sorts of people and forms and notions, and we are quite sick of affectation and insincerity. We are done with it forever. We profess to love only those who are natural and genuine, and real. So, all of you in the world (it is presumed the whole world will read and devour this letter) who have been at Trifleton House, take warning!

Doubtless it is a little dull, at present, at Trifleton House! But I have no intention of moping. Stubs continues faithful, and I have Pat. still. You see her once, and you know her, as you know the sun or the stars after having once seen them. You don't require to be constantly asking yourself, " Is this the person I thought I knew and understood ? " She is a *fact*, — a fixed fact; and I rather like facts. Fictions are well enough in their place, but they only illustrate. They really prove nothing.

In plain terms, the story about the tomatoes is just this. We expected *enough* in our garden, but (confidentially) they didn't come. So, I said to the expressman, " Won't you please to go to Mr. Forestaller and Treble Profit in the Quincy Market, and get the tomatoes. I don't know how many, but get quite a number of bushels, an indefinite quantity, if you please, and fetch them to Trifleton House, because Pat. wishes to ' put 'em up ' for the winter ! "

Such were my orders ; but the expressman didn't go. And when he did go, he didn't get the tomatoes, and I had to go myself; and when he did get 'em, they were in a process of decay — incipient, but progressive. The expressman (as he told it to me) remonstrated with the marketman, and confided the fact to me that that functionary was a " devilish fool ! " I give you his exact words, and I can't help it, how expressmen talk ; — but the indignant marketman hotly exclaimed : " What do I care for this Trifle ? Tomatoes is tomatoes, and if a man buys 'em to-day, I doesn't guarantee nothin' 'bout their keepin' forever."

This severe but accurate reasoning, no expressman could have the stamina or the authority to gainsay. Hence we had the tomatoes, and I had what I should be inclined to call in English to you, privately, a minute upbraiding from Pat.

"Trifle," said she, "here I have been 'tucked up' these two days (*she* said '*this* two days'), slighting that baby, and making blackberry jam, and preserves, and pickles, and waiting for those tomatoes, neglecting to return several calls which I owe, not to mention the buttons on your shirts and strings on your drawers, and you go to town and forget all about the tomatoes. But next winter you'll be saying, 'Why didn't we have some tomatoes put up?' That's just like men!"

When it is considered what a difficulty I had with the expressman; — that I paid several dollars for the *cans*; — that I lost ten dollars by being away from my business in order to traffic with the marketman; — that I lost my tomatoes, and came slightly near losing my equanimity, you must say that I am by no means weak when I ask for your sympathy. But what did I do? Do! Why, I took my big trunk to town, bought a fresh lot of tomatoes, had them checked as baggage, rode from the depot to Trifleton House in a carriage, and set Pat. to crying under the hallucination that her mother was coming to pay her a visit. And instead of being tenderly embraced, I was saluted with "How disappointed I am. I thought you were mother!" But it is to be always borne in mind that Pat. is so exquisitely simple.

Our Niagara notion has exploded, and Stubs and I have been busy with our guns. We have exhausted considerable ammunition, and with about the same degree of success as has distinguished the allied forces before Sebastopol. Please write me when you hear of the "taking" of that interesting place. I take it, it is expected "very soon," and I assure you we expect considerable game "soon."

The gaming ground is many miles from Trifleton House. It's a most remarkable fact that, go where you will, the birds are always several miles further on. If I were to go to the other side of the Rocky Mountains for them, I should expect to be told by the oldest inhabitant that there were "plenty out there — on the flats of the Pacific! They go there to feed!"

Not many days since, on one of our gunning excursions, Stubs and I had a conversation which I think ought to be communicated. We had just set our *decoys*, which pleasant occupation carried us both knee deep in mud and water, of which a real gunner should never be afraid. How the accomplished Trifle looked, I cannot tell. I know, though, that Stubs looked very much like an Irish laborer just from digging in a canal. We lighted our cigars and "lay low" for "black breasters" and "yellow legs."

We puffed in silence. I was gazing at the decoys, thinking what fools the birds were to be deceived by them (I afterwards discovered, though, that they were not such fools as I took them for), when Stubs inquired —

"Trifle, how is it to be ascertained if a woman really loves you? Which are most reliable, her words or her actions? How much is a man to believe, and how much to doubt? Can you *ever* doubt the woman that truly loves you? Is not affection so involuntarily demonstrative as to disarm doubt and convert suspicion even into trust? Is a woman justified——"

"Down, Stubs, down! There they come — black

breasters!" (Here followed a tremendous duet of whistling for the birds, which I can't very well put on paper.) "They see the decoys. Now! now!"

Bang! bang! bang! ba—a—

"Well, by Jupiter, if *that* isn't great shooting. Four barrels, and not a bird!"

"Why, they were not within two gun shots, Trifle! What should you say? Is a woman —— Confound my gun; one barrel didn't go. I don't see what's the matter with her! She must be foul. Ought a woman —— Pshaw!"

"Set a new cap, man, and let her go. Off with her! Don't bother forever. When you have a good chance, she'll interfere —— Hark! a couple of 'yellow legs.' They answer my call. If I can get loaded."

Ram, ram—a moment and my caps are on—*click, click* go my hammers. They come like the wind. They dart down towards the decoys—swoop off. Whack! whack! this side and that.

"I took 'em—one with each barrel! What do you think of *that*?"

"Capital, Trifle. Now load up, and then sit down and keep a little cool, if you can."

I did so. Stubs discharged his recreant barrel, reloaded, and, if I remember correctly, we both examined our *pistols* at this point, to see what condition they were in. The examination proved satisfactory, and Stubs continued:

"Ought a woman to act so from impulse, as to make a man, who acts from reason, unhappy?"

"Impulse is generous, but not safe. I like judgment better. But then I'm an old married man, you know."

"*Money!* is that anything?" said he. (Here let me say, to satisfy curiosity on that point, that Stubs is not only rich, as you have seen, but he has plenty of money; which is remarkable, for few rich men have much money. It is chiefly sterile, barren individuals who abound in that article.)

"Nothing more than a means, and a slight one at that, with sensible people. A real man is superior to money; and all circumstances yield to him, or ought to. Else is he not a man. A *man* will always have money enough. Money is much with women, though. It turns their heads ——"

"Suppose a woman, by language — caresses — warmth — fire, indicated that she was yours; and then —— should be foolish, cold, irresolute, and almost despicable. How then?"

"I think I should let her go. But, Stubs, you have never told me. How is it? are you really *engaged* to Pink?"

"No."

"Rumor says so."

"Rumor lies, then."

"Have you ever been?"

"No!"

"Do you expect to be?"

A cloud passed over his face; —*passed*, you will observe. For he has educated himself, and has nearly conquered. He is quite under his own control.

"Let's go home, Trifle. There are no birds. A profitless pursuit is enervating."

Both of us grew silent and abstracted, and before long we went home. Stubs came with me to tea. As we entered the hall, the musical voice of Pat. was heard crying, " Tri-fle ! " — " *Tri*-fle ! "

" Well, Pat. ? "

" I've got a letter from Pink. She is coming home soon."

Almost unconsciously I turned to Stubs. He was pale and shivering. His game-bag had dropped from his hand, — he stood like a statue.

I read, most critically, this letter from Pink. It indicated intellectual capacity — nay, more, absolute talent. It was pungent, pointed, at times satirical. It hit off the frivolities of Hotel life at Newport. It was sufficiently piquant and racy, and real in one sense, but it was not womanly. I read on and on, till my eyes were clouded — looking, O, how eagerly! for Pink's heart. It was not there. In silence and in grief I folded the letter, and threw it back to Pat., saying to myself, " Alas, for Stubs! How he must suffer and struggle, to have mistaken such a character as *this* for his ideal. His discipline is fearful; but he will conquer. He will bend, but he will never break." The concluding paragraph of the letter was in these words:

" Love to Trifle and to Stubs. Is the latter as sober as usual — not to say forlorn? How different *he* and Stubs are. He finds something to laugh at in everybody and everything, and converts everything into ridicule. He is too funny. He is the exact opposite of Stubs. What a figure Stubs would cut down here! Are we never to laugh? My diamonds have evidently attracted attention, and I think provoked remark. It's rather inconvenient, though, this appearing in them at breakfast. But no more.

"N. B. I have much to tell you when I return."

X.

THE ARM CHAIR,
As shines the harvest moon.

ROMPY-DOMPY, the pet of the house, has gone to pleasant slumbers. As she said "good night," her large blue eyes gazed up at the full orbed moon, just rising over the hill, and wondered how it could look so bright, and just get up when she, tired of play, was ready to go to bed. She loved the moon and wished it would shine in the day time. Alas! so inopportune seem many pleasures as we journey on. Happy we, if, like the sweet child, we are content that they should come to others though we enjoy them not. She has gone to the land of pleasant dreams, and may angels guard her pillow.

While her sweet accents and merry laugh still linger on our ear, we turn to you, most rare Trifle, for a short space, cutting even the delightful moonlight, which with mystic art enhances beauty, and conceals defects, in the scenery. Isn't love or friendship like the moonlight, softening and adorning the character of those we prize, throwing a shadowy veil over the depressions and inequalities, and beautifying with a silver light the prominent and striking traits? Few are the clear sighted friends or lovers who can penetrate the veil into the recesses where hide, sometimes unprized loveliness, and sometimes hideous deformity.

Speaking of friendship, recalls the melancholy introduction of your last epistle. We should rather think that you had a little suspicion of the friendship of some of the visitors at Trifleton House. Else why those lamentations in advance, over the loss of friends? To be sure you try to keep "a stiff upper lip," and to be a man about it, and profess that Stubs and the ever faithful Pat. (our choicest wishes to her) are enough for you. But you don't feel quite so well about it, after all; — there's a little swelling of the heart, a little regret — little? nay, *we* cannot measure it, — because you fear that change, in some one, which is worse than absence or death. And you are right — your heart, not your professions — for Pat. and Stubs, faithful and firm though they be, are not enough in the long run, and even the self-reliant Trifle cannot afford to lose friends.

So, pray you, keep a warm welcome at Trifleton House for those you prize, and they shall not change. Entertain them well, flatter them, please them at any cost, and they shall cling to you — as long as the chains of hospitality, flattery and pleasure shall endure. Is it possible that the sagacious Trifle, with all his world wisdom, with all the delights of Trifleton, its productive garden and its wondrous breakfasts, has made the sad mistake, the egregious blunder of not so entertaining his company that they may wish to renew the pleasure! Rural influences, again. But courage, man; we'll count you one more friend, — so long as you write letters, tell the truth, don't disparage woman, and earnestly cultivate virtuous plants in the garden of Trifleton House.

It is just as we expected about the tomatoes, when you played the braggart over your garden. We knew they wouldn't come, and you confess, at last, a little ashamed, that they "didn't come," — neither from the bed, nor from the scattered single plants. But why didn't you come to us in your dilemma? — *We* could have shown you tomatoes, "a number of bushels," awaiting a summons to usefulness. We could have *shown* them to you, but — are you fond of picking them?

To tell the truth, fellow-sufferer, we sometimes have a grief of this sort, ourself. Didn't we expect to have such a varied and startling display of fruit, this year, that we should throw the veterans in horticulture, Wilder, Hovey, Walker, and other men of culture, utterly into the shade? Didn't we! Hadn't the "gold medal," "the society's plate," the "first premium," been constantly in our vision, so that in dreams our very back was broken by the mingled weight of great prizes and mammoth apples? Didn't we fancy the commotion among presidents and committee men, the envious look of distanced competitors, as we came along, the conquerer on this field of peaceful strife? Didn't we? —— O, didn't we expect great things and get confoundedly disappointed! Well — we are pretty sure we did.

Just think of it; hear our woes and pity them. In the first place some envious fellow (we don't call names, mind you) stole our best and biggest Bartletts; — we trust they stuck in his throat with all their obesity. In the next place a mischievous devil in the wind plucked our largest and most rotund Flemish

Beauties, that would have been a delight to the artists of Flanders. Then our Van Mons Leon le Clerc — what bad spirit got into the sap of that tree to prevent its nourishing the pears? Perhaps *you* can tell, philosophical Trifle. And our Duchesse, why that promising tree became insolvent and only yielded us a dividend on the magnificence which we expected, is more than we can tell. As for our Belle Lucrative and Seckle, by some means Shrimp contrived to find all the best ones on the ground, among his potatoes. The Golden Beurré of Bilboa, a thrifty dwarf, didn't grow tall enough to keep its fruit out of the reach of our neighbor's hens. Our —— but enough; — the Doyennés and the Beurrés, the autumn pears and the winter pears, the melting and the buttery, the whole tribe seemed determined that we shouldn't have the prize. They wouldn't grow, or if they did they would fall or be eaten. And so, here we are, no more distinguished for our pears than you for your tomatoes.

The fact is, this is a terrible disappointment to hopes and expectations cherished and growing (much faster than the pears) ever since blossom time. We were as confident of success as the allies before Sebastopol,* — and we've got it in about the same proportion.

* Sebastopol! There we are with our heels tripped up again. The Allies ought not to have spoiled our comparison in such an uncivil, blustering and sanguinary manner. Sebastopol is taken! Do you hear? You asked us to inform you when that "interesting event takes place," and so we do now. Sebastopol has fallen, and you can condole with the Russian bear, if you choose. Sebastopol is down, and so are our hopes of the first prize.

Isn't this an affliction to grow melancholy under? Perhaps Stubs can afford some sympathy. Shrimp only laughs at us, — but we shall see who laughs last when he digs his potatoes.

The Hards have returned from Newport, Madame a little more worldly than ever, and Miss Bel wretchedly languid, — terribly disappointed perhaps, because mamma's manœuvres and her charms did not succeed in detaching him of the "corn-colored" gloves from your friend, the brilliant Pink. Madame thinks that Pink is altogether too forward, free and dashing, too bold to be pretty and too pert to please. Bel wonders why she will persist in that outre style of head dress, and thinks her wit too keen and unlady like. They are agreed that she can't be a good match for *him*. But what's to be done about it now that "Newport is over," they can't quite settle.

As for young Hard, Abel, he would have been in a state of despair, had he remained a week longer at Newport. But now he is a new man. He has actually accomplished something, done some good — that is, probable good — having saved the life of a poor woman's child. The little fellow had fallen from the wharf, and Hard, who was aboard the steamer just on the eve of departure, plunged in and manfully saved him, while others looked on to see the poor boy drown if he might. The dandies shrugged their shoulders, the young ladies were in ecstasies over "the hero," the matrons were terribly shocked about their nerves, Madame Hard, herself, was supposed to faint, though she looked ruddier than ever, and Miss Bel was in a pet that her brother should get himself into such a horrid plight. But there were two, besides the little boy, who were really happy, — the mother and Abel Hard. The former came rushing down the wharf just as the two were drawn up, almost beside herself with fear and joy; and when she at last found her boy was living, she divided her caresses between him and his deliverer, upon whom with all the fervency of a mother's heart she called down the blessings of Heaven.

It was "a scene" for the worldlings on the boat, and Hard tells me he could perceive the different emotions which it produced. Some — ay, the many, were disposed heartlessly to laugh and joke over the matter, but here and there was one in whose eyes were tears, bright witnesses to the existence of their hearts. These Hard would, at the time, have embraced as friends; and between him and the others the gulf grew wider. But it could not last long; the steamer must depart in spite of foolish, drowning little boys, or rash young men; and Hard, who had no idea of becoming a lion, merman, or other wonderful animal in that company, insisted upon remaining. And so the steamer with its freight of fashionables departed, and Madame Hard and Bel — much to their chagrin, for they had reckoned on a last chance of attaching the "corn-colored gloves" to Miss Bel's suite — went ashore with their luggage and returned to the Ocean House.

One generous action leads to another. Hard, finding that the boy's mother was poor, took measures to relieve her wants before leaving Newport, the day after his adventure. And not content with that, he has just taken a sudden start back to the place which he so recently detested, intending to do something more for the boy, who, he says, is a bright little fellow and is destined to better things than his circumstances now promise. And this is Abel Hard; a month ago a sad, unhappy fellow, who looked through a veil of gloom on everything. He has at last discovered that a life of idleness is a curse to one like him, and that he must break through his "surroundings" that his generous impulses and real worth may vindicate themselves.

Two pretty "peeps" you and Stubs must have been, lying in wait for "yellow-legs" and "black-breasters," with foul guns — *fowling* pieces you call them, do you not? — and pistols. Did the pistols bring down any game? Fine sportsmen, truly, to be there, out on the marshes, discussing female character and thinking about Pink! Your game it seems was far away, attracted by such a decoy as you did not set — though scarcely better, if all accounts be true. As for Stubs, we can hardly pity him; for why should a man of his sense, a man of sober, quiet thought, noble and generous withal, suffer himself to be enslaved by a selfish and heartless creature, be she ever so beautiful? He is a man for a gentle and loving nature to cling to and make happy; an oak which affords a sturdy support whereon the tender vine may grow, making the rugged trunk beautiful with its foliage and flowers.

The days shorten, Trifle, have you noted it? The sun has grown chary of his hours, the twilight quickly fades and the night comes on. Long evenings are in store for you — and pray what shall you do, you who have so long revelled by gas light in city amusements? Is it not a dismal prospect for you, these long evenings when the clouds hang heavily over the earth, and the sere leaves are damp and still, and the crickets have ceased their song, and the wind howls and moans through the naked trees? Ah, let not the darkness and gloom of the outward world then settle on your heart. But may the warm light of domestic joy shine round the hearth of Trifleton House, and through the clouds gleam ever a star, to guide you onward and upward.

XI.

TRIFLETON HOUSE,
In time of the "Equinoctial."

THE Equinoctial is, indeed, upon us. The rain is pouring in floods, and the wind screams piteously among the trees. My peach trees have yielded to the violence of the storm and are quite prostrate, and the elm by the south parlor window reels to and fro like a drunken man. The pattering of the rain on the windows, — the rattling and "snapping" of the blinds, — the mournful voices of the night wind, — all together, conspire to make it gloomy enough at Trifleton House.

My soul is sad to-night, and the mysteries and responsibilities of life, the associations of my Past, and the uncertainties of my Future, press heavily upon me. I am talking with myself, and I discover in myself much that is vague, unreal, and difficult to understand. Sometimes I am consoled by myself, but, oftentimes, much disheartened. In this particular, doubtless, I illustrate my kind.

But enough of this. My duty is to recount incidents. Listen!

The sea has been so fierce as to have carried away our bathing houses. The oldest inhabitant remembers nothing like it. It heaves, and toils, and screams, and rages, and does all sorts of tragic and mournful things.

A brave thing, a fine thing, an all glorious thing is God's mighty sea! It never grows old. It has constantly new beauties, grandeurs, terrors! It tranquilizes, alarms, — excites, soothes, — plays and fights forever, and forever, and forever. Through the lapse of Time, — quite to the verge of Eternity, — up to the Judgment, it will be thus. For God's powers diminish not, and the sea is one of His chiefest. Possibly it is His right arm. Men pass over it, — and the products of their toil. Hence is commerce; — and commerce influences, and largely controls the world. The sea separates, and ties the nations.

Again. Pestilence walks on the land, as, for example, in case of Egypt in Pharaoh's time; as in Norfolk (oh, pity, pity, Father!) or Portsmouth in our own. But death is quite at home on the sea; — to wit, case of Arctic, case of President, and the like. There is a *locus* selected for me in Mount Auburn; but don't bury me there! Oh no! Ye future generations, I give you notice, and I request you! If practicable, and *perfectly convenient* and *agreeable* to you, let Trifle's coffin be the sea! The sea likes him, and he likes the sea.

Stubs and I were smoking in the south parlor. It was a howly night. The chaste harvest moon was sailing calmly along; but the winds were abroad and were angry, to say nothing of clouds and rain. But from our south-east window the lighthouse was palpable. Its revolving light gleamed like a suggestive and oft-recurring hope.

Pat. was "up stairs" with Prig. He was breathing heavily, and I didn't like the look about his eyes. They *glared*, in a word. I said to Pat., "The Doctor should come!" But she said, "No! it's nothing. It will pass." So I was comforted and went down to smoke with Stubs.

"Trifle," said Stubs (most confidentially and rather demurely), "I have been writing verses!"

Parenthetically — for aught I know — he had been writing poetry, though I'd never heard of his capacity in that line. The capacity of a talented man is not perceptible at once; it is ascertained, — and by degrees. Fools and "brilliant" women alone show all they know in an hour — or in less time.

"Subject?" said I.

"Look!" he replied.

I looked. But all I saw was the passionate sea. Away in the distance, however, stood the lighthouse. It touched me so tenderly, that I said,

"I see nothing but the lighthouse. How suggestive it is of hope or expectation. Its light gleams, kindles, burns. It goes out, though, or seems to, periodically. It is like Faith. It fades and droops and comes near dying, if you please, but it never dies. It shines, — shines eternally. Brighter, or dimmer, now and forever it shines, and shines, and shines! But read, Stubs."

He read as follows:

I.

Lo! where the Lighthouse lifts its piercing eye,
  And gazes on the horrors of the storm,
Calm and unmoved, while winds rush screaming by,
  And lightnings flash around its stately form.

II.

So noble spirits look upon the strife
  Of human kind by angry passions riven ;
And, unconcerned amid the storms of life,
  Serenely wait for perfect rest in Heaven.

III.

Oh, grandest Lighthouse, founded on a rock ! —
  Oh, largest souls, upheld by Faith divine ! —
Superior to trial and to shock,
  You educate weak natures likest mine.

I made no comment, but the verses subdued me. Had they been written by some one else than Stubs, — some well-known poet, for instance, — I should have said they were very natural and fine, and all that. Indeed, the way to judge of poetry is not from the effect it has on your feelings, but from the fact of its having been written by this or that poet of established reputation. If the well-known A. B. wrote it, it must be good, as a matter of course. If C. D., it should be unquestionably very fine.

This valuable idea was one I acquired when I lived in town, — in *society ;* and I have no notion of losing all the useful acquirements I made there. Hence I smoked on in silence, without a word of praise or criticism, while Stubs proceeded to say that he had another piece, in a somewhat different vein, and read as follows :

How bitterly I've strove
  To justify my fate !
Oh Heaven, that I should ever love
  The woman that I hate !

— Down, devilish spirit, down ! —
I'll conquer, or I'll die ;
Far nobler souls, — who've won their crown, —
Have suffered here than I.

Here ! — this is not my home,
This place of rotten lies ;
The world is but a Styx of gloom,
This side of paradise.

Nor ferryman, nor boat
I need. I'll go alone ; —
With but *myself*, — Suspicion, — Doubt, —
I'll, sorrowing, press on.

— Forbear, rash fool ! thy God,
With Faith, can bear thee up : —
Christ drooped, but — kissed the rod, —
Drank, — drained the fearful cup.

Temptation rends thy soul,
But discipline is sure ;
While calm Religion's sweet control
Alone can make thee pure.

Down on thy knees to prayer,
Bid earthly hopes farewell !
And cling to Heaven, whose blessings are
Dearer than tongue can tell.

The rich tones of his voice, as he read, fell on my ear with a sort of fascination, and made me feel as I have sometimes felt when I have heard a voluntary played on an organ in an empty church. One listens, but with a feeling of sadness and desolation. The deep-toned cadences seem half unreal, and you appreciate them only from the lasting effect they produce. They sound too sad to be pleasant in the actual hearing.

He ceased reading, and we smoked on in silence again. Cigars are extremely useful in such cases.

"How is Pink ?" said I, at length, and very abruptly. "Have you heard from her or written to her recently ?"

"Both ; but I shall discontinue any further correspondence or connection with her," he replied, and then got up and walked about the room nervously.

I scrutinized him carefully, and saw that he looked haggard and wan. I felt very uneasy, but said nothing. I ask you, what could I say ?

"I will read you an extract from her last letter, and you can judge for yourself," he said, in a few moments.

His hand trembled as he held the letter, and his voice trembled as he read it.

It ran as follows: "It is quite uncertain when we shall return. There is time enough, and I am not over anxious. We shall come *via* New York city, where we intend stopping a week or two. The Ts. insist on our coming, and besides, Pa is desirous that I should see Rachel, who is just about to appear. We are told she must be seen several times to be appreciated. Your *lecture* was quite thrown away upon me. We can never agree. Our natures are too dissimilar, and you regard life in too dingy a sort. With your permission, I shall continue what you call 'the pursuit of pleasure,' within moderate bounds. My hair has not yet begun to turn gray, and I have no intention, just at present, of going into a convent, or on a mission. So, Mr. Stubs! —— How intimate I am with *him*, is a question. Would you *really* like to know? Are we growing a little *jealous*, I wonder? The tone of your letter does not please me. If it be not *dictatorial*, it's *pokish*, or old man-ish, — or patriarchal, or some such thing. I should suppose it was my grandfather talking to me. Good bye and don't mope!

N. B. — I am knitting a purse, which you shall have, *perhaps*, if you —— *behave*, that is."

He folded the letter and put it in his pocket. A long pause. —— The silence was becoming painful, and I ventured to remark, finally,

"There can be no doubt that Pink is sincerely attached to you. She is frivolous, but she will improve. She is generous at heart, and her nature is, after all, a deep one. She is too impressible, though, and —— "

He interrupted me, furiously, notwithstanding my words evidently carried some balm to his hurt spirit, with

"Her generosity! Her heart!" — with a most bitter emphasis on the last word. "She was born without a heart. I have wasted my nature on her long enough, and now she may go — forever!"

I had never known him so excited before, and it was terrible to see this strong man thus stricken with passion.

"I have suffered in silence," he continued, "and without a murmur, the —— "

When hark! Pat. called loudly and sharply,

"Come up here, Trifle! — quick!"

I rushed up stairs, and it was as I had all along apprehended. Prig was in convulsions. He tossed his little arms wildly about and moaned most piteously. I did what I could. Pat. and Mary hastened to get him into a warm bath, and I started for the Doctor. I looked in at the parlor for Stubs. His head was buried in his hands. He had forgotten me and mine. One thought was driving him mad.

I told him what had happened. What an instantaneous change! he lived out of himself again, and thus became himself again.

" Stay," said he, and do what you can. I will go. Bob can harness Kate in a few minutes. It's but a mile, and I will have the Doctor here in a half hour or less."

He pressed my hand, and through the wind and the rain departed. No strongest Hercules or Goliath could have stopped him, and I let him go; and I thought to myself as I had thought often before, how eagerly and how gratefully I loved him.

The Doctor came and said the trouble was in the brain. It was too large, &c. . . .

We shuddered.

The next day it was the same, and worse. And the next. — Dear, poor little Prig! We had ice about his head and temples constantly, and that was all, principally. Said I, " Give him something or he will die!" The answer was, " It would kill him."

I rushed to Boston for a consulting physician. He came and — went.

There was no hope. This I gathered from mysterious looks, anxious expressions, &c. No such thing was said. It was plainly hinted, though.

" The result is in *His* hands, then," I reflected; and

I thought I would fall back upon my Faith, but I had none. I was neither hopeful nor submissive.

I went out into the garden. The dead leaves were all around, and I said to myself, " What a miserable world this is ! "

Some inward voice appeared to reply, and this conversation ensued :

" The world is better than you think."

" I deny it. There is my best friend, who has talents, and virtues, and character, and station, and wealth, — and what are they all ? He is perfectly wretched, and *I* —— am to lose my boy. But I will not. I will keep him. I want him. He is my chief hope. If he dies, my heart will break. Oh, it's a splendid world ! "

" Your friend's character is not complete, nor is yours. You are proud and rebellious, and it may be you are to be 'sifted like wheat.' Who are you that you should not suffer ? Your boy ! — He is not yours, and never was. Take care. He is passing rapidly. Go and save him, if you can. You are simply a weak, feeble fool, and have regarded 'your boy,' as you call him, with too much complacency. You have built too many castles about developing his mind, — moulding him, — impressing on him your own imperfect nature, and habitudes of thought, feeling and action, and reproducing yourself in him. One such as you is quite sufficient. It is probable he will die, and you would better be humble and penitent, and ask God to forgive your sins, and surrender him and yourself into His keeping. You will find it very hard and very useless to 'kick against the pricks !' "

I could bear this no longer, and I returned to the house. As I went in, little White-y came skipping towards me, and tenderly kissed my hand. He seemed to indicate that he missed Prig from the garden, and wished to sympathize with me. It made my heart ache to see him.

I went to Prig's chamber. I had left Pat. there, — and Stubs, for a moment, bathing the dear boy's temples. Nobody else.

There was another person just flying into the room before me, — unannounced. It was Pink. With her usual precipitancy, she rushed into Pat.'s arms, and with a passionate burst of tears, exclaimed,

"My poor, darling Pat., how my heart bleeds for you. Can you forgive me? I hate and despise myself for being away at such a time! Why did you not send for me? It was because you considered me too unworthy."

And she wept *bitterly*.

Pat. soothed and comforted her, and they mingled their tears together.

Prig lay perfectly senseless.

Stubs stood speechless.

Again I said to myself, "What a world this is!"

XII.

THE ARM-CHAIR,
In the Indian Summer.

OUR hearty sympathies are with you, afflicted Trifle, in the sorrows which shadow your dwelling. Happy, indeed, are you, that through the clouds shines so brightly the sun of Friendship, — that you have the large-hearted, firm and generous Stubs ready, with something more than words to aid you. Ah, Heaven be with you through the long, anxious hours that come and go, with solemn steps and slow, in the dark, silent room. God be with you and your cherished hopes!

Your letter recalls a time, when one to us as dear as Prig to you, struggled through the dark cloud of sickness. The night came on black with thick vapors; but darker was the gloom of doubt and dread within the dim, still chamber, where the little sufferer gasped. Hope sunk, and flickered — rose and sunk again, till it became fear and dread. Oh! we remember well how, as the gloom fell like a pall upon that vanishing hope, we drew aside the curtain to look out upon the night, — and what a thrill the ray of a star, beaming through a broken cloud, shot to our heart. It was like a messenger from Heaven in answer to the prayerful agony of the hour, and it brought peace and hope and gratitude. The morning came at last. Night fled before the approaching day, and with it fled the clouds, and the fears that were darker clouds upon the heart. The morning came; morning upon the hill-tops and in the golden sky, — morning in our hearts and over the dear child, — morning and thanksgiving.

And so Trifle would be buried in the sea. Have you calculated that it is any better to become "food for fishes" than "food for worms"? Do you like the picture which Clarence painted? —

> —— "a thousand fearful wrecks;
> A thousand men, that fishes gnawed upon;
> Wedges of gold, great anchors, heaps of pearl,
> Inestimable stones, unvalued jewels,
> All scattered in the bottom of the sea.
> Some lay in dead men's skulls; and, in those holes
> Where eyes did once inhabit, there were crept
> (As 'twere in scorn of eyes) reflecting gems,
> That wooed the slimy bottom of the deep,
> And mocked the dead bones that lay scattered by."

Have the treasures of the deep such a hold upon your fancy, or upon your habits of trade, that you would fain sleep the last sleep in that slimy bed where such things are? And then the Ocean's mighty, restless currents, look you! would you have them swinging and tossing your worn body to and fro forever? The surface of the sea hath many voices as its waves break and roar; a solemn, grand, majestic music along its beaches and its hollow rocks. But in those depths the echoes come not, nor near or distant harmonies, but silence and motion forever.

Let *us* say rather "Dust to dust," far in the green retreat of the wooded sanctuary, where the sun's rays may sometimes softly linger on the grassy slope, and where the deep-toned forest organ sounds its soft or grand and ever-changing symphonies, and solemn requiems swell and die forever. But what matters it whether your decaying body rot in the "slimy bottom" of the deep sea, or ours crumble at the roots of the giant oak, if our souls shall have passed the dark portal, with heavenward hope and faith, into the bright fields beyond?

Stubs — well, we pity him; but let him not know it, lest he scorn our sympathy. How deeply must run the current of his love; else such a nature as his could scarcely have been moved to verse-writing, and poetry had found no expression through him. But as it is, the secret depths of his heart have been brought to the surface, in the earthquake struggle which rends it, and feelings which were scarcely acknowledged to himself have become active, demonstrative. With the feelings is aroused the talent to express them; — how well, let those fine lines on the lighthouse testify.

The stately Autumn marches slowly on with his rich burden of sheaves and fruits, and the forests have put on their gorgeous robes — flung out their banners of crimson and gold, to gleam in the clear sunlight of the year's holidays. O, how rich in beauty and how rich in thought is the bright season of the ripened leaf!

Behold the varied tints of the woods, — the ruddy brown of the oak, the scarlet of the maple beside the deep green of the pine, the deeper crimson of the sumach contrasting with the emerald sward, the yellow of the elm and birch and the light brown of the walnut, all mingled in rich masses, such as the painter in vain may attempt to imitate. And over all is the soft sunlight of a mild, clear day of the Indian summer. Such beauty ever tempts us forth to gaze, and to receive the gentle influences that steal through eye and ear into the heart.

But let us narrate. It was such a day, just gone by, that we visited a spot whose beauty has lingered in our memory from childhood. On the one side, the many-tinted woods half circled a quiet retreat where the turf lay partly in sunlight, partly in shadow; and on the other were groups of noble trees in brilliant array, standing on little knolls whose sides sloped down to the still water's edge. Beneath one of these groups were cattle standing, or reclining in picturesque positions. Ah, it was such a scene as Poussin would have loved, and such as you might wish for a companion to that "still life" of Durand.

We were delighting in these untiring beauties, as you delight in the sea. But an indistinct murmur of voices, swelling once into a musical laugh, told us we were not alone, and must therefore indulge in no mad transports. So we watched to see the excitement of others, whoever they might be, who evidently enjoyed the same delicious scene. And there they were, in a lovely spot, leaning upon the rustic fence that kept those cattle subjects from straying out of the landscape. They were a man and a woman — a lady and a gentleman, if you please. Her broad-brim summer hat shaded a face whose half seen profile appeared sufficiently beautiful for the elegant form which supported it. He was like a hirsute foreigner, a little *outre* in dress, but with an eye and brow that never belonged to the dandy, nor to assuming mediocrity. He was an artist, and with sketch-book and pencil he was rapidly transferring this "study from nature," while she watched with interest the work, and listened to words which were evidently eloquent.

Incontinently we left the objects of our recent admiration — the trees and the cattle — to the artist, and made the twain our study. We'll even confess that we approached them — stole nearer to them unseen — to obtain the same point of view, of course. Passing around those sumach trees and birches, we came to a nearer and full view of them. And lo! we found the artist was none other than Umber, born hereabouts; a strange boy, who would make pictures instead of money, who went but little better than penniless to Italy some years ago, for the purpose of studying art instead of buying macaroni, and who has of late returned with just about as much money as he carried, but with a rich store of knowledge, high ideas, skill and great resolutions, — returned in truth a man and a true artist.

We could hear him now. We had some misgivings at playing the listener, but — never mind. He was gaily discoursing of artist life in Rome and Florence, now and then recalling a picture suggested by the scene he was sketching. His tones were rich and his words and manner fascinating — as we saw clearly by the attention of his companion. He was painting in glowing colors his sojourn in the land of art, when he was interrupted by an abrupt and hasty question.

"Had you no regrets for home?"

"Home! — ha, ha! — my home was where my pack or easel was, — some time in Rome, once on Mont Blanc, in the crater of Vesuvius, anywhere."

"But friends?"

"I did make friends with two, from whom I regretted to part, as I don't know that I have another friend in the world. One was a sorrowful sculptor from Germany, the other a pretty flower-girl in Rome."

"A flower-girl!"

"Beautiful as Hebe."

"O, doubtless! — and as fit to be waiting maid."

There was a little tremulous scorn in the words, and the speaker turned hastily away from the artist so as to bring her face fully before us. Was it possible! — It was, in truth, Bel Hard, and her cheek was suffused, and there was just the springing of a tear in her eye, that really flashed. Yes, it was the languid, fashionable Bel Hard. We shall have plenty of larks now, for the skies are about to fall!

With a hasty step she passed on, leaving us unnoticed. Umber had started as she spoke, looked up, and as she went away, arose from his seat and gazed after her as if doubtful whether to follow or not. Then he seated himself again and went to work. But he did not look at the landscape. We approached him cautiously, and looking on his work beheld a lively sketch of Bel Hard. So — her face lingers long in your memory, Sir Artist.

Umber and Bel had been playmates years ago, though he was a poor woman's son. But in her teens

Bel must aquire "accomplishments," in order that Madame might accomplish her ends; and Umber by hook or by crook, went to Italy. A man of genius and of travel, he is not to be passed by now, for wealth can patronize art, and not degrade itself. Besides, Abel, who is utterly regardless of propriety, esteemed his old friend. So Umber, fresh from Italy, is a welcome visitor at the Hard mansion, — Umber, the poor artist, is simply patronized.

"A beautiful scene this, Umber."

He started, and looked at us askance, and then a slight smile curled his moustache —

"*Nature* is always beautiful."

"But hereabouts nature is too often hidden by tawdry and senseless ornament."

"Still, nature is underlying."

"Remove the ornament, and you have but a barren soil."

"Perhaps, — and haply one wherein may grow the loveliest flowers."

He put up his book and pencils abstractedly, and mused awhile as we turned homewards. His thoughts were not of art. But he soon broke the spell, and turning again towards the scene he had been sketching, exclaimed with artist warmth —

"Italy can boast of nothing equal to this, either in nature or art."

And then he discoursed on, till we wondered not that under the influence of such talk even the languor of Bel Hard was dispersed. Bel Hard, — perhaps we have done her injustice. What should *she* do with a heart, though? Have not fashion and her practical mother trained her to do without one?

But Abel Hard. He has been to Newport to look after his protegé, and returned in a more sad and nervous mood than ever. He had made a discovery which threw him entirely off his balance, if his mind could ever be said to possess such a blessing. The mother of the unfortunate little diver had been a servant in the family of *her* father. Misfortune had overtaken him, and he had come to America. For a few days Hard was in miserable doubt, but at last he set out for the prairies in search of — what he expects may prove his happiness. An almost hopeless search; but we shall see. Madame is excessively annoyed, — possibly she may yet find more cause.

As evening set in, Umber made his appearance in our library — a little abstracted at first, but he soon took us to the Vatican. They talk of the Vatican at the mansion now; and Madame has hunted up Murray's Guide-book, which Abel had brought home. When one patronizes an artist from Rome, one must not be a fool. Bel has been reading Hillard's "Six Months in Italy." She borrowed ours, when Umber first made his appearance, and she still keeps it.

But, most patient Trifle, we weary you. Silence is in the house, silence and sleep. Darkness is over the earth, darkness and rest. Here and there through the broken clouds gleams a star. May it watch over the rest and peace of the dwellers in Trifleton House.

XIII.

TRIFLETON HOUSE,
As the Indian Summer advances.

THE storms, for a season, have ceased, and the serene and beautiful days pass on. Let those who will, talk of the Spring, — the balmy Spring I believe it is called, — (are there any East winds in Spring time?) but Trifle is content with the Fall. It is quite in keeping with his nature. It is a season of decay, and sadness, if you please, but with what a glory it is crowned! Sunlight shines upon the hills — a token of promise. Now suggests Hereafter. The nights are longer and the winds are chiller, but the days are clothed with a beauty that is persuasive and suggestive. It is touching as the grace and tenderness of a farewell, and seems to say, "I am lingering while I may, because I know I must pass. But it will be but for a season. The bright days will come again. There is a Death, but there is also a Resurrection."

But — of Prig! It is all over with him. Yes, my Editor, it is over. Tell every body you meet, "it is over!" Inform the world. Wherever your paper is read, — through the length and breadth of our country — on the 'change and at the hearthstone — by the land and over the seas — by mail and by telegraph — by words written and spoken, convey the intelligence, the — glad intelligence, "it is over" with Prig.

He lives!!

He rallied as rapidly as he declined.

Politics are to be forgotten. Who shall be elected Governor, is of small consequence. A more important thing is to rejoice with Pat.

If you could see her, you would forget everything else — and every body; even *Mrs.* Editor, and all the embryo Editors, for a season. Why should you not? She is excellent among women. She is, in fact a — woman.

She loves Prig more than ever. Why? He has made her suffer.

Hark! — and hold your breath. Water was forming on his brain. They said so — the Doctors. He was to die. *They* said so.

Pink was sitting by him in despondency. She was touched to the quick, and I detected her heart. It seems she has one. I was, somehow, cool and experimental. Prig lay with his eyes wide open. I waved my hand before them. He made no sign. I lifted his arm, and dropped it. It felt like lead. I turned his head this side. He did not move. — That. The result was the same. There was no sign of life. I gave him up — *almost.*

It was then that Pat. came to me. With moist eyes and a trembling voice, and, withal, very incoherently, she asked me if I had "any objections" to sending for a minister and having him "*baptized.*" I had opposed it previously because I don't like squalling *babies* in church. I wished to wait till he was a *boy.* She had known me six years, and yet she asked this question. You have known me four. Are you not surprised?

The minister came. My mother and my sister hurried from town; my sister's husband and my brother's wife. The last mentioned, indeed, has been full of kindness and sympathy from the first moment of Prig's illness, and has insured, forever, Pat.'s gratitude and mine.

She could quite appreciate our feelings, for she has lost a boy of her own, her first born.

Friends came and neighbors. How and why, I know not. But they stole in like shadows, and as I looked on them, and they on me, I noticed that their eyes fell. The women among them turned away their faces, and I could hear their sobs.

Stubs stood like a guardian angel at the door, and Pink sat by the bedside holding the hand of Pat. in her own. *He* would scarcely have known her. She looked like one who had been chastened and subdued — who had struggled with herself, and, at least for the time, conquered. A little sick child that she loved had done more for her than Stubs and all the rest of the world. He had made her think, and feel.

Last of all came in the servants — our own, and those of our neighbors who had played with the boy at intervals, and had become interested in him and attached to him. It was current that he was to die in a few brief hours, and they came, partially from curiosity I presume. They were, most of them, strangers to us, but they were, all of them, in tears.

Prig lay with his eyes wide open, but he could not see, nor hear, nor speak, nor feel. He was like one dead, except for the feeblest and faintest beating of his pulse. He didn't move, and he couldn't.

"Let us pray!" said the minister.

He prayed.

I stood erect, with my eyes fixed on my child. I looked upon him as long as I could see. The minister prayed, but I was talking all the time with some one who was not there, and yet was there.

" The offering is a poor one ; such a mere fragment of his life. It is too late."

" He will die, then, you think ? "

" He will."

" Are you willing ? "

" I believe I am."

" You are changed then. You were disposed to rebel not many hours since."

" It is true. But I have been able to see that 'whomsoever the Lord loveth He chasteneth.' It makes me happy to think the Lord loves me."

" How have you been brought to this way of thinking ? You evidently did not seek it yourself ; besides, you love your boy."

" I know it ; and my heart is bleeding even now ; still I defer to His will. He knows best what is for my happiness and good."

" This is no answer to the inquiry, '*why* do you think and feel thus ? ' "

" I cannot tell. If I did not, my heart would break. I want to feel so — and try to."

" Why ? "

" Oh ! how I am perplexed and tried ! Because it is my duty."

" Why ? "

" Because God created all things ; me and mine with the rest ; and all things are inferior to Him and dependent on Him."

"Is duty, then, so important?"

"Yes! Duty perfectly accomplished makes perfect happiness; and exactly in the proportion of duty accomplished is the happiness of man, be it less or more."

"How do you know?"

"By experience."

"Your child may rally."

"I think not."

"Still he may."

"I see no reason for expecting it."

"But God may. You saw no reason for his becoming sick. You are, you perceive, far more weak and insignificant than you supposed. Very little has occurred as you would have it. But God knows better than you what is for your good, as you have admitted. He disciplines His children, but He loves them also. He has brought your boy to the edge of the grave, but He can return him to you. Yet remember! Never consider him yours again. You have given him up — in every sense, given him up."

The prayer was over. I had heard every word, and felt it even while I was carrying on the conversation above recorded.

The holy rite was then administered, and as the words, "I baptize this child," &c., were uttered — "in the name of the Father and the Son and the Holy Ghost" — you could have heard a pin drop.

Palpably to all, there was a *presence* in that room, unseen, but none the less appreciable.

And we gave him up forever and forever.

The ceremony was over. Those who had come to

witness it, gradually departed, as noiselessly as they came. I said, I believe, that they stole in like shadows. They went out like beams and rays; — with a glow on their faces.

It was but a little sick boy, after all.

True, but he had an immortal spirit, and he was about to depart with the angels. The angels had come to meet him, and, evidently, all believed they were there. They bore him —— *not* away.

The hours passed on. I took no note of them. All was quiet and peaceful at Trifleton House. I looked out upon the sea. Its great heart was beating regularly and slowly and calmly. There was peace on the sea.

I looked forth upon the hills. They were robed in the same attire, nearly, as was so beautifully described by you, my dear friend, in your last letter. Not a leaf stirred upon the trees. The afternoon sunshine lingered and played amid their branches. There was peace on the hills.

I looked in upon my heart. The sharpness of my grief was over. I had met it face to face, measured it, drooped under it — well nigh broken; but now —

There was peace in my heart.

From the sheer force of habit, I went to Prig's bedside, and, leaning down close to him, I said, as I had said a hundred times during his sickness, and got no answer, "Do you love your Papa?"

I listened, but expected no reply from those chill, clammy lips. Faintly, faintly, but oh! how softly and sweetly, he whispered —

"Ye-e-es."

I have heard birds sing, and Jenny Lind warble. I have listened to the accents of friendship and the promises of love; but I never heard music like the music of that one little word, "Yes." It thrilled through and through me, and made my heart leap, and my pulses quiver. He could speak, and had his reason! — And the angels of Hope and Gratitude came and "supped" with me, and "took up their abode" with me.

From that moment he began to mend. As is always the case with children, he came up as fast as he went down, and, at this present writing, he is quite well, quite himself, except that he is a little thin.

The doctors say it is almost a miracle, and that we must be extremely careful of him. All of which is very well, but, — he is in better hands.

Let us live more humbly, my Editor. Let us have done with pride and haughtiness, and all such things! Let us be simple-minded, sincere and earnest in all good thoughts, words and actions. Let us think better of humanity, and reflect that there are many in all ranks and stations of life who love us, but are too timid or artificial to be demonstrative except when their sympathies are provoked by seeing us in affliction!

Most of all, let us believe, and act, hereafter, upon the principle that people of low degree — even our servants — are not to be despised; but that they feel as keenly and tenderly and as affectionately as we, whom adventitious circumstances have placed above them; — as we, who have been better cultured; — as we, who have more blessings without, oftentimes, appreciating their source, — as we, who must respond in proportion as we are endowed; — as we, who think and talk of "society," and "our set," and spend much of our time in "growling" because we are not "better off;" — as we, who are apt to think we are burdened by cares and anxieties beyond account, and that our case is peculiarly a hard one!

Could we but run our brief career without so many murmurs, how much more nearly should we approach him who suffered as never man suffered — spake as "never man spake."

Think of it! Think of it!

XIV.

THE ARM-CHAIR,
Under the Clouds.

WE rejoice with you, happy Trifle, that your boy is spared to you,—that the hour of darkness and doubt, of dread and despair, is past, and that the sunlight of hope and joy has come to you,—ay, that the rebellious spirit is become meek, and rejoices humbly in the sunlight.

Clouds are over the earth. Dampness is in the valleys, and over the hill-tops the mist hangs heavily. The wind with fitful breath rustles the fading leaves, and one by one they slowly fall into their damp, cold grave. The autumnal flowers look sad under the shadows and amid the decay of summer's beauties. The harvest is gathered, and the fields look desolate. Gloom gathers over all, and darkness comes on early, the starless, murky night. Happy we, if the hearth-stone is bright, and cheerfulness beams out from sunny hearts. Alas! how many hearts are shadowed by heavier clouds and murkier gloom than that which darkens the earth. Those whom we met this day,—how many were free from the clouds of sorrow, sin, or remorse? He who went bustling by to drive a 'thriving trade,' was not care and anxious throught in his brain? She who smiled sweetly as she displayed the costly fabric from Hovey's or Stewart's, wrought into fashion's latest conception, was there not an uneasiness about her heart, a fear, a regret? — envy, and bitter hate, perhaps? He, the man of reputed piety and worth, were there no misgivings in *his* heart? May there not have been there the deep shadow of unknown sin? And they whose goodness none may doubt, in their true humility, were there no inward struggles and sorrowful regrets for them? But not for us is it to read our fellow-mortals' hearts.

Clouds are over the heart of Bel Hard. A few years ago she was a light-hearted girl, in whom nature was ever expressive. But 'education' smothered nature, chilled the warm springs of generous affection, and made her the creature of pride and fashion. Ductile in the hands of her managing mother, she has been a mere machine for the display of wealth and the performance of folly's masquerade. The return of an old playmate, the remembrance of those sweeter joys of unfrozen youth, the influence of his noble nature, had softened the ice. The sunlight shone in upon her heart, forgotten dreams returned, hope began to beam, and love, scarce recognized, found a secret dwelling-place there. The change was sudden, and the heart, thus bursting from chains and frosts, was all undisciplined. A few words had raised there a dark and angry spirit, and there are clouds of doubt, and fear, and jealous dread, over her heart. She seeks relief in her old routine of hollow pleasure, but it is not there. She may seek to resume the apathy of her recent life, or even its *ennui*, but it is too late; for the time being, at least, the discontented spirit rules, and the clouds will not depart.

Over the heart of Umber, too, are clouds. In his long sojourn abroad, the remembrance of his old playmate never yielded to more recent impressions. He had returned to find her changed; but underneath the acquired habits and coldness and follies of fashion, he had discerned the existence — faint and struggling — of a heart, and natural, generous sympathies. But ere he dared attempt to cherish these into stronger life, ere he dared hope what most he desired to hope, a word had separated them. And now he felt the difference of their positions. She was wealthy, and he was penniless; and here, in the land of democracy and equality, to be penniless was to be worthless, friendless, hopeless. Clouds might well overhang his heart for a time, but in his art he shall find sunshine to dispel them, and riches in his mind which gold and silver and bank-notes, stocks and real estate, can never buy, or borrow, or rival, except in the estimation of — nearly the whole world. Well, if the world *will* think so, — that dollars and cents and treasures that rust and corrupt are better than the treasures, rich, but immaterial and unvalued, which last and grow forever and ever, — why, let it; Umber, possibly Trifle, shall not care, save now and then when the world is insolent in its opinion.

There has been, of late, a new guest at the Hard mansion, the *Hon.* Mr. Weed from the South, a man of money and — nothing else, save some vices, perhaps. Not having his history and pedigree, we cannot say how he acquired his *title.* But mysterious orders have suddenly made great men out of even less material; and men who delight in the vocabulary of Billingsgate, to say nothing of jockey parsons and other rogues, have the term *Hon.* prefixed to their names. So, why not the Hon. Mr. Weed? He saw Bel at Newport, and he concluded that she should be the future Mrs. Weed; but among the "matches" at the fashionable watering-place, he was not so prominent as to stand foremost in Madame Hard's list. He had that however, on which he could rely for ultimate success somewhere, even if his pride should be mortified by one refusal. But Bel would best grace his establishment, and Bel at home might find no greater attraction than himself—or his wealth. So he spends a month and much money in Boston, going daily to the Mansion, riding with Bel and ingratiating himself with Madame Hard. And so Umber daily feels that he is poor, and of no account in the world.

Yet is he not forgotten at the Mansion. O, no! Bel — but no matter. Madame Hard mentions a young artist, just from Rome, whom she would recommend to her friends. We were present when he was named to the Hon. Mr. Weed. The Hon. Mr. Weed thinks he "must patronize him." He even desires that this artist may be permitted to paint Bel's portrait, "if he is competent." Bel's portrait for the Hon. Mr. Weed! Madame thinks that very promising. What an excellent man, too, to patronize so willingly the poor artist. It must be done.

But Bel objects. In her heart she feels she cannot trust herself near that easel, yet she desires it. Madame intercedes. The Hon. Mr. Weed "begs this great favor, which will be most highly prized." He intimates something about possessing the original, in a rather confused sentence, but perfectly intelligible to Madame, and startling to the heart of Bel — gratifying to her pride. And Bel consents to the portrait, for she feels that a crisis is coming. She consents — and goes to weep. Umber goes not to the Mansion now, and so Madame invites us to introduce the Hon. Mr. Weed, who offers the commission with the air of a patron.

The artist hesitates, — an icy hand seems laid upon his brow, and the blood presses at his heart. Has it come to this? Well, well. It will be a solace to paint that face, though the sittings will be painful. So the Hon. Mr. Weed is informed that Umber is not a portrait painter, but that he will consent to paint *this* picture "for the future husband of his old playmate." The Hon. Mr. Weed is a little staggered at the artist's manner and his language, but he takes refuge in his money and consequent superiority to "such folks." And so, Bel is to sit, after the Rachel season.

Rachel has come, and the *beau monde* is in ecstasies — the *beau monde* and Frenchmen. The latter naturally and properly, the former fashionably and foolishly. Snobs and parvenues with their white kids turn the leaves of Rachel's plays, and are of course able to appreciate and criticize! They may know as much about French as they do Choctaw, but — it is all the same; truly, '*tis* all the same to them. You and we have read Racine, Trifle, but we should find those stately lines and troublesome rhymes quite a new thing as recited by Rachel. But the books, (such books!) like the librettos of operas, may they not make it all easy and intelligible? Of course they do, for do not even the snobs and dandies applaud? *They* can follow the text, blunders and all, appreciate the intonation and expression, and smile approval. The great tragedienne has a fearful ordeal. Paris has grown cold, but if the Yankees approve, what need she care? As for the French classical drama, that will be delightful to those who "can't bear Shakspeare."

Of course the Hards and the Hon. Mr. Weed have taken seats for the season. He displayed his magnificence and presence on the first night, as he waited upon the ladies into the balcony. Very deferential was he to Madame, quite kindly familiar towards Bel, explaining what she knew better than he. He applauded when others did, and Madame smiled approval and looked appreciation. But Bel was silent, undemonstrative, sad. Her eye often wandered from the passionate face and classical *poses* of the tragedienne to an unobtrusive seat, where Umber, the artist, a perfect French scholar, was renewing the pleasure he had felt in Paris. Did she think how, under *his* instruction, she might have enjoyed the performance? Her thoughts wandered, too, manifestly. Was it to the artist's studio, the meetings that must take place, the conversation, the feelings which must come? Or were they with the lump of humanity by her side, whose gold is so much weightier than the artist's worth? And then she smiled a bitter smile, as if she thought how the latter would be punished if——

Ah! the smile vanished as if the thought were hopeless. Verily, we found a better study in this living scene, than in Rachel's impersonation of Corneille's heroine.

A letter from Abel Hard tells us that he is prosecuting his search beyond the Lakes, for Lily — so he calls her — and her father. The place whither he was directed by his poor Newport friend contained them not, and he gets no trace of them; but among English emigrants and at land offices, he makes ceaseless inquiries, anxious and troubled ever. The activity of his life alone preserves the health of mind and body. But when will this mad search end?

But even so do we all — wandering away in search of happiness, or what we foolishly deem such, regardless of what lies close about us, in our daily paths, — the sympathies and affections, which we may discover or awaken and cultivate, and which will yield a hundred-fold of joys. So we wander away to perform imagined duties, forgetful of those humbler ones at home, and ever present, which, if well performed, will bring a richer and surer reward. Ah! Trifle, when shall we learn to live the true life, cultivating our own gardens, rooting out the weeds, cherishing the flowers, and reaping the fruits, grateful for dews and life-giving airs, rejoicing in the clear heavens, and knowing that above the darkest clouds shineth God's Sun forevermore!

XV.

TRIFLETON HOUSE,
In time of Buckwheat Cakes.

YES, *sir!* Buckwheats have come, and Pat. may have the "chivalric" corn cake all to herself now. I have been trying to learn to like it, it is so eternally on our breakfast table. Every morning — no matter how much or how little of any thing else we may have — there looms the everlasting corn cake. But I find I can't quite "go it." I'm not enough like a hen, not sufficiently *hen pecked*, I suppose, to appreciate it. But buckwheats! — Well, I'm of the opinion that they are pretty good — for breakfast. I'm certain, in fact, that I "like 'em;" and you know when Trifle likes anybody or anything, there's no half way about it. He likes or he don't like. It's out and out. There's no "tolerably," or "comparatively well," or "so, so," respecting the matter. It's "yes," or "no." And so it should be with everybody. Diamonds are better than rubies, but the greatest of jewels is sincerity; — unlying, undeceiving sincerity. Commend me to people who've got brains enough to know for themselves what they like, and what they don't, and courage enough to say so.

I tell you, man, I know I like buckwheats, if you must be told. Don't begin your breakfast on 'em.

Don't spoil 'em by eating 'em with your beef steak and fried potatoes, or what not. But wait awhile, and when you're about three-quarters through your breakfast, ring Mary in and give her the word. Now then! — Commencing, as it were, *de novo*, but actually finishing, in point of fact, forget what you have previously eaten, and surrender yourself to buckwheats. Two at a time, small, thick, spongy, light, hot, with plenty of Vermont butter, and the least bit of syrup or refined molasses, with a fresh cup of coffee, (very much sweetened to atone for the molasses,) attack them in a quiet, serene, gentlemanlike way, and tell your Pat., or your Mrs. Editor, or your Mrs. "smart subscriber," that you've read all that Charles Lamb says about "roast pig," a hundred times, but it is not to be believed. It's all fancy, madam! "Roast pig" is nothing, madam, absolutely nothing to buckwheats!

If, then, oh Editor, in spite of all previous warnings, you will come and "see" one of our breakfasts, come and criticize our buckwheats, and discuss — Rachel.

We've seen her once, which is quite enough to satisfy us.

When I say *we've* seen her, I mean Stubs and myself. We went Saturday afternoon, like honest country folks, who can go at no other time. We attracted considerable attention, doubtless, on account of our costume. Mine, I suppose, looked as you might imagine such a shabby, unpolished person as Trifle would naturally wear, and Stubs' about ditto. Why, we got over corn-colored gloves and "genteel" coats some years ago, — before we left town even.

Several young ladies of extremely engaging manners and pleasant little ways, which can only be acquired in town, who were probably *French*, as they talked that exquisitely euphonious tongue exclusively, turned up their "turn up" noses—which, *mirabile dictu*, they all had, excepting one "snub" and another proboscis—at my thick boots and Stubs' long-waisted coat with short tails, as I thought, but this may have been imagination. I ought to remark, perhaps, that we had had the audacity to purchase seats in the same box with them; and it is clear that young ladies of "style" and "breeding," who can talk French, are entitled in public to do as they please. What astounds me now, is our assurance in supposing that we had a right to sit in the same theatre, much less the same box.

I do admire young ladies, particularly in public, they are so winning, so undisguised;—*they show so readily what they are;*—they have so little reserve, which is but a poor, weak, maidenly thing after all.

This coterie of lovely creatures, as I said, talked French, which was evidently intended as a "crusher" to us. We were considerably overwhelmed, as you may conceive. We have had but the slim facilities of Cambridge, under Longfellow, in that delicious language;—have merely *read* the best French authors, in a word.

It is quite true Stubs resided a year in Paris, and I have been an indifferent traveller; but we don't pretend to *talk* French. We consider it quite a feat to speak good English, and indeed we hear very little of that. These fascinating creatures of the feminine gender, who know French, seldom use good English. Why, I could never tell, and it puzzles Stubs, too.

The young ladies who sat near us, I have no doubt, were French; but their language bore little resemblance to the kind one hears in Paris, considered in regard either to its elegance, pronunciation, or even grammar. Still, it was very charming, and I don't know when I have been so much enraptured — astonished I think I may say — as I was in listening to it. I had to listen, you see, because they didn't talk in whispers. I think when Trifle has some daughters, it will be of small consequence whether they learn English or Latin. No, sir; they shall be taught French, and sent to concerts, operas, theatres, and so on. For why should they know it, if they are never to exhibit it, I pray to know.

One thing I could not help observing. These sweet young ladies astonishingly resembled certain men we know in town. In fact, I could almost swear that I knew their *Pas* — worthy tradesmen in the great city. Possibly I could asseverate that I had seen them in company with their Pas, in the street and elsewhere; but in this I am probably mistaken. They were incontestably French. Their excessive politeness and "style" proved that.

Amid the conversation of these stupendously accomplished creatures, (French is the greatest of achievements!) we caught, occasionally, a little of Rachel. I wouldn't have you suppose, for a moment, that we caught much. How could we, bewildered thus by beauty and accomplishment, in the closest proximity; — crowded by it, and overwhelmed by it, I might say?

The play was Adrienne Lecouvreur. We were,

in plain *English*, disappointed. We were constantly waiting for something which did not come. We are told, however, that this play does n't call into requisition Rachel's distinguishing traits to any extent; — that it is only in the fourth and fifth acts that she indicates her power.

It is very possible; but we are satisfied that a capital prerequisite to appreciating her is an entire familiarity with the language. Hence the ecstasy of the French ladies who sat with us. They thought it was "splendid." It seems they could talk a little English.

We should wish to see Rachel in a different play before passing our judgment upon her, though we remember how fascinated we were with even Miss Davenport in the translation of the same play — from beginning to end.

Pink was considerably indignant at our being disappointed, and with a sweet serenity remarked that it was what might be expected from two such "old fogies," for we neither of us were judges of good acting. Perhaps not. But we have seen, often, Booth's Lear — which *we* call acting; and his Sir Giles and his Iago. But we shall never see any such acting again. We have seen, next, Brooke's Othello, and *that* we call acting. We have seen Macready again and again, and after Booth and Brooke we call *him* an actor. His Virginius is by no means despicable, and his Hamlet will quite do. We call the elder Vandenhoff in Coriolanus and Brutus, too, "some pumpkins." Forrest, indeed, though not to our taste generally, is an actor in his William

Tell and his Richelieu. We will say nothing of such players as Anderson, Charles Kean, and so on.

True, we know very little of acting, but we have seen among women, Grisi, Mrs. Charles Kean, Miss Vandenhoff and Miss Cushman, and heard "Mrs. Butler" read. We have also seen Biscaccianti in Lucia, and Miss Davenport and Miss Logan in their respective *rôles*, with once or twice Mrs. Barrow. We might mention Mrs. Barrett, "Miss Dean," and "Mrs. Mowatt," but enough is as good as a feast. We have wasted more time at theatres, and money and patience than we shall again, although it is true, as Pink said, that we know nothing of acting. Our only means of knowing about it has been in witnessing it and studying it to a moderate extent — but we are quite done with it. It amounts to very little, after all. What is it compared with *oratory*, that first of powers, that not only influences men for the time being, but controls them for coming time; touches their springs of action, and, by a quasi magic, converts them into whatever the orator wishes to have them. A great orator is the greatest of human impulses. He indicates, and creates, and impels, and subdues, and conquers. He is likest Divinity, intellectually. He is a marvel to his kind, and an enigma to himself. He cannot quite understand how he moves the masses. It is from a fusion of two principles — incoherent and dissimilar, but still coalescive — human sympathy and human weakness, which are more nearly allied than you think. They feel *with* him so far as he feels as they feel, and yield *to* him insomuch as he is, or as they think he is superior to them. Men, in some respects, — the masses, *i. e.* — are extremely weak; that is, are impressible, whether they will or no; — that is, have no individuality; — that is, exhaust themselves in a hurrah.

Speaking of orators, we have been reading the Memoir lately of S. S. Prentiss of Mississippi, the great orator of the Southwest. We thought "Christie Johnson" was interesting — extremely so, deliciously so; we have been plunging with some curiosity into Amos Lawrence's Diary, &c. We have cut the leaves of "Bayne's Christian Life," which we understand is one of the best books of the age, but we have been intoxicated, held our breath, wondered, laughed, almost cried over the "Memoir of S. S. Prentiss."

You have read often, no doubt, Macaulay's description of the Trial of Warren Hastings, and been bewildered. You have read, probably, March's account of Webster's Speech in reply to Col. Hayne — and like a true son of Massachusetts been touched to the quick; but if you wish your pulses to quiver, and your heart to beat tumultuously, read the account of Prentiss's first speech in Congress, when he was only twenty-nine years old. The galleries were thronged to overflowing. John Quincy Adams and all the great men of the house drew round his chair, and Webster and Clay and Crittenden and Preston, the four greatest orators of America, marched in from the Senate to hear him.

With eagerness and avidity (for the book, edited by his brother, indicates that marvellous eloquence was a family trait,) devour the history of his career. See him at thirty, with a national fame as a lawyer and a statesman, and as a stump orator, influencing and controlling at his command the feelings and opinions of thousands and thousands and thousands of his countrymen. See Webster, and Crittenden, and Clay loving and idolizing him, and the masses of the people absolutely worshipping him, blocking his path as he travelled through the country, and pushing him up higher and higher towards the pinnacle of fame, — and so on through the whole of the first volume and most of the second. And during all this brilliant career, see him writing the tenderest, and sweetest, and most affectionate letters constantly to his mother and sisters at the North, where he was born and whence he emigrated when a boy, indicating that he was in nowise intoxicated, or shaken from his balance, but that his nature was still simple, childlike, generous and incorrupt.

You might suppose my tone and the tone of the book extravagant, and adulatory almost. But it is not. There is ample evidence to substantiate all that is said in regard to him. He was in very truth a great man, — one of the greatest men, in a word, that America has produced; and in character and heart the noblest of the noble. But alas! he died young, — but a little over forty.

If you can, or your "smart subscriber" can read this second volume through without moist eyes, you are very different from Trifle.

In many ways his career was marvellous beyond account, beyond imagination almost. One of Nature's noblemen, he loved everybody better than himself, and towards the latter part of his life his fortune slipped through his fingers, and his health, but not his energies faded rapidly away. He would not yield. He died, as it were, "with harness on." He tried an important law-case while he had one foot in the grave, and with his soul full of love to his poor heart-broken wife and children — and to his mother and sisters, whose idol he was — he passed away from this relentless world.

Oh, it is a story full of interest and tears! All beautiful things fade, all garnered hopes are lost, all delights perish — *here.*

I never knew Mr. Prentiss, never heard him speak, never saw him. I have been influenced in writing thus about him, simply from reading the book of Memoirs. I call it one of the most intensely interesting books I ever read.

XVI.

THE ARM-CHAIR,
In November.

FROM doubtful satisfaction with Rachel, uncultivated Trifle, you turn to loud praises of Sergeant S. Prentiss. Well, perhaps you may be right. But a year ago, before you essayed rural life, would you not have followed the fashionable column into the theatre with plaudits for the great tragedienne? Now, forsooth, because you have lived six months in the country, and have there taken up your abode — for just so long as you shall be contented — you assume to be like Stubs and other country folk, and go to the theatre when Rachel is here, with thick boots and unfashionable clothes. How could you expect not to disgust and annoy young ladies of *haut ton*? Is it not a serious offence to thrust yourselves, as you and Stubs did, into such company, in such garb? How could you expect, when so dressed and entirely devoid of fashionable airs, to appreciate and admire the great French artiste?

The annoyance of such highly educated and cultivated young ladies, whom in your ignorance you took to be French, it seems was well repaid by the sense of inferiority which they produced in you. If it be any consolation to you, be assured that you and Stubs are not the only persons who have been so impressed by the presence and high breeding of charmingly dressed young ladies, delighted with Rachel. Many sufferers can condole with you.

But you dismiss Rachel quite too cavalierly. Notwithstanding all the draw-backs and disadvantages, — notwithstanding the farce played to perfection in the auditorium, you might have seen a little of the tragedy on the stage, and acknowledged something of Rachel's merits as the greatest tragedienne of the age, — as the consummate artiste, who can give the most touching and the most terrible expression to passion and all the emotions of the human heart. You might have felt her power, or at least seen her look, her bearing, and her "making up" which the French ladies, and the shallow-pated dandies, even, so warmly applaud. But alas! for Trifle, — he has buried his taste and his fashion in the garden of Trifleton House, to fertilize the soil for his tomatoes.

You extol oratory as "the first of powers," and the orator as "likest divinity, intellectually." Were it worth while to dispute about the matter, and were we able, as doubtless Stubs is, we might join issue with you on that proposition. But the praises which you chant to oratory, and the enthusiastic encomiums which you bestow upon Prentiss — the justice of which we neither admit nor deny — come with such fervency, that manifestly you are to be convinced only against your will. We have no desire to make Trifle dissatisfied with himself, but we can't quite agree with him, even in the matter of "corn bread" and "buckwheats," — nor of oratory.

What is oratory except a mode of expression? It is not an intellectual power, but a power derived or resulting from an adaptation of the physical powers to the intellectual. Eloquence is not simply and merely oratory, for the man who has none of the physical gifts of the orator may write words of the most touching and stirring eloquence. Moreover the power of oratory is transitory and limited. It moves, impels, excites, thrills and astonishes those brought directly under its influence; and this for a time only, for it is soon like a mere echo to those who have listened, and its influence diminishes and dies out as the echo recedes. The eloquence of the thought and language, however, may remain, entirely distinct from the oratory.

If you mean by oratory that comprehensive union of intellect, utterance and action, language, cultivation and grace, you understand something more — much more — than oratory literally or really is. The utterance, action and grace together with the power — a sort of magnetic telegraph — by which these are connected with and controlled by the intellect, are all that belong peculiarly to the orator; the other and greater powers or gifts are held in common by orator, poet and philosopher.

The orator's only lasting and real power, therefore, is in that which he possesses in common with other men of genius or talent, the intellect. But the powers of intellect manifested by oratory, all powerful and exciting though they may be on those brought directly under its influence, by the senses of hearing and sight, produce not so lasting or so general impressions as they may when expressed in other modes. The oratory of Demosthenes is a mere tradition. His eloquence, which, as we have said, is more than oratory, is not felt now. But the tragedies of Sophocles or Euripides are still potent in their influences, exciting the same emotions, nearly, that they did in the minds of the Greeks, astounding by their power, and delighting by their beauty. So the still more ancient epics of Homer live, and influence, and affect the reader beyond all the oratory or eloquence of Demosthenes, or Æschines, or Pericles.

What orator, in the time of Shakspeare, before or after, has so influenced the minds and feelings of men as the great bard? — has excited such deep emotions, has produced such lasting impressions on the human mind, has so led the heart captive? — or will live so long as a great master over human passions? Sheridan, a splendid orator, is better known now as a dramatist than as an orator, though by no means in fact so extraordinary in his dramas as in his oratory.

No, the poet in his closet may send forth words more potent and more enduring in their power than the greatest orator. The power of the orator seems greater because it is exerted on numbers simultaneously, and the effect of his influence is manifested to a certain extent by a sympathy in his audience, whereby they act upon each other, or by which he intensifies his influence for the time being. The poet, through his written eloquence, touches, arouses, moves, one at a time, separately, a wider circle. Were there any other means, besides the voice, of reaching the hearts of men simultaneously, of conveying the same ideas and producing the same emotions at the same time, the power of the great poet would be even more manifest by the enthusiasm, the excitement, the tears of those brought into the magic circle, than that of the orator.

Moreover, the powers of the orator are generally addressed to transitory subjects. State policy, political events, topics of temporary or local interest, for the most part, are subjects which call forth the powers of the best orators of any nation or age. Even pulpit oratory, which has the advantage that it *may* dwell upon the immortal truths of religion, often makes its greatest and most striking displays on subjects of minor consequence, but haply of more exciting present interest. So we may see that, after all, oratory owes not a little of its power and influence to the interest of the subject-matter and the excitement of the auditory. The speeches of Kossuth, for instance, owed their enthusiastic response to sympathy with his cause, felt by the delighted and deeply moved audiences.

Of Prentiss, whom you so highly — perhaps justly — extol, we cannot presume to speak. We know how his eloquence thrilled, and moved, and influenced those who were brought under its magic spell, — that he was, in truth, an orator gifted in some respects beyond most other men. But is it not true that even his eloquence has died away into a faint echo in the memories of those who heard him? And now its influence on you, is it not as much through the eloquent affection of a brother who describes the triumphs of the orator.

But enough of this. Thank yourself, most provoking Trifle, for thus leading us off into an essay on oratory, which after all is only the result of "kissing the Blarney stone." Who knows that we, or Trifle or Stubs might not become orators, gifted as we are, had we but the good fortune to salute that wondrous geological specimen.

You are an admirer of the genius of De Quincey, and have doubtless delighted often over the pages of the Opium Eater. But have you read "Klosterheim," recently republished? It is said that the author considers it a *juvenile* effort, but it was written some ten years after the "Confessions," and in the full maturity of his powers. It is not altogether such a book as one might expect from De Quincey in an extended work of fiction, and belongs to the class of novels now out of date. It is a work of passion, mystery and terror, of secret passages and mysterious assassinations, the whole machinery of which impressed with superstitious awe the minds of the actors in the story, although it is all explained and unravelled in a very natural and reasonable way. The author delights in the *appearance* of the supernatural by a mysterious development of the real and actual, and while the reader feels the force of the circumstances which to a superstitious people might seem something more than human and natural, yet he is assured that the line of probability is not overstepped.

The scene selected for the story is in Germany, and the period during the Thirty Years' War; time and place, you will admit, affording ample opportunity for the novelist, and especially for one disposed to write in this particular vein. The characters are such as would be likely to be thrown upon the stage during the continuance of such a war, — men and women who could act in a terrible drama. Some of them are developed with striking personality, but others are like shadows stalking across the scene. The book is written for the most part in the clear, rich and captivating style of the author, who is called the best master of the English language. It is, indeed, free from some of the defects of most of his narrative writings, and the reader is not often led off into digressions from the story, which, however agreeable in an essay or simple narrative, would be a serious drawback in a novel. It is a story of great dramatic power, and abounds in " scenes " of a striking character.

"Klosterheim" is not a book to be written at this day; and if now first published by an author of less eminence than De Quincey, would find readers only among that class who delight in the supernatural and extravagant; notwithstanding its literary and artistic merits. But it is a book which will be re-read because De Quincey wrote it. And so we will place it beside the Opium Eater's other works, that it may complete that varied, and in some respects wonderful collection of writings, and show what he could do — rather what he *did*, in his only attempt at an extended story. Pray you, read " Klosterheim."

November! Look you, Trifle, how time goes apace. It is in November, and the year is getting into its dotage, — sinking into a lethargy, and waking up only from its long naps to short and cloudy days. The short days may be an excuse to Umber for the slow progress of Bel Hard's picture. After Rachel's first week it was begun — that is, the canvas was put upon the easel, and Bel had a sitting. The Hon. Mr. Weed was there, so it was a chilly, November day, and it was all over for that time. But — they met again.

Yes, — it is November, the month of fogs — and suicides by the Thames and the Seine — thank Heaven, not very generally, here. Why should the mists that fill the valleys and shroud the hills create fogs in men's brains, and so darken their way that they must needs step over the brink into the ocean of eternity? Can the philosophic Trifle solve us that? November in the heart is more dismal than the November of the year. Alas, that there should be a perpetual November in some hearts! Yet can we wonder that from a perpetual November aching human hearts should sometimes seek relief? Thank God, Trifle, that the dismal fogs hang not about your life and your heart.

We don't mind November. That is, we don't *always* "knock under" to it, and feel grouty, and have the blues. We didn't when, some years ago, we scribbled the following lines, and unlike the politicians, we subscribe to the same sentiments still.

There's pleasure in the rainy night,
  The dark November night,
As the drops come pattering on the pane
  With footsteps quick and light

And I sit musing quietly
By my hearthstone warm and bright.

The leaves are withered, crisp and dead,
On the yellow ground they lie, —
The clouds are stooping down to weep
Their loss right grievously,
And the night wind o'er the robeless bough
Heaveth a mournful sigh.

But though 'tis starless gloom without,
'Tis bright and warm within,
And my heart is light as if it knew
No sorrow, doubt or sin,
Or as if the watcher, conscience,
Could not come peering in.

A night for fond remembrances!
My friends, I greet *you* here;
I see you sitting by my side,
Each face well known and dear;
A smile is wreathed round every lip,
Bedims no eye a tear.

Our days have lightly flown since last
We parted years ago;
We've culled full many a blossom
In its beauty's brightest glow,
And we've quaffed from many a fountain
Where sparkling pleasures flow.

Then let us all be merry now,
Though the clouds without do weep,
And o'er the leafless boughs the winds
Sigh mournfully and deep, —
Our thoughts are amaranthine leaves,
That know not death's cold sleep.

We'll gather them about us now,
  To tell of days gone by,
And twining wreaths we'll bid the hours
  Fly as they erst did fly,
While we heed not the sad cloud's tears,
  Nor the sorrowing wind's low sigh.

XVII.

TRIFLETON HOUSE,
In November.

PRIG IS in town, with his grandma and grandpa, (of whom more anon,) and we are in — *November.* There's no doubt about it. It's the genuine and the veritable — there's no mistaking it; it's *the* month, of — *November;* and Tom Hood will tell you all about November, if you don't know already. I've no doubt the sunshine would seem very pleasant once more. Have you faith to believe it will come? — What do you think now, with this leaden sky — this drizzle, fog, mud? Do you discover any promise in these dingy mornings and starless nights? If it's a fair question, do you consider it likely the sun will ever shine again?

Don't despair, my Editor! It's dubious enough, but

"Some days must be dark and dreary."

We've had an arrival and a departure. *Ellen* has come — with the best of recommendations; and *Mary* has gone — with our best wishes for her happiness. It was not an abrupt departure. It was a thing understood and inevitable. She has no objection to serving at Trifleton House, but she is looking forward to reigning in her own. She would be queen where Robert is king.

She was one of Prig's earliest friends, and has been, ever, one of his most faithful. Many a weary night has she watched over him, with Pat., when he has been sick, in times past. When we have had sorrows she has grieved for us and with us; and when we have had joys she has cordially rejoiced. And you are requested to inform the world through the columns of your valuable paper, that Pat. has promised to attend her wedding, and that I have serious thoughts of bewildering her with some spoons.

It's very natural, I'm willing to admit, that you should be anxious to hear more about our baby. But then there's no occasion for your so bursting with curiosity in regard to it. You're very deep, very deep indeed, to say nothing upon the subject. But I understand it. It's a sly game to draw me out, sir, and I would resent it — I would foil you at your own weapons, and be "mum," were it not that "there never was such a baby!" Quotation marks, you perceive. The words are Pat.'s. Unless I'm mistaken, she has thus remarked to me *more than once*. I've done what I could for *you*. I have said repeatedly, "Mr. and Mrs. Editor have got a baby as well as we, and they think "there never was such a baby" as theirs. Pat.'s exact words have always been in reply — if, as a veracious historian, I must recount facts — "Well, Trifle, let them think so. It can do no harm. All I can say is, I *know* 'there never was such a baby' as ours." And, in addition to this, she is of the opinion that he is "a lamb." She says, a hundred times a day to him, "you sweet lamb; — you pet lamb, you!" She has had no means of knowing whether I concurred in this opinion, and so she asked me a few days since, in rather a sheepish way:

"Don't you think he's a perfect lamb, Trifle?"

"Yes, Pat., I think he is. I'm reminded of his lamb-like qualities about a dozen times every night, when he cries so sweetly that the idea of one's going to sleep is quite out of the question."

"Well," said she, with a fling of her head, "I like to see a 'wide awake boy.'"

"Oh, you do," I observed, astonished at this brilliant remark from Pat., as you may readily conceive. "Has Pink been here to-day?"

"Yes, Trifle, and she said, *too*, that there was nothing like having "a wide awake boy."

"Why, how queer!"

"So I think; but I was telling her, you know, that we thought the baby cried, considerably, nights."

"Oh! — and so she thinks just as you do about it. Well, that's clever."

I think, my hungry Editor, that you would better come and try the *preserves*, for who is (or are) to eat them, unless it be the coming generations, I'm at a loss to know. Why, sir, Pat. has the morbidest passion for *preserving*. There's nothing she hasn't preserved, and nothing she won't preserve. She intends to preserve this correspondence, even.

I think I informed you in regard to the tomatoes. Well, sir, it was the same with the grapes. The indifferent bunches Pat. bribed a small boy to pluck for our table; but upon one vine, in particular, hung high and tempting a peck or two, as I should "reckon," (to use one of Pat.'s elegant words,) of as fine, large, handsome grapes as you ever saw. I said to myself, "I will let these ripen well, and then I will send them to the Editor. He and Mrs. Editor will be pleased, and (you perceive my cunning) he will write most gorgeous accounts of them in his paper, and thus the fame of the Trifleton grapes will extend throughout the world.

Day after day I watched them — eagerly, proudly watched them, till, on a certain occasion, I found the vine entirely stripped. It was as naked of grapes as young ladies past twenty-five are of hopes of conquest and marriage. It turned out that the small boy had earned another quarter, and Pat. had been all day engaged in *preserving*.

And so with the quinces. I aimed at drawing a prize at some horticultural fair with them. But they shared the same fate. I was permitted to gaze at them after they were "done." But only for a moment. They are now buried in relentless jars, and hid away in our cellar, to grow hard and mouldy for the coming generations.

Not only did our fall pears go the same way, but Pat. said they were "too few." Hence we purchased more in order to have "enough." And we've got enough, I assure you.

I'm aware that there is a necessity for your paper's going all over the world; but I think it would be well to withhold the issue which shall contain this letter — from the Crimea. I want no Russian army at my doors in search of supplies. It is pleasant for me to reflect that posterity will pass judgment on Pat.'s preserves.

It would be entirely useless to attempt to tell you of the pickles. From minutest cucumbers up, and immense mangoes down to —— I can't tell what, we have "enough" — for a host; and therefore I will let them pass.

It seems Pink has informed Pat. of a conversation she has recently had with Stubs, which is of such a character that, as a chronicler of important events, I feel bound to communicate it. Pink narrated it to Pat. under the injunction of strict secrecy, which is, doubtless, her reason for having imparted it to me; — for they do say, (or used to, in town,) that a secret burns in a woman's keeping, as much as a shilling burns in a boy's pocket.

Pink was in the act of reading a letter from *him*. It was an interesting letter, inasmuch as it was an offer of his *hand* — corn-colored gloves and all. It descanted upon her attractions, and hinted at an establishment in the Fifth Avenue, with an equipage, livery, etc. in the winter, and a cottage at Newport in the summer. It abounded in the common-places of devotion and what not, and wound up with an extract from some unknown poet, which, being interpreted, signified that somebody was very wretched, and would continue to be so unless somebody came to the rescue. In a word, the letter was touching to a degree, except that there was no heart in it, as Pink readily observed. Like a true woman she felt hurt and insulted. Stubs entered the room, and found her flushed and excited. He was himself pale, fidgetty, and evidently off his guard. He didn't perceive that his visit was inopportune. He began, abruptly, as he always does —

"Pink, I am going away from home soon, as you know, and I want to talk with you seriously."

"You are always talking seriously. What do you wish to say? Has any thing new occurred?"

"No, but I am about to leave you for some time. I am perplexed and anxious. I need your sympathy, affection — love."

"Well!"

"Upon certain conditions, that is."

"Such as ——"

"That you will meet me with your real nature, and promise me ——"

"What?"

"Nothing if you choose to adopt this tone."

"You are critical to-day, as, indeed, when are you not? But I am not bound to please you."

He was hurt at this remark, but continued,

"You can please me when you try to."

"I can please many without trying." (Proudly.)

"True. Everybody admires you that sees you, but they do not see your faults. I admire everything about you but your faults."

"Indeed! You are quick to perceive faults. — Have you none of your own?"

"Many, but I strive to conquer them. When I fail, nobody deplores it more bitterly than myself. Life is a discipline, and character a struggle. Paul and David were true men, but they accomplished a great victory by conflict with themselves."

"What is the point of this preaching?"

"The point is simply this. You know how tenderly I love you when you are yourself. Will you promise me to be yourself — to have done with all that is not simple and natural — to be, as you are capable of being, a true and genuine woman? For my sake, will you do this? I have asked you often before. I have told you my views of life again and again. You have conformed to them, and then acted in opposition to them; — made me happy and made me wretched. I believe you love me, and I am ready to devote my whole existence to you: but I must tell you once more, and I hope for the last time, that I love you more for what I think you are capable of being, rather than for what you are now. During Prig's illness you seemed lovely beyond account, and I wore you in my heart of hearts. Why can you not be always thus? Why persist in causing those who love you best to make your life and your opinions the subject of continued criticism? — Why unsay to-day what you said yesterday: — appear to-day full of feeling, generosity, and nobleness of nature, and to-morrow giddy, frivolous, heartless almost! Why contradict yourself constantly and forever?"

She heard him through. As I have said, she was in no mood to be talked to in such a manner; and completely losing her self-control, she rose from her seat, and, with a flashing eye, said,

"When I need your instructions, I will ask for them. When you need my sympathy, you can ask for it in fit terms. My affection you never had, and never can have. It is already engaged. Your affection you can bestow where it will be appreciated;

but when you find the woman who attaches the same value to it that your own conceit does, you will find a person whom you are authorized to address in such a manner, and in such language, as you cannot afford to address to me ;" — and then swept out of the room.

Thus it was they parted.

So she told it to Pat., and so Pat. told it to me. And said Pat., moreover,

" After she told me, poor girl, she cried as if her heart would break, which I can't quite understand, as, true it is, that immediately after leaving Stubs, (which I forgot to mention before,) she rushed to her room, and dashed off a letter accepting the offer of the house in the Fifth Avenue and the cottage at Newport."

I have always supposed before that an *engagement* was a subject for congratulation and rejoicing — not tears. However, I have been directed to say never a word about it to Pink, and therefore I do not. But if a house in the Fifth Avenue, and a cottage at Newport, and a husband with corn-colored gloves be not enough to make a woman happy, for goodness sake what is?

" I will teach him who I am. I will sweep by him in a carriage such as his whole fortune cannot buy. I'm glad his property is involved in a lawsuit. I hope he will lose it all. I detest him, and hate him."

All this she said, as Pat. informs me, and she told her also that Stubs would be humbled to the dust, and she would be elevated herself to the front rank in York society.

Stubs has left us, and will probably spend most of the winter in Washington City. He left abruptly.

I have been reading Longfellow's new poem, "The Song of Hiawatha." I read it at one sitting — every word of it. But I don't think it will ever be a *popular* poem, in the ordinary acceptation of that word. It hasn't the scope and completeness of his "Evangeline." It is rather a string of Indian legends, which hang well enough together, but which, several of them, would be quite as good and as perfect by themselves. The story underlying them is well told, but not so skilfully as it might be. The fragments of "Hiawatha's" life are somewhat too detached. In a word it don't travel so continuously from its beginning to its close as it might. Its growth is not steady enough. It jumps by fits and starts. However, this is of small consequence, and a more careful reading might satisfy me that my criticism would not apply.

There's a freshness, and gush, and tenderness about this poem that there is in all Longfellow writes. It may not make you wiser to read it, but it will make you better, if you read it through, that is. — There's the same story of life that is everywhere apparent in this sad world; the same toil and struggle, the same sunshine and shade, the same grief and pleasure, the same hope and disappointment, the same death and tears; beautifully depicted in this Indian tale.

To be fully appreciated it should be read out in the woods, of a hot summer's day, under the branches of the forest trees, by the banks of gushing streams, and amid the murmuring of brooks and fountains. As you read it in your study, even, you seem to be listening to the sighing of the pine trees, the voice of falling water, and the music of singing birds — the "Owaisa," the blue bird, and the "Opechee," the robin — and almost fancy you hear the chattering of the squirrel (Adjidaumo), and see the rabbit (Wabasso) leaping and scampering before you.

The rhythm of the poem is very quaint, musical and sweet. In fact, I think, as Pink once said, "Longfellow is painfully sweet and more than sufficiently tender. A little of Tennyson's sourness and snappishness would do him good." But he is always chaste, pure and religious. You will never become worse by reading what he writes, but if you are affected at all, you will be made better. He is not, thank God, of the miserable and detestable school of "Childe Harold" and "Maud."

I wish I had time and room to say more of this poem, and to make some extracts, but I have not. It seems to me, though, to indicate a thorough study and appreciation of Ossian. In "Chibiabos" (the musician), we are reminded of Ovid's "Orpheus;" and in the story of "Osseo" and "Oweenee," we have Ovid's exquisite "Philemon and Baucis" in some sense reproduced.

I shall put this poem where you cannot find "Maud" — in my library; — and some of these days, under the Trifleton trees, I shall take my afternoon cigar — when the summer comes again — and read or rather sing, its gushing and oftentimes plaintive measures to Prig, whose ear is full of music, and whose soul is full of poetry. I can tell by him whether it be simple and natural. I *know* he will drink in every word of Hiawatha's first hunting expedition, will be absorbed in the story of his wedding tour, and stand dumb with grief at the last words of his beautiful bride, "the dying Minnehaha."

On the whole, I should say the poem is musical and beautiful — "*nothing shorter*" — and, of its kind, admirable. But it is not of a high order. There have been three *poets* in the world, — Shakspeare — Milton — Motherwell."

XVIII.

THE ARM CHAIR,
As Thanksgiving approaches. }

WE are not quite sure, most sapient Trifle, that we shall be able to digest all your remarkable sayings in season for our Thanksgiving dinner. We hardly know which to dispose of first, but the serious and weighty observation that "there have been three poets in the world," has troubled us most, being much like the incubus resulting from a hearty supper.

But "*three poets in the world!*" Shades of Homer and Virgil! of Dante, Petrarch, and Tasso! of Chaucer and Spenser! of Wordsworth and Campbell! of Shelley, and Keats, and Byron! is this to be forgiven! And if *you* forgive it, will the unnamed poets — not few nor nameless — will they all forgive a judgment like that? "Three poets in the world!" Ah, ye living aspirants for a crown on the summit of Parnassus, what shall you do? Three poets in the world, and Motherwell the third. Oh! — we assent. There *have* been *three* poets, Shakspeare, Milton and Motherwell — *and several others.*

But of the Song of Hiawatha. Pray, are you afraid lest you commend too freely? Some there are who think criticism is fault-finding, and value an opinion on a book only as it dissects it and throws it to the dogs. Was it for such reason that you commend with qualifications in your commendations? As you go on, you turn the leaves of the poem, and its beauties beam forth so that you forget your allowances, and speak as the heart feels.

You say it lacks the scope and completeness of Evangeline, which is all true enough, from the very nature of the subject. But because it is "a string of Indian legends," some of which would be as perfect by themselves, does not detract from the merit of the poem as a whole. Its purpose was to collate and idealize a series of such legends, and we think that the poet has given us, in truth, a string of gems. It would not have been difficult for him to have told the story of Hiawatha's life more *skillfully* — that is, a more continuous, detailed story, which should run on from beginning to end smoothly and connectedly. But it would have been necessary to have supplied from the imagination what is wanting in the legends, so that the story would have lost half its interest and its beauty. It was the poet's purpose simply to give us those old legends of the aborigines, in the language of poetry, which is so well adapted to them. Idealizing as the poet should, adorning with his fancy, adapting language to the thought, but making no new story, it seems to us that Mr. Longfellow has admirably accomplished his purpose, and has given us a poem of rare and peculiar beauty. Not without its faults is it; but when we have a feast of good things let us not single out some spice, or sauce, or mode of dressing, which does not exactly suit our taste; — let us rather delight in and be thankful for so much that is pleasant to us.

Now is not the whole of Hiawatha's childhood beautiful? Well may you read it to Prig, for if he is what you say he is, — and parents are never deceived, you know,— he will tell you how the rhythm, and the choice and quaint yet simple language, convey to him the story of the wondrous boy of the Indian legend. He will feel the spirit of the time and place — the wilderness in the age of the hunter — as he hears how sang the Owaissa and the Opechee, "Hiawatha's chickens," and how gamboled the squirrel, rabbit, beaver and deer, "Hiawatha's brothers."

Still more beautiful is "Hiawatha's wooing," wherein he seeks

> "Minnehaha, Laughing Water,
> Loveliest of Dacotah women."

And having wooed as the red man wooed, and won the ancient arrow-maker's daughter, how

> "Pleasant was the journey homeward
> Through interminable forests,"

where everything in nature seemed to smile upon and bless them.

The story of Mondamin — the origin of maize — has been told in verse by Bayard Taylor, but not in a style so adapted to the legend, or so beautiful as this by Longfellow. It is one of the most pleasing of Indian legends, and loses none of its grace in these lines.

One of the most touching portions of the poem is

"The Famine," in which there is a sound of foreboding, of sadness, of sorrowful tenderness — even in the music of the words. We see Hiawatha, heavy-hearted, in the desolate forest seeking hopelessly for food for Minnehaha, and we hear the echoes answering his cry of agony, "Minnehaha, Minnehaha!" And in the desolate wigwam we almost feel the presence of the weird shaaows, that in his absence had crossed the darkened threshold, sitting by the dying Minnehaha. Solemn and sad and low come to us her words, as she passes away

"To the Islands of the Blessed,
To the Kingdom of Ponemah,
To the Land of the Hereafter."

Doubtless, to enjoy this song of Hiawatha, you must yield yourself to the spirit of the legend, and suffer the poet, using the quaint language which the theme suggests to him, to carry you far back into the shadowy Past. Critics who sit themselves down in the present, who measure lines and weigh words by modern standard weights and measures, can no more appreciate the real beauties of Hiawatha, than they could were it chanted in the language of the Dacotahs. It was not written for such, and the music, the spirit, the thought of the song are wasted on them.

It is all very well for you, vainglorious Trifle, to talk about that baby, now that your garden at Trifleton House is desolate, and you have no more tomatoes to praise. But after all, your thoughts seem to dwell as much with those jars of preserves, hid away in the recesses of your cellar — beside those silver-tops, doubtless — as with the little Trifle that disturbs your slumbers. And your praises of this young scion on your family tree, why, they are absolutely *nothing* to those which neighbor Timmins's wife bestows on her child, the very homeliest of plain babies, who was offered for a prize at the baby show. We are not to be scared by such glorification — but it is quite pardonable in you to think we should be. No, sir — we don't believe *all* you say.

Pickles, preserves and babies! Well, Trifle, we should think you might be prepared for Thanksgiving. Thanksgiving, the Pilgrim "institution," the festival of the fireside, around which cluster so many hopes and joys in the *un*fashionable world of New England, is coming. The trees are leafless, the gardens are desolate, the snowflakes, avant-couriers of old winter, are falling lightly on the dry leaves. The out-door pleasures of summer and early autumn are gone, but around the hearth-stone there are new and more genial pleasures, bright, warm, lasting. The harvests are gathered, and are plentiful, notwithstanding high prices deny it; peace is here — albeit the London Times attempted to break it; pestilential airs have not blown hitherwards. For all which, and for the blessings innumerable that have fallen like gentle showers, let there be thanksgivings, — thanksgivings in the highways and by-ways, in unbroken circles from rich to poor. Even in the desolate chamber of pinched poverty, let there be thanksgiving, O, thou fortunate neighbor of the suffering! that there may be truer thanksgiving around thine own hearth. And more than all, let there be thanksgiving in the heart, for bounties and blessings, for mercies and joys,—thanksgiving that shall crown the past, garland the passing hours, and bring serenest slumbers to the pillow. Such be Thanksgiving at Trifleton House.

If your expect us — you and the inquisitive Mrs. Trifle — to "tell all about" the Hards, you must send us a supply of stationery. In the meantime we have only an item or two to mention. And in the first place, Abel Hard has, at last, ended his search. Umber has received a letter from him in which he relates how, by chance, he found that those whom he sought, Lily and her father, had left the land of the prairie to dwell on English soil. Republican airs did not suit the old, but broken down and disheartened aristocrat, so well as the more accustomed fogs of monarchy; so they had gone to Canada West, and on the borders of Lake Erie they had found a home, where he hoped to hide — not to forget — his sorrows, and she hoped — nothing, save to devote herself to the comfort of the parent whom she followed from friends and luxuries and joys, to the hardships of the wilderness. Thus Hard writes:

"I have found her, the dream of years, at last. You remember her beauty at Florence, — that beauty beaming with the light of a pure soul, which entered my heart and dwelt there ever after; it still is hers, only it is more spiritual now, and softened by sadness. That musical voice — you heard it once — which charmed my ear in Italy, with all its well remembered sweetness, but with a tone more touching for the sorrows she has known, greeted me — *welcomed* me to her humble home on the shores of Erie. Welcomed me ; — tones utter more than words, and there was something — it might be gratitude — which gave a tenderness to her salutation.

"Not to have forgotten me was something, but to remember with emotion was more than I had dared to hope. Nay, more than this have I learned, even in so brief an intercourse. My love for her had been to me so old a thing that I forgot 'twas new to her, and abrubtly hinted it — confessed — explained — I know not what. Was it altogether gratitude that received the story with such gentleness and maiden modesty — such looks, such tears ? On a beautiful spot, overlooking the blue waters of Lake Erie, hope beamed upon a love born on the banks of the Arno. But alas! clouds are even here, and disappointment may tread roughly on the heels of hope. Her father's will — more imperious under his misfortunes — is uncertain. The hold which her delicate health, under new scenes and hardships, has upon life, is yet more uncertain."

Thus much we read of Abel Hard's letter in Umber's Studio. On the easel before us was a portrait, not yet finished, but beautiful. It was the face of Bel Hard — not clouded with a look of languor or of discontent or of sorrow, nor cold with the heartlessness of fashion — but her beautiful features lit up with the light of youthful happiness, the expression of her girlhood, long since departed. In short, it was her face idealized by the memory of Umber, to whom her girlhood is an ever present thought, and who had painted her as she *was*, or as she might have been. Umber was slowly and thoughtfully putting a few touches to the picture. He was silent and sad, and as he was manifestly in no mood for conversation, we involuntarily passed off into a reverie on the picture before us. From this we were suddenly startled by the entrance of Madame Hard, Bel, and the Hon. Mr. Weed. What followed we may tell another time.

XIX.

In Town,
Thanksgiving week.

"Bag and baggage, Trifle and Pat., and baby and Kate, with all but Ellen, who is indigenous to the Trifleton House whereabouts, and hates to leave (and whom we have therefore left in charge of the Trifleton forks and spoons), we have come up to town for the Thanksgiving Jubilee. Prig has been here these two weeks, and has become quite "city-fied." I am getting on, myself. I have already visited "the club," and played a few *match* games of billiards by way of recalling old times, and because we "country folks" have a very natural desire to "look around a little," when we visit the great city. I was warmly welcomed with "Trifle, how are you?" and "Why, bless me, Trifle, what a stranger!" and "Glad to see you back my boy!" &c., &c., &c.

I was immediately pressed into a *match* with three of the best players in the club, and there was a most piquant curiosity to see how I would play. You remember, probably, that I used to play what was considered rather a "strong game," and asked no points from anybody.

As I seized my cue, I confess I shared somewhat

the anxiety of my partner, who paid me the compliment of demanding odds from our opponents, on the ground of my being "out of play," — which I refused in the most dignified manner. However, the first time my hand was in, I made a run of thirty-one, "round the table" and "without scratching." I should have made more if the balls hadn't "kissed," (what nuisances these *kisses* are), and my partner began to feel easier. I will "only add," as the young ladies say in their postscript, that the side Trifle was on beat "the rubber."

On going home, I informed Pat. of this instance of tremendous dissipation, and expected a huge "curtain lecture," but was let off without one. As a compensation, I am to take her and Prig to the Museum some Saturday P. M., to witness one of those "*Spectacles*" Kimball is constantly getting up for such simple and untutored "country folks" as we are. Mr. Kimball is a very kind man.

I received this morning the following missive:

"RESPECTED SIR, —

Having been apprized of your arrival in Boston, we are desirous of extending to you the freedom of the city. We would, therefore, take the liberty to ask you, at your earliest convenience, to indicate to us the hour and place most acceptable to you for meeting your fellow-citizens.

Most obsequiously yours,
SEVERAL WIRE PULLERS, AND
SOLID MEN OF BOSTON."

In the absence of Stubs, I asked Pat. what this meant. She said, "Why, that's the way they always do, when distinguished men travel. The wire pullers and the noodles invite them to public dinners, &c., for the sake of extorting a letter out of them, and glorifying themselves. So Mr. Clay used to tell us, long before I knew you. You must write a letter declining the invitation, which will indicate, you know, that, though possibly you may be half crazy about it, you consider it a small matter for a person of your consideration. Make it as pompous and ridiculous as possible, or it will not be apropos and in keeping with what the 'great men' usually do in such circumstances.

The fact is, Mr. Editor, Pat. lived in the atmosphere of Washington too long, and saw too many "great men," not to find them out. Hence her sharpness upon them, I suppose.

With her assistance, I drafted the following letter, which I am about to despatch at once:

"SOLID MEN OF BOSTON :—

GENTLEMEN: Impressed as I am with the conviction that you are solid as solid can be, from head to foot, (if I may use the expression,) I hasten to reply to your favor, offering to me the freedom of your city. I remember how cordially you threw open the doors of Faneuil Hall to the late lamented statesman of the North, on a certain occasion; and how unwilling you were — men, women and children — to take any notice of — to look at, even — the distinguished Mr. Charles Dickens, on his arrival in your midst, so that he was obliged to write a book in order to depict your extreme reserve.

These capital instances, with many others I might mention, show you to be a people capable of great self-respect, simple in your tastes, not likely to run after foreigners, and disposed to appreciate the men in your midst.

The freedom of a city like yours, I need not tell you, I regard as invaluable; but I regret to say that I shall not have time to attend to the receiving it from your hands.

Pat. wishes me to suggest, that public honors are, doubtless, far preferable to domestic quiet and enjoyment, or you would not have extended to me this unmerited invitation, and that we shall, therefore, try to fitly appreciate your invitation and — yourselves.

I remain, Gentlemen,

With the most distinguished consideration,

Your obedient servant,

Trifle, of Trifleton House."

In order that you may know how we, distinguished men, do these things, I will inform you that I wrote the above, and asked and accepted Pat's criticism upon my draft. She said she thought it was silly enough, and therefore would do. That she didn't imbue it with her own cleverness, to some extent, I will not attempt to maintain.

There's nothing like consulting your wife. I have the best authority for knowing that the lamented Chancellor Kent got puzzled in deciding his first equity cause, and went home and asked "ma'am" what she thought, and decided as she said was right. If she was as "smart" as Pat., she was a good wife. Most of my consequence I owe to Pat.

We have had invitations to several parties, but intend to decline them all. We are told that it is considered indispensable, now, for the men at parties to walk on their toes, and "*wriggle*" about in the most absurd manner, and for the women to "waddle" in huge hoops, which, even if Pat. approved them, I should be tempted, almost, to flatly interdict.

Are you informed whether or not there is a degree of absurdity which women are incapable of approaching, in matters of dress? This is no inquiry of mine, but of a cynical old bachelor I was talking with yesterday. With huge profanity, he said — " these hoops look like the d——l!" Are you not shocked?

But, chiefly and mostly, my present duty is to speak of our having come " home " for Thanksgiving.

This is a great gathering with us, for the Trifles are as distinguished for their numbers as for other things, and we all come " home " and dine with " father and mother " on Thanksgiving day. — The boys and the girls, (for such we are still to each other, though several of us are past forty,) with their Prigs, babies and servants, all come home and live the past over again on that festive occasion. For many years, we met with unbroken ranks, and numbers constantly increasing. But in this sad world there must be deaths as well as births, and if you walk down —— Avenue, in Mount Auburn, you will find where " Stella " is buried. She was the first to leave us, and our hearts are now more in Heaven, for did not the Master affirm " where your treasures are, there will your hearts be also," and she is now there, as we trust. Our youngest brother, too, is away — in a land beyond the seas. Our prayers are with him, and we know his are with us. We shall miss his pleasant face at the table, to-morrow, and listen to his cheerful laugh in fancy only. May God bless him, and after a brief season, bring him home in safety to our midst!

Stella's *children* will be with us. They love nobody better than "grandma" and "Aunt Louise," which is scarcely saying much, for I never saw anybody who didn't love *them.* The heart of the latter has been the repository of all her brother's secrets, anxieties and yearnings for years, (she is capable of keeping a secret, in spite of her sex,) and the heart of the former is large enough to comprehend a host. In fact, "mother" is a wonderful peacemaker and union preserver. She has managed to keep us all united in affection and interest thus far in life, and the Union of these States would never be in danger if she were in the President's Cabinet. Her mission is, indeed, a noble one, but, as diplomatists shine best when treating the most difficult and hazardous questions, so is she most herself when family cares and perplexities thicken. When she has nothing to trouble her, she appears to be least happy.

If you wish to be informed in regard to my father, you must ask Prig. He knows him best. I find nothing in my daily walks, more grateful to me, (and to Pat., too, for that matter,) than the affection subsisting between Prig and his "Grandpa."

There are some pleasant features in this life, after all. I like to see them "take a walk" together. After tea, the Journal and Transcript having been despatched, advertisements and all, my father takes a couple of canes from the entry, and handing one to Prig says, "Come, Prig, let's walk down about as far as the "Old South," or "the Insurance Office," or "Mr. Pardy's!"

Prig's fancy is addressed, and off they start. They talk a little at first, but, after a while, they grow silent, and my father becomes abstracted and lost. I understand it all. His early associations come back, as he passes, in imagination, this spot and that. The shadows of the past hover about him, and the companions of his boyhood and early manhood — they who have one after another gone before him, seem to surround him, and accompany him. But soon he clasps, involuntarily, the hand of my boy more tightly, and as I look at him with a carefully guarded scrutiny, which he don't observe, I can see that his eyes are swimming, and he is thinking within himself, as Charles Lamb so exquisitely says, —

"All, all are gone, the old familiar faces."

And then, some remark of Prig's, such as, for instance, "Why, Grandpa, you hurt my hand so!" puts an end to his reflections and the walk.

And yet he is a cheerful man. All the young girls like him, — "he is," they say "so funny." When we are all together at our family gatherings, he finds it difficult to keep quite cool. He rubs his left elbow with his right hand which we all know is a sure sign of his feeling very happy, informs us usually which way the wind is, and if any one happens to ring the door bell, we expect instantly (and we are seldom disappointed) to hear him cry, "Come in!" notwithstanding two or three servants are rushing precipitately to the door. My mother, on such occasions, gently seizes him by the arm and says, — "Don't alarm the neighbors;" at which he replies very vigorously, "Who cares for the neighbors? It's a free country."

One thing we can truly say. He is, has always

been, a conscientious, sincere and single-hearted man, and with some eccentricities of character, the kindest and best of fathers. Our prayer is, that he may live to see and rejoice in the successes and respectability of his children. All his best thoughts are absorbed in them, just as all his life has been devoted to them.

We look forward to a happy Thanksgiving. Commend me to Mrs. Editor, and tell her I shall think of you all on that day.

Item. — Before we left Trifleton House, as Pat. tells me, Pink informed her that *he* was expected at her father's house, to spend Thanksgiving and make a visit, and she was full of regret that Pat. couldn't stay and help entertain him. Entertain him, indeed! If Pink, with all her powers of fascinating, finds it difficult to entertain him before they marry, how will it be after?

N. B. Just, as I was folding this letter, the following telegraphic despatch came from Stubs:

BALTIMORE, Nov. 28th, '55.

"Please provide fat Thanksgiving turkey for Goody Green, *to-day, without fail.*"

This is the poor old woman of whom I wrote you in the early part of this correspondence, who said Stubs was "as good as a minister," you recollect, and also that he was "too good for her," referring to Pink.

Privately, though, which please don't mention, there was no occasion for the despatch, for I ordered the turkey myself before I left for Boston, for I supposed Stubs might have forgotten it in the hurry of his departure.

Said *Bob* to me — (Stubs' man) — "I'm afraid he is troubled in his mind, sir. He seemed very sad when he left, and as he shook hands with me and said, 'Good-bye, Bob; God bless you!' which were *jest* (just) his words, sir, I could hardly help crying. He's always been very kind to me, sir, and I shall be glad when his troubles is (are) over."

XX.

The Arm Chair,
In Winter.

How many lucky stars were in the ascendant when you were born, Trifle? We verily believe that the stars didn't shine at that important epoch of our life. Or if they did, they must have been far down towards the western horizon, so that they couldn't see us. We must write from the arm-chair still. We can't "pack up our duds" and be off, like you, — bag, baggage and babies, — to town or anywhere else. If we stroll away for half a day, the passing hours bring us back again to the arm-chair, by the window under the cherry tree. The cherry tree is disrobed now, and is like any other tree. We can only see its old gray limbs, which stand out stiff and stark against the cold sky, defying the storms and the howling winds. Underneath we look out upon cheerless fields, which but a short time since were "with verdure clad." But it is the same window and the same arm-chair, where we write. Possibly we may go to see the double murder of Duncan and Macbeth, or to delight in the wondrous powers of Lagrange and the rich tones of Didiée, but before the long chimes of the night have sounded, here we are back again; the chair extends its arms to embrace us, and the shadows on the wall tremble a welcome.

As for the Hegira from Trifleton House, why don't you "own up" to its real cause? You talk about going to town for the "Thanksgiving Jubilee," which may be accepted by the verdant and such as don't know you; but we put no faith in such a story, — it is all sham. Go to town to "spend Thanksgiving!" Why, sir, everybody who *goes* to spend Thanksgiving, goes into the country. The truth is, your departure from Trifleton House was a cowardly retreat, notwithstanding, like Gortschakoff or Menschikoff, you call it something else. You looked out from the windows and saw blue devils — call them goblins or spirits, if you choose — playing about your garden, dancing over the frozen clods or the dead plants, and scowling and mocking at you from the grim old trees. You heard them howl and laugh as the blast came off the sea. You shuddered and were vanquished. You packed up and hurried away to the railroad station. You besought the engineer to put on all steam, and hardly ventured to look from the car-window, lest some goblin might have tracked you, and be sitting there, grinning horribly, even at your elbow. You did not feel safe till you found yourself rattling over the pavement of the great city, where noise and gas-light might affright even the bluest goblin of them all. Then you began to be relieved, to talk, to laugh even, and to glorify the comforts of town. Thanksgiving! — doubtless you were thankful at your escape, — but the "jubilee" was only a very convenient cover for your inglorious retreat.

You needn't deny it, and in truth you have shown more pluck than many city folk. We have neighbors,

— for three months in the year — who leave the city when all the beauties of spring are past, and who think of returning when the swallows disappear, (which is about the twenty-fifth of August, mark you, Trifle) and are not to be caught out of town, when the first ripened leaf falls. You have done better than they, and kept the enemy at bay until winter brought up the reserve; then you fled. But do not despair; a campaign or two will strengthen you, and in time you will conquer.

But behold the rural Trifle in town again! We said something about *habits* once, and you took offence at our allusion to your old coat. But as easily as the old coat the city habits are slipped on, it seems, and sit as comfortably. The first thing you do is to go to the club and play billards, asking no odds of anybody and bragging of the game you play. The game at billiards finished, you sit down to other "game," doubtless, and your old fondness for discussing "canvas-backs," "grouse" and "venison," with the "fixins," returned undiminished. Since you are so fond of game, why didn't you "die game," before quitting Trifleton House? For your dissipation you were conscious of deserving a "curtain lecture," but the innocent and amiable Mrs. Trifle has evidently relied too much upon the good influences of Trifleton garden, and couldn't imagine that Trifle would so far "forget himself," as to return to that "vile club" and to — his old game, at the very first opportunity.

We cannot but admire the self denial with which you decline the honors tendered to you by the "wire pullers" and "solid men" of Boston. We have no doubt that the offer was really as delightful to you as the incense of poor pigmy mortals might be to some snuffing Olympian divinity, and we can only wonder that your conceit permitted you to decline so distinguished and urgent and unusual an invitation. Dinners and presentations and testimonials were wont, a long time ago, to be quite common, and the honor was of no account; but now they are of very rare occurrence and are only "extended" to the most distinguished men of the day, such as the very greatest defaulters, pugilists and other operators, or, now and then, to a famous policeman — famous on the principle of "setting a rogue to catch a rogue," — and sometimes to some plucky runner with the "machine." As such honors are bestowed only upon the most distinguished characters of this sort, they are so much the more to be prized. While, therefore, we commend the unexpected modesty which has seemed to govern your conduct in this matter, we are all the more surprised that it should have triumphed over your conceit when so severely tempted. However, as you say, you have a good wife, and owe much besides your "consequence" to her.

There are several matters to which you seem to invite attention, but they are subjects such as engross the thoughts of city folk only, and we shall not enter into any such barren fields, notwithstanding you so invitingly "leave down the bars." As for the inquiry of your cynical old bachelor, "whether or not there is a degree of absurdity which women are incapable of approaching, in matters of dress," — if the amiable and sagacious Mrs. Trifle can't answer it, we refer you to the first long-skirted dandy that you meet, one of those individuals who seem so anxious to assume petticoats.

We were telling you how Madame Hard, and Bel, and the Hon. Mr. Weed came into Umber's studio, to inspect the picture. As he heard their step, Umber retired behind a curtain into a little room adjoining the studio, and we were left alone to welcome the visitors, which was done after the city fashion that we acquired from you, — that is, as well as we could attempt so stupendous a lesson. The formalities being over, they turned towards the easel. Madame first spoke.

"Ah, here is Bel. But really, I should scarcely recognize my daughter. It has a resemblance, — the features are like, but it lacks expression." (Ah! Madame, there is a most expressive smile on that face.) "It does not show the maturity and bearing of Bell; it is too like a school girl."

The Hon. Mr. Weed looked at the picture with a face expressive of a prolonged "Humph!" Then he glanced at Bel, who was flushed, and bit her lip. He thought she was indignant, so he uttered his criticism.

"It is not at all like the original. It wants the air of a high-bred lady." (Of course it does, for the heart — a good one too — is in the face, and high-bred ladies never reveal that.) "It lacks character, too. It is quite unfortunate that this young artist does not succeed better."

And the Hon. Mr. Weed's face resumed its half contemptuous look, as he and Madame both turned to Bel to inquire her opinion. While Bel had been looking at the picture she had been struggling with some emotions which had caused, as we observed, her face to flush and grow pale. But she responded quickly and somewhat bitterly to the inquiring looks —

"No, it is not like me, or I know not my own features and expression."

Just then Umber returned and courteously saluting his visitors, gave them no time to speak of the picture or to apologize for the criticisms.

"Pardon me for leaving this ideal head upon the easel. We sometimes, for a study, attempt to give to portraits which we paint, — especially beautiful faces, — an expression entirely different from, and sometimes in strong contrast with that of the original, showing the force of character and feeling in changing the self-same features. *This* is Miss Hard's portrait."

And he placed another canvas beside the condemned picture. He spoke pleasantly and quietly, as he usually does, but with just a slight tone which might reach accustomed ears. Here was the portrait of Bel Hard, indeed, and so it was greeted by Madame Hard and and the Hon. Mr. Weed.

"Excellent, — Bel herself!"

"An admirable likeness."

"The features are very correct, and the expression life-like."

"The bearing and air of the original. A charming picture!"

Bel was silent. Her eye turned from one picture to the other, and she evidently contrasted the two. The new picture was perfect in its portrayal of features, and they wore the proud, cold expression which *she* wears, with a slight shadow of discontent or unhappiness. In this last respect the artist has flattered her, for the shadow on her face is deeper than in the portrait, — deeper than it was under the summer foliage. To her the words of Umber were full of a meaning which did not reach the apprehension of the others; and she must have been pondering them or the contrast between the two pictures, else why did she start so when Madame asked her what she thought of the portrait?

"It must be good, since you and Mr. Weed find it so excellent. The artist best knows whether he has done justice to his subject. But if the picture is satisfactory to the one who ordered it — I am content."

There was a peculiar tone to her voice, as if she intended something more than her words. Possibly Umber noticed it, but the Hon. Mr. Weed evidently did not, judging from his words —

"It gives me great pleasure to commend the artist's fidelity, and my admiration for the picture is only second to that for the original."

Bel bowed coldly to this formal compliment, and Umber deigned no notice of his share of it. It was rather awkward for us to witness the embarrassment of the parties in the silence which followed. But it was soon relieved by the Hon. Mr. Weed condescending to request Umber to finish the portrait, which being done in due form, as we suppose, the visitors departed. They had been gone but a moment, however, when the door opened again and Bel Hard reappeared, somewhat impetuously. There was a flush of anger in her face, but there was the softness of tears in her eyes. But perhaps it was not anger. She spoke in a suppressed but passionate tone to Umber who met her.

"Why have you done this?"

"What?"

"These pictures — have you not painted them to make me hateful to myself? — to show to all beholders the *contrast* — that was your word — between me as I am, cold hearted and miserable, — for such you make me, — and what I should be if *you* could form my character, and display it in my face?"

"Have I not painted your portrait to meet the approbation of those who see you oftenest?"

"And know me least, — you have."

"That portrait was for their eyes."

"And the other was to show the virtues and graces which I have not."

"No. It was a study — of *memory* and *hope*, intended some time, perhaps, for your own eye, but chiefly for my——"

"Amusement! But why then was it displayed here?"

"Not by my desire. You surprised it, and your friends summarily condemned it. It had no meaning except to your eye, — and since to you alone it possessed meaning, I can scarcely regret that it was left there to produce impressions."

"And read me a lesson on my deficiencies! That is a new province for your art, and an assumption on your part of duties which belong to you by no right or privilege. You do no good in your attempt. You simply make me *miserable*. If that be a pleasure to you, you are richly rewarded."

"Bel!"

But she was gone.

XXI.

Still in Town,
About the time of the Winter Solstice.

Yes, the Winter of 1855 has come. It absolutely startled me to see the heading of your last letter — "In Winter;" but Time lapses, whether you and I are conscious of it or not. Since this correspondence commenced, the Summer and the Autumn of '55 have passed over our heads, and, as you say, we have crossed the threshold of Winter. When we were boys, a half a year seemed like an Eternity almost. What is it now? Immersed as we are in the anxieties and small frettings of life, the seasons pass by us, and

> "—— overcome us like a Summer's cloud,
> Without our special wonder."

We grow older, but do we grow better — more generous, simple, truthful, self-denying? That single word "self-denial" chiefly describes life. Do you, then, live, my Editor? Do you *brace up* against difficulties, and carry a vigorous heart against the world, saying, "Confessedly, oh world, you bear pretty hard. You are sufficiently relentless. You fight against me rather sharply, and at times I'm disposed to cry for quarter; but then, you see, there's Mrs. Editor and all the little editors. — I'll beat you yet, and carry the glory home, for I've discovered how to 'put the world under my feet,' and I will show you 'what's what' before we get through!" Do you put it on to the world thus, my Editor?

We are about making preparations to return to Trifleton House. We have seen the "folks" and they have seen us. We have dined out sufficiently, and everywhere we have been, Pat.'s good looks have created a sensation. They say she's grown hearty and ruddy. Who denies it? They say she never looked so well before in her life. It's no lie. Her lips are red and her teeth white (notwithstanding these days of degenerate teeth,) and her eyes sparkle with the vivacity of excellent health.

"Why is it, sir?"—"why is it?" I'm astonished to hear you ask. It's because we live at Trifleton House, and we are determined to go back there. A little of "town" will do, but too much of it is very like too much champagne. *Headache*, you perceive. Everything not perfectly plain and simple, must be indulged in sparingly.

Good bye, Town!

I have had a letter from Stubs, which I enclose. It seems, which I have only learned recently, that there is a lawsuit now pending in the Supreme Court of the United States, involving the validity of the title of the principal part of his property. I have known all the while during the Summer, that he was interested in the result of this suit, but not to what extent. For some good reasons, no doubt, he has been uncommunicative respecting it. He usually tells me everything and desires my sympathy and advice. But perhaps he thought it would be foolish (as doubtless it would be) to talk with such a person as Trifle respecting anything so dry and musty as law.

Like many rich young men, Stubs has studied for the profession of law, and been admitted to the bar. But he has never cared to practice, except to take care of his own property, &c. He has capacity enough. Indeed, if his inclination were equal to his capacity, he would shine at the bar. But here you have his letter: —

"WASHINGTON CITY, DEC. 1855.

My dear Trifle:—

I have been dawdling in this rendezvous of squabbling politicians, for some days. It is sufficiently stupid. The wrangle for the Speakership progresses.

The place hasn't changed much since we were here last. Pennsylvania Avenue wears the same look. The same four-legged donkeys flourish on one side of it, and the same two-legged ones, if anything a little more *blasé*, strut on the other. The same exquisite Republican simplicity of costume distinguishes the fair sex, as they trip along the pavement, or gossip in and about the Capitol. Can there be any danger to the safety of our country, so long as the women are so serenely simple, and so little addicted to show, outdoors, and luxury, in-doors?

If the wife of a Congressman, who gets eight dollars a day, and sells all his self-respect oftentimes for even that, 'admires' feathers, and silks, and what not, why, it's none of my business. Let her wear them. Women in England and France dress somewhat differently, it is true, at least in the street. But, then, that's nothing. They are not Republicans, you know.

The accessions to the Capitol are progressing quite rapidly, and will vastly improve its appearance. As I have wandered about the Rotunda, looking at the pictures, I have thought a good deal of times past, when we stood in the same place with Pat. and ——, before Pat. became your better half! You remember the old leaky omnibus and the drive in the rain, when, *horribile dictu*, Pat.'s bonnet got soaked doubtless. We have lived years since then, Trifle. At least I have, and experience has been my teacher. I have idled enough of my life away, and I am resolved to go to work. I find the older I grow, that I am more inclined to judge men by what they have done, and that I have very little respect for such as merely exist, with no definite aim in life, and accomplish nothing. Energy is a great trait in a man, or a woman. Whoso is at work has no time to sentimentalize and — grumble.

After some conversation with my counsel, I have resolved to open our case, myself. I do not appear as a party on the record, so that the world will not know that I have a 'fool for a client,' although I shall be practically arguing my own case, because the Court's decision in the case we propose to argue, will settle all the law points in which I am interested. The docket is much crowded, and we shall not be reached for some weeks, probably. I spend most of my time examining the authorities cited in the respective briefs. You can judge somewhat of the work, when I tell you they number more than five hundred. Lawyers from every part of the United States are constantly rushing in and out of the Law Library, where I am now sitting. They are mostly men of distinction at home; but I can see their nervousness as they are preparing their arguments for the Court here — the highest in the land. They feel, probably, that they must sustain that reputation which they have labored so hard and so long to acquire elsewhere.

I have an advantage over most of them in this respect, because I have no reputation to lose. I have one to make.

I go into the court room every day. There's a charm about the place which is almost sacred. There is something in the appearance of the nine venerable judges, in that little chamber, removed from all the world, which reminds one of the Roman senators in the palmiest days of the Republic. They look like men who have lived down all the hot anxieties and wretched frivolities of life, and have conquered themselves. I think there is more benignity and childlike simplicity of character expressed in the countenance of Mr. Justice McLean, than I have ever seen in any other man. Did you ever remark that all great men are exceedingly gentle and simple, both in looks and manners?

I have listened to some of the arguments before the Court with great satisfaction. A masterly one from the distinguished Attorney General of the United States, excited in me the same mingled feelings of 'admiration and despair,' which Chancellor Kent said he always felt in reading Blackstone's lucid chapter upon Contingent Remainders. Not many abler men live than Caleb Cushing. I have been admitted as a member of the Court upon his motion.

I have looked in upon the Senate occasionally, but with feelings of pain. I saw neither Webster, nor Clay, nor Calhoun there; and I thought of the time gone by when we heard these great men in the debate upon the Compromises of 1850.

We shall never hear again such eloquence as we heard then, and we shall never see again living in this country such men as these men were. In their loss, the prestige of the Senate seems to have been lost.

In the great political struggles impending over our country, which will, in my judgment, shake more terribly than ever before the union of these States to its centre, who and where are the men to lead and guide us with safety? God grant that they may appear when the crisis comes, as it must inevitably sooner or later! If we were only more intensely *American*, and *National*, and *Republican*; if we would only appreciate the contrast between the condition of the rest of the world, immersed in war as it is, and our own blessed country, it seems to me we should have none of these sectional animosities and bickerings which threaten our peace and salvation, and these States might remain forever united and compacted in bonds of fraternal affection.

I need not tell you how much I miss you, and dear Pat., to whom please give my warmest regards. I am, indeed, very lonely, and am much weighed down with anxiety and responsibility. I care very little in regard to the result of this lawsuit in a pecuniary point of view. I ought to earn my own living, and I respect in one sense, the mere day laborer who toils for bread by which to feed his wife and children, more than the rich man who idles his life away. I will be, henceforth, no 'cumberer of the ground.' I will do what I can for myself and my kind. I need to live more out of myself. I have been too selfish and inert, and I look upon my effort here as promising to furnish my initiary step to a more manly and useful career. I feel ashamed when I think how little I have accomplished in life, and how little of real humanity there is in my nature. My discipline should make me better, and yet, dear Trifle, I am very rebellious. You have your devoted and affectionate wife and children to soothe you, and soften you, and make you happy. I have —— *nobody*. I am *all alone*. My life is becoming dreary and desolate. This I tell *you*, because I must tell somebody. Else I should quite break up. It is unnecessary that I should ask you to keep my weak complainings secret. You are my second self. But farewell, and God bless you!

The enclosed verses I wrote last night.

Your sincerely attached STUBS."

"When will this weary heart find rest,
These strugglings all be done;
When learn that 'all that is, is best,'
When be the victory won?

When grow insensible to grief,
And learn — no more to *feel*;
When have no yearnings for relief,
No sufferings to conceal?

When will this fearful weight of care
Cease to oppress my soul? —
This fierce, relentless, black despair
Loose me from its control?

Peace! babbling child of sin: not thine
Life's mysteries to explain;
'Mid night, and dark, the stars still shine,
And rainbows follow rain."

I have no comment to make upon this letter. It needs none.

XXII.

THE ARM CHAIR,
As Christmas comes. }

IT is not in vain, then, that you have lived at Trifleton House a few months. The town tires you. You confess it is like champagne — a little too sparkling and exciting, and brings the headache. Yet are we a little astonished at your fickleness. Undeniably you ran away from the blues when they first attacked you at Trifleton House, and when once in town you made a "dead rush" to the club, to the theatre, to parties, to dinners. But now you seem to be surfeited, and propose a return to the quiet of rural life, which has unfitted you for the continuance of that round of pleasure, a year ago an absolute necessity for your existence. But pray carry back all your courage, and ample store of munitions for the war which you are to wage against your unsubstantial foes. Most potent of such munitions will be the prattle of Prig and the smiles of Pat. But even these will prove ineffectual, unless you have an abundant supply of content. Back to Trifleton House, then, and forget all else of the town save Thanksgiving, and home, and friends.

The Winter has indeed come, though with more genial smiles than is his wont. But what an unwelcome guest he is in some dwellings, as he thrusts himself in, and seats himself at the very hearthstone, and looks coldly and sadly into the eyes of the poor, and lays his icy fingers on their hearts! None the less unwelcome is he in some more comfortable dwellings, where with harsh aspect he stands guard over prisoners who are sighing for pleasures far away. Such dwellings are in the country, mostly, and the prisoners are summer birds from the city. Ah, Trifle, be on your guard lest Winter prove such an unwelcome sentry over you. Ay, follow him, even, if you can, into some of those less fortunate homes whither he goes to carry want, and suffering, and despair, — follow him with faggots, if need be, with fire and — food, and cheerful, hopeful words. So shall you carry the war into Africa, and drive the chilly sentry from your own door.

Winter finds little to tempt him at the Hard Mansion now. He has sometimes apparently gloated over the sullen looks he found there, and has called to his aid the storm wind and his whole train of fierce and cruel satellites. But Madame, and Bel, and the Hon. Mr. Weed have gone to Washington. We have not inquired whether the latter is one of the gentlemen who have been amusing themselves and the country by two or three weeks balloting for a speaker. Madame wrote to Abel to meet them on the way, or to hurry after them. But Abel didn't get the letter till it was sent home after him, he having arrived here a few days after the departure of the party for Washington. There is a sort of whisper among the domestics at the mansion, which came to our ears after the usual fashion, that Miss Bel was very unhappy about going, although she is to be married soon. But you can't depend on such stories, you know. As for Abel, he seems in no hurry to go, and is evidently gratified to find a little chance for the indulgence of his own fancies without being too closely questioned about them. He is happier than formerly, but there is still a shadow on his brow, sometimes, and his heart is not altogether at rest. A few evenings since we visited him, with Umber. It was a dark and cheerless night, and the north wind brought snow and sleet to tell us that Winter is reigning prince over these regions. But as we entered Abel Hard's library we found a cheerful contrast to the cold storm without. The Cannel hissed and flamed in the grate, shedding a ruddy light over the rich drapery, and the dark cases, and one or two fine paintings. Abel's face glowed in the cheerful beams as he welcomed us to that bright and genial room. Next to the almost forgotten hickory-wood fire, give us the brilliant, glowing, earnest Cannel. It warms the soul as well as the fingers. It addresses the sense of sight and hearing as well as touch. It cheers and enlivens everything and everybody that comes within its light and influence. Let us have for real, cheerful warmth, no furnaces, and registers emitting hot air like breaths from Tartarus.

We disposed ourselves at ease about that beneficent fire, and joined Abel in the enjoyment of cigars, one of which (contrary to the ordinary rules of the mansion, he said) he was already discussing. The weather was nothing to us now, so we didn't talk about that. The shadows on the wall were more attractive than the clouds. Doubtless Umber thought — he *said* no such thing — that the brightest light of the house was gone — and its darkest shadow. We followed them a moment to Washington, and thence we hurried westward, to tarry awhile with Abel by the shores of Erie. Then we congratulated our host upon his return to that pleasant room and upon — we scarcely know what. At this point of the random interlocution — it wasn't conversation — there was a pause, which we severally improved to watch the smoke curling gracefully from our cigars, and possibly to think. To think deeply, however, at such a time, would have been a burden and a bore. But there was no occasion for it, as Abel quietly assumed the talk himself, and Umber and we smoked in silence.

"It is two years since I first met Lily at Florence, — two years the very day I found her on the shores of Lake Erie. It was in the Cascine, where all the beauty and fashion of Florence is wont to display itself. She was riding with her father, and an aunt, or some other elderly female who took the place of aunt, for her mother was dead. By some means — I remember the result better than the means — an accident happened by which their horses were affrighted. The ladies were still more alarmed, and really there was some danger which I had the good fortune, by being near, to avert. But the gentleman sprained an ancle in jumping from his carriage, and the carriage was broken, so here was an opportunity for further service, and to see whom I had served."

Umber's eye twinkled a little, but we smoked on in silence.

"I assisted the gentleman into his carriage again, tendering the use of my light trotting wagon — a genuine Yankee carriage — so far as it could be of service. I cannot describe, though indelibly fixed in my mind, the look of mingled alarm, anxiety and gratitude of the one lovely face in that carriage. But the result of my offer was that I had the privilege of carrying home the aunt — an accomplished lady I found — instead of the lame gentleman or his beautiful daughter. It served the purpose, however, for I discovered their residence and name, and acquired the privilege of calling again."

We knocked the ashes from our cigars and smoked on.

"We met — Lily and I — not unfrequently after that. I can't remember or tell all the details; but we met, — and her father being confined to the house for some time by his lameness, I sometimes rode in the Cascine with the ladies, or took a drive into the beautiful country about Florence. I went to the Uffizii galleries, with them, to the Pitti Palace, and to the churches; and while we gazed at the almost divine beauty of Raphael's paintings, and I listened to Lily's gentle voice, uttering pure and beautiful thoughts, — I should have been heartless, indeed, had I not loved her."

We looked in the fire and smoked on.

"I loved her, as a young man of sensibility if not sense, who had led the life of a student, reading poetry and having nothing else to think of, might be expected to indulge in the passion — for the first time, and under such circumstances. I never breathed it aloud, nor hoped that Lily responded to my love. But somehow she, or the aunt, discovered that I was going mad—and so they took steps to cure me, or make me more mad. The old gentleman got about, and then Lily could not often be seen. Christmas and Twelfth Night we met at one of the churches. Lily's manner was constrained, the aunt's was formally polite, and the father's was haughtily civil. Florence soon became dull for me, for I could only take pleasure in the works of art which we had visited together; and they only served to remind me the more forcibly of my loss."

Umber unconsciously—sighed, but we silently smoked on.

"I went to Rome, and with the fiercest industry visited galleries, churches and ruins, studied frescoes and statuary and gazed at pictures—all with a most admirable unconsciousness of what was before me. On the last day of the Carnival—an excellent illustration of things in general as presented to my mind—I saw Lily and her father again. Again, and for the last time, but it was sufficient to add something to my feelings and not a little to my folly, probably. I sought for them, but I found that they preferred to pass Lent in Naples. I wasn't fool enough to follow them, but I went to Venice, when I had finished Rome. But the seal was on me, and neither Venice, nor Greece, nor Germany offered anything to take the place of Lily in my mind or memory. On my way home, I ventured to call in London at their house, but it was not in the season and they were out of town. And so I came home, a little melancholy, perhaps, and found nothing here, or in society, at watering, places or in town, to take the place of the past.

"Are you surprised that I posted off at the first information that Lily was in the country and under circumstances so changed?"

Of course not, but we replied only by a whiff.

"After a long search I found them. Lily's father had lost his estates by the turning up of an heir supposed to have died in India. Mortified and despondent, he had come with a moderate fortune to this country, seeking a home sufficiently distant from the new heir and his lost property. Lily, though pressed by many friends to remain in England, felt it her duty to follow and comfort her father. She still remembered our meetings in Florence, and has —"

He paused, and Umber, after a puff or two, finished the sentence:

"Crowned your Italian adventures with happiness. You are more fortunate than I am. I met in Rome a beautiful flower girl. The flower girls there are not often beautiful, so she was the more remarkable. Her gentleness and good will to me in a severe sickness demanded my gratitude, and the only favor she asked was, that I should sketch her face to send to her lover. That of course put an end to the possibility of romance on my part. But she was very grateful, and was still more so, some months later, when I succeeded in getting her lover, who was a 'patriot' and was wounded, out of the way of the French as they entered the city. She would have suffered much to serve me. But the very first time I spoke of her friendship after my return hither, I disgusted a fair lady, and have painted more clouds than sunshine ever since."

Thus we enjoyed our cigars by the bright Cannel

fire in Abel Hard's library. For our part we had no personal adventures to relate, so we told of Trifle and Trifleton House, of Stubs, and Pink, and "corn-colored gloves." Umber and we were about to depart, notwithstanding a bottle of Rhenish wine invited our stay, when a servant announced that a poor woman with a little boy desired to see our host. We passed out into the dismal night and Umber went home in silence.

Christmas comes, Trifle, and so we date our letter, for even the anticipation of a great event is worthy of record. Yes, Christmas comes, and in a few hours will commence the glad peals from church and campanile, — the deep-mouthed clangor and the sweet silvery chimes, sounding on in an unbroken circle around the world, — proclaiming the return of the holy night when the shepherds on the eastern hills saw the star that stood over Bethlehem, and angels sang, "On earth peace, and good will towards men." From mighty cathedral and from humble chapel shall swell the songs of praise and the solemn mass. In hall and cot shall be happiness and love, and young and old shall rejoice in the festal day of Christendom.

"A merry Christmas" at Trifleton House!

XXIII.

TRIFLETON HOUSE,
Christmas week.

HOME again, the whole bunch of us! A great many sympathizing friends in the great city (considerate souls) have said, and are constantly saying to me, "You must find it rather tough at Trifleton House in the winter. You'll freeze to death. You'll die with the blues!" But we have been home a week or two, and I'm afraid, for the sake of those who regard us with such tender compassion, that we shall neither freeze nor pine.

The truth is, my Editor, we think tolerably well of Trifleton House — it seems very much like *home* to us, so that you perceive, in that point of view, it's not such a very gloomy place. Still, I go for sympathy. It's a very generous trait, and when I'm condoled with so undeservedly, I always say to myself, "Trifle, my hearty, never find fault with the world again; don't you perceive how many are interested in your welfare!"

My own idea is, though, that the atmosphere of Trifleton House is such as to warm people up, — even those who are pretty cold. If I don't find any colder people elsewhere than I do there, I shall be disposed to call it rather a mild winter. Prig expresses himself as absolutely pleased at getting home. He says he don't think he shall go to Boston again for a great while; but "I'll let Grandpa come here, and see me," he considerately added, — I have given you his exact words. He inclines to the opinion that his White-y is making a very long visit away from Trifleton. In fact, it slightly puzzles me, where he has gone. He departed in good health and spirits, one evening, just before we all left for town, without even saying "good-bye," and he hasn't been seen since. I tell Prig I think he's gone off with some dog or cat, perhaps, to *stay* — all the time, but he persists in the assertion that he's "on a visit," and will come home "by and by."

Oh, human faith!

That "by and by," how many tears it has dried up, how many yearnings soothed, how many drooping hearts encouraged, and how very many cheated and disappointed! Still, let us not quarrel with it, my Editor. It's a very pretty phrase. Let us take courage and hasten on. We shall be perfectly happy — "by and by."

What I wish to say in regard to sunrises, sir, is this: When we were on our visit in town we didn't see many, for I believe they are not very beautiful at quarter past eight of the clock. In town it's a mere question of night and day with one, — and the day begins in the winter season somewhere between eight and nine. To be sure, there are coffee and the morning papers, which are the two most romantic and important considerations which ever occurred to me there on "getting up;" but at Trifleton, sir, we see the sun rise every morning of our lives, when he can be seen anywhere, that is. On several occasions I have seen him come up from the sea, and merely penetrate the line of dark, gloomy, wintry, slate-colored clouds upon the edge of the horizon with a white light, and then advance up into the clear sky without a semblance, even, of crimson, golden, or pink, being perceptible, but, at other times, lately, he has come up with a glory I have never seen surpassed, if equalled.

This morning I asked Pat. to describe the colors for me; he appeared in such a remarkable manner. "How beautiful, how transcendently beautiful," I was saying while buttoning one of my suspenders, (the green silk ones, which cost me two dollars, and in the purchase of which I got shabbily imposed upon, sir,) Pat. concurred with me in opinion, in spite of the knot she was trying to unravel in the strings of her — *night-cap* — I was actually going to say, if I hadn't stopped to think how extremely improper it would be; and she began immediately to describe the colors. Below is her description. Before buttoning the other suspender, I seized my pencil and took it down from her lips.

"First, — line of dark, rich purple clouds; next line above, golden; next, a line of blue; next, a line of *flaky*, pink clouds."

"What kind of pink, Pat?"

"Flaky," she replied, "Flaky."

"What's that?"

"Why Flaky is, —— why Flaky means — Flaky, — what's the matter with this string, for patience sake?" (with a twitch at it.)

After this lucid definition, I wrote it down "flaky," as in duty bound.

"Next," she continued, "comes a long, wide space of light yellow; and, directly above this space, a pile of rich, gorgeous, crimson clouds, tinged with blue."

"And the sea," I exclaimed, "how magnificently it looks!"

"Yes," she said, "of a dark purple color, with the reflection of all the other colors I have mentioned blended upon it. How very beautiful!"

"What's beautiful? I want to see," and out came Prig from his trundle bed into the dressing room, staggering and tottering in his flannel night drawers, drawn up and tied at the feet "to prevent his getting cold," as Pat. says, "when he kicks the clothes off."

"The sun, boy, look!"

He clasped his hands in ecstasy, and said he liked "all beautiful things." At this juncture, the baby began to crow in concurrence, and thus, sir, you have the opinion of Trifle and his whole family upon the subject of that sunrise. I wish you could *see* such an one, but, as "the years of a man's life," in this mundane condition, are only "threescore years and ten," and calculating the chances of your being "up" in time within thirty or forty years to come, I consider it extremely improbable that you will.

I forgot to say that Pat. upon reflection, concluded she would say "flaky *salmon colored*," on the whole, rather than "flaky pink." After fishing for it a long time she said that that was just the word. When you consider, sir, that this description was taken down from the lips of a young woman with white teeth, which teeth were employed in snapping and biting at that knot in that—*night cap*, as I came very near saying again — during the whole time, and that it was written by a man of the extreme dignity of character of Trifle, in his shirt sleeves, I trust you will regard it as "one of the sunrises you read about," henceforth and forever. I laughed a good deal while I was taking minutes, and so did Prig, but, the moment I buttoned the other suspender, it flashed upon me that I had compromised my dignity immeasurably, and as I looked at myself in the mirror, while tying my cravat, I practised an indignant frown which I adopted for the rest of the morning. I considered it due to myself and proper for the education of my household that I should wear it. If you continually laugh in the presence of women and children, they take advantage of you, my Editor. They put their arms round your neck, and sit on your knee, and pull your whiskers, and kiss you, and all such things. Pat. and Prig, and even the baby are extremely addicted to this sort of thing with me. Did you ever hear of such monstrous familiarity? They require very much to be educated on this point, as you perceive.

But, of Pink!

I havn't much to tell you in regard to her, for I have seen very little of her since our return. I suspect she is slightly offended with me, but I think without cause. She came to Trifleton House to tea, and was pouring forth a torrent of asseverations about it's being "so lonely" in our absence.

"Lonely! Has not *he* been here?" I inquired.

"Yes," said she, demurely.

"And are you not *engaged*?" I continued.

"Yes," almost snapped she in reply.

"When Pat. and I were engaged," I stupidly narrated, "whenever we were most lonely, we were happiest. We were society to each other, and when any one else was by, the cold obtruding world seemed thrusting itself upon us, destroying the delicious romance and sweet poetry of our natures. When alone, we conjured an idea of heaven, and chiefly then. Those who are 'tenderly attached,'" I added, I'm afraid somewhat warmly, "like to be alone,"— and yet, why afraid? Affection is not a thing to be ashamed of, nor are its habits or demonstrations. It carrieth its own reward. It refresheth the soul that is full of it. Oh, ye who love Trifle, and whom Trifle loves, he is better and fitter for heaven for *your* sake.

She waived the discussion, and began to ask me about Thackeray's lectures. Upon a purely intellectual topic she can always fascinate me, and I forgot *him*, corn-colored gloves and all, in listening to her admirable parallel between Thackeray and Dickens.

While she talked, I drew a parallel also in my own mind between herself and Pat. I thought of her surpassing beauty, her clever wit, and powerful grasp of intellect, but I thought how far higher, and purer, and more admirable, because more womanly, was Pat.'s warm, gushing, affectionate nature, and sincere, generous heart. A woman without a heart is a libel upon her sex.

"Poor girl," said Pat. after she had gone home that evening, "she is very much to be pitied." I inquired anxiously why, but I was not enlightened. It seems she and Pat. have long and mysterious confabs almost daily, but upon what subjects is quite beyond me. I presume, though, that the number of bridesmaids and the quality and cut of the wedding dress for the approaching ceremony, are among the most important. It is to come off in the spring, and it is clear that three or four months are quite a short space of time for the discussion of these momentous questions. Consider, too, what an undertaking it will be to "go to housekeeping" in the Fifth Avenue. It should be expected, doubtless, that a woman would break somewhat in anticipating such a thing. I give you the benefit of these suggestions.

Item. — I was passing by Goody Green's yesterday, and she called me in. "Mr. Trifle," said she, "what a world we live in. I hear tell that good Mr. Stubs is going to lose all of his property." She clasped her bony hands, reminding me of Goody Blake when she prayed in the snow. But not as Goody Blake prayed for Harry Gill did she pray for Stubs. She raised her eyes to heaven, while the tears poured from them like rain, and, with tremulous accents, murmured "may he never know what it is to want. May he be rewarded for all his kindness to the poor and needy, and find as faithful friends as he has always been to them!"

"I have faith to believe," she continued, turning again to me, "that the Lord will take care of him." She was strangely agitated, but grew calmer as I informed her, as well as I could, for my own voice began to falter, that he would probably in no event ever become destitute, for he could earn his living even if he lost his property, a thought which seemed not to have occurred to her. I asked her who gave her her information.

"Why, Miss Pink," she replied, almost gaily, "she han't got no pride, now. She comes and is very kind to me, just as Mr. Stubs was. She reads the Bible for me, just as he did. Sometimes I tell her the chapters he likes,—them as he said were good for poor lonely women, whom the Lord tempted with tribulations in this world, or some such hard word, to try their faith. She reads 'em, but I don't know what makes her turn her face away from me so, when she does; and then she stops so often, too. When she picks out a chapter herself, she reads the best; for then she looks right at me, and reads right straight along, and don't mind the periods and commas, and such like. I like her better than I used to, and I told her so the other day, but she said, 'Dear Goody, I am very unworthy of affection.' Think of her saying *dear* Goody. Well, it's a strange world. I told her I supposed she felt more kind like to me, 'cause she was so happy about being married to such a fine rich man. 'But,' says I, 'Miss Pink,' says I, 'I always thought that you and Mr. Stubs would be married to each other. But there's a Providence in such things, and I 'spose it's all for the best, tho' he'll make a good husband for somebody, don't you think so?'

"'Yes, Goody,' said she, 'he will.'

"'Well then,' I was going on to say, but just at that moment she turned very pale, and began to shiver all over, so I did not talk any more, but told her she must go home and keep house, for she had a very bad cold. 'Pears to me she's getting very delicate. She don't seem so strong as she used to. She's not so gay as she was, nor so proud neither. God is dealing with her, for she sighs very deep sometimes when she reads the Bible to me."

She is human, then, and has a *heart*, after all, I thought to myself once more.

I trust that you all had a happy Christmas. Prig and the baby hung up their stockings, which produced from Santa Claus, in the most mysterious manner, all sorts of things for the former, and a nice, beautiful silver cup for the latter.

Kind, considerate Santa Claus.

XXIV.

THE ARM CHAIR,
In the last hours of '55.

NOTWITHSTANDING the old maxim, which you may have heard, that "*Ignorantia* (*legis*) *neminem excusat*," we are of opinion that ignorance must be an excuse for many things, even for some of the sayings of the sapient Trifle. You think we never see the sun rise! Having escaped from the brick walls which imprisoned you for so many years — the amiable Pat. must not know that we say *many* years — you have at last seen the glories of sunrise, and you imagine they have never been witnessed by any one else. As we have been familiarized with such sights from the cradle, it is a little too absurd that you should tax your mathematics by a calculation of the probabilities of our beholding this daily event.

Yes, sir, we do see the sun rise, and not only that, but in these short days we see his rising on other people before he shines on us. We watch the shadow of the horizon slowly sinking down the western sky till the sunlight crowns the distant hill, and then the top of the church spire. It creeps down the hill and across the plain, brightens the exterior of dwellings and sends smiles of gladness into the windows, — startling many a sleeper, doubtless — and then comes slowly on through the valley towards us. When it reaches the chimney tops of our nearest neighbor we turn to see the sun itself come up beyond the dark cedars that crown the hill in the south-east, in splendor perfect to our human vision.

But the 'splendor of a life time' was that which met the eye a few days since, when the sun's rays were broken and reflected in myriads of dazzling flashes by the icy robes of the trees, — the robes all glittering with jewels which the winter had cast upon them in a single night, as if to rival the foliage of summer. Did that wondrous spectacle pass unnoticed at Trifleton House? — that glory which surpassed the dreams of fairy land? — that shimmering blaze of light, bursting and trembling about every branch of every tree? When the sun came up with the ruddy glow of morning, and when he went down with golden drapery about him, was Trifle taking down from the lips of Pat. words to describe the shining tints that leapt and sparkled over the whole earth? Make a note of it, for but few such sights, so intense in brightness and beauty, are permitted to one lifetime. But it passes away, like all the beauties of earth, — perchance into infinite and everlasting beauty, as time passes into eternity.

Time passes! Ay, look you, 1855 is near its end — will have passed away ere we shall finish this writing. The sad Old Year is drawing his latest breaths, and the happy New Year comes close upon his last sigh. The New Year cometh out of the east, under the clear, cold starlight. But the stars, heedless of him, as of the long train of which he is but an atom, roll on and shine the same as on that morn when first they sung together. Already, in other lands, has he been greeted with joyous shouts and merry-makings, and now he is on his way over the sea whose dark waves roll, forever the same — unmindful of the departure of the Old and the advent of the New.

The New Year cometh over the sea — nearer and nearer. The Old year breathes shorter — the clock seems to tick faster, and half past the eleventh hour has already struck. Twelve months ago and this Old Year was young, and fresh, and full of promise, — bringing joys, and hopes, and high purposes. He passed on through the seasons in his allotted course, and now he lies at the end of it. Ah! he has brought many sorrows as well as joys, — sorrows to those who least expected it. But for sorrows or joys he is alike almost forgotten now, for the many sleep unmindful of his departure, and those who wake are watching to hail the new king that comes so quickly. But let us reverently watch his end, recounting his benefits and remembering the lessons he has taught us.

How we have wronged the poor Old Year! — When he has offered us precious gifts that might have added to our treasure — not gold and silver; few indeed neglect to acquire that if they can — we have refused the boon. We have turned us coldly away from golden opportunities which he brought, and wasted the hours which were his life blood. He led us by the door of the afflicted, — the hungry and the naked, yet we clothed and fed them not, — the broken hearted, but we comforted them not, — the erring, yet we guided them not homeward. He brought us sage counsels from his fathers, and pointed us to bright examples of steadfast virtue and earnest purpose, too often in vain. And now, 'tis too late. He has no more gifts to offer us — only a brief retrospection; he has lavished all upon us, and now, poor and weak, he is about to depart forever. In vain we suffer regret now, in vain we implore forgiveness, for he grows not young again, and what *he* was none other shall be forever. . . . .

The New Year cometh over the sea — yet nearer. The Old Year breathes fainter. The third quarter past eleven has been chimed, and the minutes — the moments — assume an individuality and importance as they pass by now. Crowded into each are the ghosts of things past — shadows which appear for the last time, and shadows that, haply, on such a night, again may come knocking at the heart's door. The long train floats by to the quick measure of the fast swinging pendulum, and in vain the soul cries "stay!" The hands on the dial are near together, and we count the minutes — almost the seconds — downward to nothing. Ten, nine, eight, — how short the time for regrets, and penitence, and resolutions. And so the Old Year departs in silence.

The New Year cometh over the sea in silence — stealing nearer and nearer. Hark, the bells chime — and to their music the Old Year passes, floating away like those wild sounds into the great formless gulf of the past. The music of the bells dies away, and now the clock strikes one, two — on, on, to *twelve.* The Old Year has gone forever, and the New Year has come over the sea.

"Ring out wild bells to the wild sky,
The flying cloud, the frosty light;
The year is dying in the night;
Ring out, wild bells, and let him die.

Ring out the old, ring in the new,
Ring, happy bells, across the snow;
The year is going, let him go;
Ring out the false, ring in the true.

. . . . . .

Ring out old shapes of foul disease,
Ring out the narrowing lust of gold;
Ring out the thousand wars of old,
Ring in the thousand years of peace.

Ring in the valiant man and free,
The larger heart, the kindlier hand;
Ring out the darkness of the land,
Ring in the Christ that is to be."

A "Happy New Year" to the dwellers in Trifleton House.

Among the new books to charm away the dulness of the hours at Trifleton House — don't deny that there are such — pray you read Robert Browning's new volume of poems, "Men and Women," and Hillard's selections from the writings of Walter Savage Landor. Perhaps you may be familiar with the works of Landor. But if you are, you will find in the volume we speak of a most admirable selection of fine things, and true things, and pointed things, here brought together in most convenient form, — just such extracts, for the most part, as you would yourself like to make; and if you are not on intimate terms with Landor, through his books, you will find these extracts just so many graceful invitations to open the entire works of the author.

In looking through these leaves you cannot but ask "from what other author, of the present day, could so many gems and brilliants be collected?"

In "Men and Women" you will find some of the poet's best music. Browning writes not so much for the multitude as for the few who love true poetry, and for the future. He has looked deeply into the human heart, and writes with a passionate vigor the most subtile thought, and of the most delicate emotions. Sometimes, perhaps, his words seem a little mystic or his thought obscure, but even then we feel the poetry, and everywhere there shines through his chosen words a luminous beauty, which is like the bright soul animating a lovely form. Reading such books you shall forget to wear even the "practised frown," and though you thereby do not educate your family to less familiarity, you may yourself learn to tolerate and pardon their endearments, and the result will be the same, — in the country, that is, where "deportment" is of less consequence than it is in town.

Perhaps you are not aware that Mrs. Trifle, in pencil marks on your last letter, inquired for news about the Hards. Or was it a device of your own, to cover your curiosity? Now permit us to intimate, very gently, that we have no gossips about the arm chair, and we are not familiar with *all* the sayings and doings of our neighbors, even, and the Hards are not *very* near neighbors. Occasionally we by chance hear of something, or see something — but it is altogether casual. From tea drinking old maids we keep aloof, and as for stories which are bandied about from kitchen to kitchen, we give no heed to them.

Did we not say that when Umber and we left Abel Hard, a woman and a little boy were announced? Well, that was true enough, and it seems that the boy was Abel's young duck, whom he picked out of the sea at Newport, and the woman was his mother. Lily having learned from Abel that Dawson — so they call her — was a widow at Newport, had written to her to come to their new home. Dawson was glad enough to go to the young lady whom she had found so gentle a mistress, but ignorant and inexperienced in travelling she had by some means found her way to Abel Hard, whom she looks upon as a benefactor and friend, trusting that he would send her safely through. He was glad enough to serve Lily, and commended Dawson's prudence for coming to him.

"But the young lady writes down-hearted, sir — one of the neighbors read me the letter. She feels lonesome, sir, and says as how she doesn't feel as if she should live long, and it would kind o' be a comfort to her to have an old servant like me with her now."

So Abel told Umber that Dawson spoke, and what an icy dread stole over him as he heard her. And the dread has not departed, but seems to have gathered new gloom about his heart and hopes. He is darker than ever. He sent Dawson forward as soon as possible, making her the bearer of missives, of course. But the boy, Dicky Dawson, was not able to proceed, having the symptoms of serious illness about him. Dawson objected to leaving him, but Abel would listen neither to her delay or his departure. The boy was his protegé, he said, and he would take care of him, better than she could. So with many tears on the part of the mother and boy, she was finally persuaded to go. But the day she departed, Dicky was put to bed in a fever, and the doctor called. Abel had him placed in his own room, and has watched him with a care which seems to owe something to his love for Lily, and the circumstances by which the boy is associated with her. He finds relief from his anxiety for her, even while he nourishes it, in nursing this poor sick boy. Haply he shall find something better.

XXV.

TRIFLETON HOUSE,
Sunday, in the new year of '56.

IN all this correspondence, I have written you no word on Sunday, though I have often thought of you on that day.

But this Sunday has been a remarkable one, and, at this present writing, Trifleton House is completely buried up in snow. Huge drifts lie scattered all around, I don't know how many feet deep, and if we were to see you a stone's throw off, and were to beckon you to come in, you would find it quite impossible, by wading even, to reach our door. No paths are broken, and everywhere, as far as the eye can reach, extend largest fields of snow.

I have seen nothing like it since I was a boy. It has indeed been one of the "old-fashioned snow storms." We have been in-doors all day long, watching the progress of the storm, and listening to the voices of the wind, and to those other "still small voices" that speak to our souls in such a day as this.

It is the Lord's day, and He has shown us His power and majesty. "The heavens declare the glory of God," and "He hangeth the earth upon nothing." Moreover, " He saith to the snow, be thou on the earth," and, as He spoke to Job, so He speaks to us, " out of the whirlwind," saying to each one of us, " hast thou entered into the treasures of the snow?" — and " the hoary frost of heaven who hath gendered it?"

But as the day has drawn to its close, the fury of the storm has subsided, and the evening is still, calm, and beautiful! I remembered just such another Sunday, and just such another storm, and looked over my old manuscripts to find some lines I wrote in commemoration of it. I give them to you in *ipsissimis verbis.*

The weary sun has well nigh reached his home!
His course to-day has been a gloomy one.
Dull, leaden clouds have girt his chariot round,
The azure track obscuring, while the winds,
Urged on impetuous by the winter king,
The bonds unloosed that fettered them awhile,
Have, mad with license, waged incessant war,
Their shrill voice echoing athwart the sky,
Rising above the tempest, like the moan
Of wounded men amid the battle's din.
But, with the close of day, the storm subsides;
Twilight's soft hand smooths down its ruffled wings,
And opes the gate of evening, whence proceeds
The sweet, soft harmony of heaven's stars.
This day a lesson teaches, oh my soul!
While all was gloom around, the sun's career
Was nobler none the less, although obscured.
He stayed not in his purpose for the storm,
Nor, for a moment, wandered from his course.
So, thou, in passing down the vale of life,
Press ever on, pure in temptation's spite,
Breasting the storms of sorrow and distress,

True to thyself, and trusting that the hand
Of Christ, who died for all, shall, at the last,
Open the gate of paradise to thee.

I find these lines under date of Sunday evening, Feb. 15th, 1846 — almost ten years ago; and they would have slumbered quietly ten years more, in manuscript, if the day just passed, and the thoughts occasioned by it, had not called them forth to light. Pat., who, it seems, pores over such things of mine, says she has read them often before, but that "they never seemed so real and genuine as this evening." You are therefore indebted to her for them, entirely, my Editor.

Ten years ago I was somewhat addicted to writing verses, but I seldom write anything of the sort now. Good, plain, substantial prose is best for all such indifferent writers as Trifle. Genuine poetry, it is true, is always admirable; but how little of that does the world see, or has it ever seen.

Ten years gone, and another year just entered upon! Well, let them pass, my friend. We have nothing to do with their lapse, except to gain experience and wisdom, and to *keep* instead of breaking, constantly, the good resolutions we are so apt, all of us, in making. Let us live for the happiness of others, and we shall thus be happy ourselves — *here*, and we can keep a pretty clear look out for that hereafter which will call into requisition all our capacities for enjoyment. Let us travel on. What matter for the years.

I have read nothing to-day of any consequence, but have thought much upon my past, present, and future. Books and sermons do not constitute everything. Each man should study, and know himself. He may find more agreeable subjects for study, but he can certainly find none more important. Look yourself boldly in the face, my Editor. Don't shrink! — How do you find yourself — a little selfish, proud, discontented, disposed to murmur, &c., &c.? — Well, I know several others troubled in the same way. It's quite human, but it will never do, sir! — There's a cure and a balm for it. We can all become, if we will, more pure, gentle, affectionate, childlike, charitable. We are starting on a new year, and let us, therefore, try.

Monday, P. M.

The roads are so blocked with snow that all travelling is practically interdicted. Hence I have not travelled to town to-day. I have, rather, been taking a general survey of things here at Trifleton House. I have procured a small boy to dig us out of the drifts, and Trifleton House can now be approximated.

How different it seems from last summer. Then we had birds and flowers in the garden, and friends in the house; but now the garden is buried in a frigid shroud, and our friends are far away. Be it so. We should be independent of friends. We should find resources in ourselves, and we do. I speak the truth when I tell you that I feel absolutely merry to-day at Trifleton House. The shadows of last summer, it is true, are somewhat about me, but what then? That summer is fled, and my Hail is for the Future. I care not for the Past. Have we hopes, expectations, friends? Let them appear in the Future, and prove themselves real. I care not for the Past. It is gone, with its joys and its sorrows. Cling to it, you who sentimentalize. Good-bye to it, say I. It has become a ghost and a shadow. There is what is real -- there is work in the Future. Better brood no longer, ye dreamers, but awake, shake off your sloth and work, and, when you work, look to it that you work in the right direction! Care not too much for gold, for it will disappoint you. Nor for fame, for it will cheat you. Nor for what you call happiness, for it will slip from your grasp. Ascertain your *duty*, and discharge it!

Another most remarkable feature about yesterday and to-day, in addition to the snow, has been my being allowed to taste the *tomatoes* which Pat. put up for the winter; and *entre nous*, though it is by no means to be told in Gath, or to be published anywhere, I consider them an open question. Pat. says *she* don't think they've any too much *salt;* but that she " put in *considerable* to make them keep ; " and that I would better not mention it anywhere. So don't publish this part of my letter — I beg you not to. She says I'm no judge of tomatoes. I am not. The longer I live the more I am persuaded that I am rather fresh.

The quinces are a triumph, as are likewise your grapes. I'm much obliged to you for them. Editors, though, ought not to expect grapes.

I send you an extract from Stub's last letter:

" Our case has been reached and argued, and I feel satisfied that we have made all we can of it and brought out its whole strength. We stand now fairly before the Court, and I shall remain here until the opinion is given. I cannot speak in too high terms of the ability displayed by my associate counsel, and by the gentlemen on the other side also. A pure legal argument, pointed and vigorous, adorned by little rhetoric and weakened by less illustration, but marked by a severe simplicity, and pronounced in chaste and nervous English, and supported by principles and authorities, in such a manner as to enchain the interest and command the attention of the Court, is a lawyer's test and triumph.

"I was quite aware of all this when I ventured upon my opening. I trembled, at first, at the sound of my own voice, for I had for auditors men of ripe experience and mature judgment, while I myself was simply in my novitiate, and was, as it were, essaying an experiment. Still I knew by whom I was to be followed and sustained. This thought encouraged me; but, as I proceeded, I saw that the Court were honoring me with their attention, and their calm and dignified bearing and gentleman-like consideration for what even I might have to present, inspired me with a self-reliance such as I have seldom felt, and I spoke steadily on for an hour or two without further embarrassment, until I had quite gone through our brief, and discussed the several points contained in it.

"The kindness of the Court, of whose whole demeanor, in fact, I can never speak in terms of sufficient admiration, and the invaluable method and arrangement of my associate counsel, in the preparation of our brief, were the chief causes of my managing to push along as well as I did. I do not regard, then, my effort as entirely a failure; but I would not have spoken of it as freely as I have, except to gratify what I believe to be more than an idle curiosity on your part. I know that you are interested in all that I do.

"What the result shall be is of small moment to me, so far as it will affect my property, as I have said before. I care nothing for money or station, if I can but educate myself and benefit my kind, as I pass through life. I have nothing else to live for, my dear friend. For what the world calls happiness I do not look. The flush of my youth has passed, and my enthusiasm has become merged in experience and discipline. My hope has changed its name to disappointment, and my fine resolutions to work and accomplish, are fast fading away. I am growing inert and sluggish, for what have I to strive after? Who cares for me? I invest things and persons with virtues they never had, and the bitter reaction which follows the discovery of my mistake, makes me hate everybody. I am far from happy, and the amount of confidence I once reposed in a single woman, who has proved unworthy of it, I can only reflect upon with a shudder. It is unphilosophical and weak, I know, but I will never trust another woman. Whether it be true or false that one illustrate all, I know not and I care not. I wash my hands of the entire sex forever. Let them be content with their trinkets and their gossip; their small jealousies and frivolities; and their hot desires for admiration and flattery. I will not interfere with them or trouble them."

Another extract from his letter, in a different vein, is as follows:

"I have been reading Browning. We must assuredly talk him over, when I return, for the man is a marvel of his kind. Just hear him talk of 'Evelyn Hope,' who is dead:

'Her life had many a hope and aim —
Duties enough and little cares,
And now was quiet and now astir —
Till God's hand beckoned unawares,
And the sweet white brow is all of her.'

"And again, are you not startled at the irresistible appeal to the *human* passion in your composition, in the interrogatory in 'A Lover's Quarrel,' of

'Woman, and will you cast
For a word, quite off at last,
Me, your own, your *you.* —
Since, as truth is true,
I was you all the happy past —
Me do you leave aghast
With the memories we amassed?'

"The italicising is mine.

"What the following is I cannot tell, whether it be passion or poetry, or all *soul.* It is either intensely human or intensely not human — that is, something higher. Which?

'I would I could adopt your will,
See with your eyes, and set my heart
Beating by yours, and *drink my fill,*
At your soul's springs — your part, my part
In life, for good or ill.'

"Here, too, the italics are mine, as also in *this*, so full of meaning and feeling;

'Just when I seemed about to learn !
Where is the thread now ? Off again ?
The old trick ! *Only I discern*
Infinite passion and the pain
Of finite hearts that yearn.' "

We shall assuredly have to examine Browning a little, my Editor. It may be Stubs is somewhat too warm in regard to him. But don't you think the *kind* of selections he has given us a little remarkable — old married folks like us, — and besides, how are they consistent with other parts of his letter ?

I have seen nothing of Pink since my last. I occasionally ask Pat. about her : but quite all the information I get is, " Poor girl ! — Poor child ! " What this means is quite beyond me.

XXVI.

THE ARM CHAIR,
In the time of snow-banks.

WE have no doubt, most sweet-mouthed Trifle, that those grapes of which you speak with so much self-gratulation — *our* grapes you very provokingly call them — are excessively sour, even as your tomatoes are confessedly salt. We have no desire for your grapes. We have never believed in their good qualities since you told us how we were cheated — there's no use in being mealy-mouthed — absolutely *cheated* out of them, by your wife's great desire to gratify your inordinate love of "preserves." It is very refreshing to think how disappointed you must have been, when you found they were sour grapes, after all. You are fairly punished for some of your sins by this infliction on your fastidious palate.

It's all very well for you to talk so grandly about not caring for the summer, with its birds, and flowers, and friends. But of what value are words when your acts tell a different story? Shut up by snow-drifts, — to deliver you from which you call in the aid of a small boy, instead of attacking them with a vigorous arm yourself — you uncork your tomatoes, and plunge into your grapes, the only mementoes you have of the summer, and thus attempt to bring back the season which you profess to care nothing about. Do you succeed? Do the snow-drifts vanish with the taste of salt tomatoes? or are icy trees clothed with foliage as you rejoice in sour grapes?

That snow-storm *was* worthy of your notice, and certainly the deep drifts are not to be passed by without observation. Ay, is it not a glorious sight, the whole earth clad in such a spotless robe, covering its dark places, its unsightly pools, its more hideous features, as well as all its beauties, with purity? O for some moral storm thus to spread an unstained mantle over the dark places of misery, the foul pools of vice, the deformities of sin!

There are days of dazzling splendor in these seasons of snow; days whose brilliancy, and still, clear, invigorating air, more than compensate for the absence of the varied beauty of summer. The white snow everywhere, shining in the sun and blue in the shadow, with here and there a group of evergreens or the gray trunks and branches of the thick woods to relieve the eye, and over all the azure of the pure atmosphere,—cannot such a scene reconcile us to the rigors of our northern winter? The silence that seems to hang upon the still air is broken only by the crackling of dead branches in the woods, or the caw of the crow who flaps his lazy wings over the high trees, or a cheerful voice whose tones come up from the valley like music, or the distant tinkle of merry sleigh-bells, or the echoes which catch up all these sounds and repeat them softly.

So are there nights, with these midwinter snows, surpassingly beautiful, — yet of a kind of desolate beauty, which chills while it charms. The sense of solitude which comes over one where the snow stretches on every side, over hill and valley, white and shining in the moonlight in strong contrast with the dark sky, and there is no sign of human life, is really oppressive. Under no other circumstances — we have not been a Crusoe, nor at sea in an open boat, nor a solitary at the source of the Nile, nor in the great desert — have we felt so utterly alone, as in such a midwinter scene, at night. The sense of beauty is touched by the soft light, the striking contrasts and the charm of mystery which hangs over the landscape; but gradually awakens the sense of desolation and loneliness, as we look over the white plain, and hill, and valley, all cold, still and lifeless, as we hear no sound and see no living being, and feel that we stand alone above the dead earth, and in the immeasurable space above us worlds inaccessible.

We have been in this situation a few times, and experienced more than we dare — more than we can express. You have confessed to having essayed poetry in years gone by. Time was when we were guilty of the same folly, and your lines recalled to our memory some which we wrote more than "ten years" ago, suggested by an experience of such a "Winter's Night scene." We give you a part of them.

Night on the frozen earth, — night on the snow, —
Night in the dark blue sky, where the young moon,
Trailing her silver garments down the west,
Leaveth the infinite depth dotted with light,

As stars, like messengers from God, come forth.
Stillness and Night; no restless wind astir
Shakes the soft mantle of the bending boughs,
Or sighs or wails in sorrow unrelenting;
No voice nor music, chime nor echo breaks
The solemn hush, the deep, oppressive silence;
Over the pure white snow that lies, a pall,
On forms of beauty sleeping now in death,
There moves no life the solitude to waken.
The chill heart hears its own dull throbbings only,
And sinks in trembling, shivering dread before
This awful silence, solitude and death.
This solitude and death! Oh, shuddering soul,
Look up!—up from this frozen, desolate earth,
Its cold, pale, sculptured beauty, silence bound,
Into the fathomless infinite above,
Where the stars shine in ever-living light,
And chant, in full-toned heavenly harmony,
God's glory evermore.

We commended to your attention, in our last, Browning's new volume, and it seems that Stubs has done likewise. The recent death of Rogers, the veteran poet, who has so long lingered on life's stage, a representative of the past, suggests a comparison—rather a contrast—between these poets of different times and different schools. We do not propose to follow out the suggestion, but leave it for your own amusement. Perspicuity and taste are the characteristics of the author of the "Pleasures of Memory;" and his lines present a strong contrast to the frequent vagueness and obscurity of those of Browning. In poetry, and its impassioned expression, the latter is the superior of Rogers; but the clear elegance of the productions of the departed poet, their graceful harmony and polished thoughts, are sometimes more attractive than the subtile and beautiful ideas of the living one, and are, perhaps, as much to be studied and admired in these days of vague expression and meaningless words. But pray you lighten the heavy hours of a winter's evening, at Trifleton House, by comparing the two yourself. Not as Umber does, however; for though he admires Browning, with a mischievous humor he tears some of the most obscure lines from the context, and delights in showing their nonsense — when thus treated — by the side of some of the sweetest, and simplest, and most expressive of the well-studied verses of Rogers. That is the way many critics do, but, as you value your own progress by weary steps up Parnassus, be not guilty of such judgments.

At the Hard Mansion there have been some dark days. Dicky Dawson has been very ill there. The fever has run high, and for a time the doctor said the chances of recovery were very faint. And as the poor boy lay there — on Abel's bed and in his care — murmuring indistinct words, as if to his mother, and clutching at the bed-clothes, and looking up with glassy eye, it seemed that the doctor must be right, and that the course of the sufferer must be short. But the ways of Providence are not scrutable to doctors. There were kind hearts and willing hands about the sick boy, and comforts which seem sent to him providentially. The fever had its run and subsided, the mists rolled away from his brain, and the doctor has pronounced him safe. Safe! — ay, in Heaven's keeping and by God's mercy — not by virtue of physic. Yet the doctor was kind and attentive, and is skilful withal, but even the skilfulest and kindest is only an instrument. However, it is enough for the household, and the relief of the anxious, that the doctor pronounces him safe.

We went a few evenings since to the mansion, with the purpose — was it not kind of us, Trifle? — of cheering Abel's solitude a little, and relieving the monotony of his close-watching by the bedside of his sick protegé. We were surprised to learn he was not at home; but Mr. Umber, the servant said, was in the library! Umber domiciled here, and Abel gone! What has happened to bring this about? Is it a token of Umber's good fortune? So we thought as we entered the hall and were ushered into the library.

Umber was "at home," certainly. Dressing-gown and slippers and his lazy posture in an easy chair, said that very emphatically. He was at home for the evening, with no apparent intention of quitting his comfortable quarters this night, and on the contrary assuming a very host-like air, as he greeted us.

"But how is this, Umber? Have you actually become one of the family?"

"The whole of it, doing the honors of the tea table to myself, and entertaining myself after the most approved fashion, as you see. Abel has installed me here for a few days — more or less — to have a care for this boy, whom he saved from drowning to be a great trouble to him."

"And Abel?"

"Has gone again?"

"Whither?"

"To more sorrow, I fear. A letter yesterday informed him that Lily was failing rapidly, with a bad cough and other unpromising symptoms of sudden growth. A letter from Lily herself, full of gentle love — he read it to me — and a gentler spirit of resignation which triumphed over the anguish of her heart, told him that she believes her days will soon be numbered, and expressed a wish to see him again. He needed no other summons, and in his haste to comply with this request, he half conquered the misery and dread which at first overwhelmed him. He went this morning, leaving me to look after the boy whom I have just translated to dream-land by reading poetry, and now I am at your service."

"If Bel were here, now ——"

"*I* should not be."

Then Umber grew thoughtful. We fell to musing, too, checked by the grave tone of his voice; and looking into the hissing Cannel in the grate, — that fire shall ever be our delight! — we thought of the Hon. Mr. Weed, calculating how many weeks or months it might be, before Madame should make the mansion brilliant for the consummation of her plans to unite her only daughter with that piece of human — broadcloth, money and vice. Umber, perhaps, was thinking of the same thing, for he spoke, half to us, and half to himself.

"Bel is unhappy, and is waywardly, or perhaps under the pressure of circumstances, hastening her own misery. If I could but dispel the cold, unhealthy atmosphere which surrounds her heart! But I am too poor to presume to say I love her, and too proud to subject myself to scorn. Our old friendship only seems to compel her to raise a barrier between her heart and me, and as I seek to break over that barrier, and to know and make her know what her heart really is, the more sedulously she raises and preserves it. She is a paradox. She despises him whose wife she is hastening to be; she repels me whom she might love — if I were not what I am."

"Like all women, she loves display, and would marry the wealth which can afford it."

"All women?"

"Most women, then."

"Education and fashion are generally responsible for such feelings, or such actions, rather; and in Bel's case add her mother's influence. Underneath the conventional character which she assumes, I *know* there is something better, — a spirit like that expressed in the idealized portrait of her, only more passionate."

"Have you made friends with her for that offence?"

"I have not seen her since. But if I could read aright, she is too true a woman not to feel and appreciate the purpose of that picture — when she had time for thought."

"You extol her."

"Not above her worth. Yet am I a fool to dream as I do."

There was the jingle of bells in the avenue, and then a ring at the door, voices and a stir in the hall, during which Umber and we looked at each other with a due sense of the awkwardness in which we were placed as guests without a host. Before we had recovered from our surprise, the door opened, and Bel Hard entered hurriedly. We had both risen, and Bel, passing me with a gentle salutation, hastened to Umber, whom in his domestic garb she at first mistook for Abel. But she stopped suddenly.

"Ah! I thought it was my brother."

She held out her hand cordially to Umber, though her lip quivered as she spoke. He took it for a moment, but before he could say why he, and not Abel, was there, Bel burst into tears, and left the room as hastily as she entered it.

This sudden appearance and strange agitation were hardly realized, before we were made aware of the worldly presence of Madame Hard, to whom all due explanations were made, and we departed.

Women weep when they are happiest, do they not?

XXVII.

TRIFLETON HOUSE,
In the month of drained purses.

I PRESUME you have had plenty of New Year's presents; — of that kind we family men usually get, — one from the grocer, one from the butcher, one from the baker, one from the tailor; and — to sum it all up in a word — a great many from a great many others you expected nothing from; people you had almost forgotten, in fact, but who kindly remembered you, considerate souls!

There is always more or less obligation connected with this system of holiday presents, and a spirited person likes to make some return for his gifts. Hence I find it a good way to ascertain as nearly as possible, the value in money of my presents, and to force the amount, be it more or less, upon my donors. A generous grocer, or a clement butcher will waive the delicacy of the thing, and accept it at once. I have even seen those who would coolly give you a receipt, and write upon it those quaint words, "received payment;" which indicates to my mind that they actually expect to be paid in money for every present they make!

Money is a formidable agent. Men are conciliated by it, and women barter away their happiness for it. The shabby brethren of Joseph exposed themselves to eternal animadversion for a scanty amount of it; and Judas betrayed our Saviour for a few insignificant pieces of silver. And yet is a little money a most convenient thing to have in the early part of January. It is not necessarily the cause, but it is veritably the means of much happiness, in a world like this.

It's excellent to make and pay presents with.

I trust, my Editor, that you have an exuberance of it about this time. But Editors, after all, have very little need of it, for are they not supplied constantly with the choicest luxuries, with season tickets to the Theatre, and complimentary tickets to the Opera? And consider their libraries! Every new book is anxiously thrust upon them, while neither Phillips & Sampson, Ticknor & Fields, nor Whittemore, Niles & Co. ever impart a solitary volume to luckless Trifle, without compensation therefor in lucre. My real belief is that these publishers try to make all of us, who are not Editors, wretched. For we want their books. To be without them, is to be wretched; — and to be continually paying our dollars away for them, is to be wretched also. For what have we left, in order to pay our New Year's presents, withal?

Being in rather a dingy status from trains of thought somewhat kindred to these, and reflecting upon the lapse of years and the increased expenditures of living, I looked in some days since upon Goody Green, to see how the sharp severity of the new year was affecting her, and to inform her that I had ordered a few articles of fuel, clothing, &c., for her.

I found her, as usual, cheerful and happy, toasting

her shins by her stove, which answers alike for culinary purposes and for warming her apartments; and her gratitude was unbounded for my trifling donations. Mr. Editor, she is happy, poor though she be.

If you wish to know what real happiness is, she can inform you.

As she worked, with nimble fingers, upon her old shreds of list, and fragments of cloth, flannel, and what not, with which she fabricates her "rag carpets" (her usual occupation), I took occasion to ask her how she relished the idea of adventuring upon another year of life, and added that her lot was rather a hard one.

"Yes," said she, "so you folks who live in fine houses say; but I'm very comfortable, — I be."

"But you are growing old, and can't work much longer!"

"Yes, I'm almost *home*, and what mercies I've had, (I shuddered at my own ingratitude, as I looked around her wretched apartments), and how kind the Lord is that's always taken care of me! When I think o' the *poor*, this bitter weather, that ha'n't got no home, (oh, God forgive me, I inwardly prayed), I feel I have much to be thankful for."

"But do you never think that you may be worse off, and that these hard times may reduce you to a state in which you would find it difficult to sustain your present condition?" I inquired, in a very questionable if not almost mean spirit of curiosity — which I could not resist.

"Sometimes; but such thoughts is (are) pernici ous."

"The world, though, is cold and heartless, and friends are few and inconstant."

"I don't mind the world," she exclaimed, turning towards me with a glowing countenance, "and I have faith in the Lord. He is my friend."

"He may console and comfort you; but, while we live in this world, do we not need food and raiment?" said I, pushing her faith to its severest test, in spite of the conviction that I had no right thus to catechize her.

"He will give me all I wants," she replied. "Miss Pink reads to me that He commanded the ravens to feed Elijah, and about the poor widow whose barrel of meal never wasted, and whose cruise of oil never failed. I have faith to believe He will always take care o' me; and, then, our blessed Lord and Saviour said we musn't take no thought o' such things, but that we must seek fust (first) the kingdom o' Heaven, and all sich (such) things should be added unto us — or the like o' that."

And so is she happy, my Editor, from sheer *Faith.* Do you understand it? There is something certainly mysterious in this *Faith*, which is thus the sum and substance, quite, of a human life; — something which will not be gainsaid, and which utterly conquers and exorcises the temptation to despair, or even to repine and despond.

I know many cultured men who could argue this poor old woman down, but whom, in the end, she could subdue without argument.

I will not narrate to you, in detail, all the conversation I had with her. Suffice it to say I left her "a sadder and a wiser man." She said, among other things, that she couldn't understand our habits of thought and action.

She informed me that she thought Pink was unhappy (I tell it to you in my own language), because she was laboring under the idea she had wronged some one; and that she advised her to make amends for it by acknowledging her error and asking the forgiveness of the person she had wronged; that Pink said *that* was hard to do, and would cost a great sacrifice of pride and self-respect; that she told her self-respect was oftentimes only another name for what was haughty and imperious, and sinful in the sight of God, and that a chivalric and generous spirit thought not so much of what was agreeable to selfish promptings, as of what was right and just; that it was easy to do wrong, but hard to do right, according to the conventionalisms of society; but that the more we discarded these wretched conventionalisms, and the nearer we approached a state of simplicity and nature, the simpler, and purer, and holier we should become, — that we should be happier ourselves, and make those around us happier.

A very simple and ignorant woman is poor Goody Green, but she is also — very wise. Think of her advising Pink, and what is stranger still, think of Pink's asking her advice!

She says she considers that Pink is vastly changed from what she was a few months since, and that it's a great pity she is to marry the man with the corn-colored gloves; but he is impatient, and the wedding day has been fixed. It is drawing very nigh, and is only some six or eight weeks off.

Good bye, Pink.

Goody insists to me that she ought to marry Stubs; so little does she know of this world and its ways.

She has not been in *society*.

Stubs is her idol. She exaggerates his virtues. His faults she has never seen. She exhibited much concern in regard to the result of his suit. I promised her she should hear about it.

She will.

Pink took tea and spent last evening with us. It has been, as you are aware, a considerable length of time since I have seen her. I should scarcely know her. She is still surpassingly beautiful, but she looks worn and anxious. She is thinner and paler than ever before. Her cheek is not the color of the radish now.

She was sitting quietly after tea with Pat., at a small work-table. They were both engaged at their work, and interesting themselves in some private conversation, in which they evidently didn't wish me to participate. I therefore smoked my cigar and read my paper in silence. I had no desire to disturb them, and I was quite satisfied with the conversation I was holding with myself. At times, my Editor, when I am in good humor, I find myself tolerably good company — quite entertaining, in fact.

But not a great while can two feminines talk simply with each other, when there is one of us distinguished "lords of creation" in the room — and Pat. inquired —

"Trifle, what's the news from town?"

"Not much," I replied, "except —— let me think

— ah ! yes, except this letter which I received to-day from — Stubs."

I glanced at Pink. She seemed in no way interested, but went on with her work. She didn't even look up.

I read the following extract : —

"The *opinion* of the Court has been given ; it is *against* us. I shall come immediately home."

"Oh, how sorry I am ! " exclaimed Pat. "Stubs will be so unhappy, stripped of his property. I pity him from my heart."

Pink still worked on most vigorously. It so happened that a book I wanted was lying on the work-table, and as I was unwilling to trouble her to hand it to me, I walked up to the table and took it myself, and how could I avoid seeing her tears falling like rain upon her worsted, or what not, which she was vainly attempting to get out of the snarl in which she had entangled it. She had been working all the time with great assiduity, and I was surprised to see the kind of progress she had made ; and why she selected such a moment for crying, is more than I know. But who can understand women ? — Without noticing her embarrassment (and neither she nor Pat. knew I observed it), I remarked carelessly, —

"I am glad Stubs has lost his case."

As in the olden time, Pink turned towards me, her head no longer drooping, but thrown back proudly, her eyes kindling and blazing with fire, and the tears, which were still swimming in them, glaring like diamonds, and inquired —

"Is such, then, a man's view of his friend's misfortune? How charitable it is!" (with a slight curl of the lip.)

"It is," said I, quite satisfied with my experiment, "and it is also a charitable view. In both particulars you are correct — as you generally are."

A shudder again — a struggle, and the fire in her eyes went out, and she was meekness illustrated.

"Pardon me, dear Trifle, but I do not quite understand you."

"Stubs has been a fool most of his life."

"How? what do you mean? are you jesting?"

These questions came all in a breath, with great rapidity — vehemence almost. She looked up in my face with a gaze of such beaming, earnest inquiry, of such radiant, sparkling intelligence, that I thought it was not only not surprising that Stubs should have loved her so, but surprising, rather, that the whole world did not.

"I never jest," I answered, "upon subjects of this character. What I mean is, that Stubs, who has capacity, only wanted necessity to provoke it into action in order to make his mark. That necessity has come."

She replied with a smile, such as no woman I ever saw could command, and was eagerly putting another interrogatory, when I interrupted her with —

"But I ask your pardon for saying so much of my absent friend. You will think I have no interest in *you.* Come, let's hear about the great event. Is the dress selected? Are we quite ready, Pink, and how does *he* feel about it? Does he write most tender letters, urging you to have compassion on his impatience?"

"Why, how foolish you are, Trifle," said my interesting Pat.

I'm sure I could see no impropriety in what I had said, and I looked to ascertain if Pink were at all hurt. I was startled — shocked, I may say. A look of wretchedness was on her face, such as I have never seen except on the countenance of Mrs. Fanny Kemble, when representing Queen Catherine, in one of her readings. I said nothing further. A long pause ensued, when, presently, a voice was heard crying, in eager, almost jubilant tones, "Trifle, Pat., I am home again!" and my hand was wrung, and Pat.'s lips were warmly kissed before we could scarcely collect our senses at the sight of —— Stubs.

My duty is to record facts, and disguise nothing in this most veracious history.

Pink started. Evidently struggling with emotions she found it impossible to resist, she rose from her seat, and, bowing, attempted to speak; when, turning very pale, she began to tremble, and would, I think, have fallen to the floor, if he had not caught her in his arms. He laid her on the sofa, and forgetful of time, place, and circumstance, kissed her like a madman — brow, cheek and lips.

Pat. and I stood spell-bound.

Once she opened her eyes, and a sweet and quasi angelic smile passed over her face. She lifted her arms involuntarily, and wound them round his neck, and — again she was like one dead.

Pat. and I were awed. A moment more and we were deluging her with restoratives.

I have told you in a former letter how Stubs and Pink parted.

It was thus they met.

Said Pat — "She has had these headaches frequently of late. They always make her faint."

There spoke the woman!

Item. — Pink's father has failed in business. He is deeply insolvent. She don't know it, as yet. But I do. What think you of the world, my Editor?

I incline more and more to the opinion that Pink has a heart.

XXVIII.

THE ARM CHAIR,
At the close of the 1st month, '56.

MONEY! That is the text of your last letter from the date thereof to the "item" which mentions the failure of Pink's father. A very suggestive subject, truly. Suggestive of misery, however, as much as pleasure and happiness, — misery to yourself, who fall into a "dingy status" (that's a queer expression,) as if Trifleton House were insolvent, and misery to your friends, who have the misfortune to lose their property and to become as poor — as we are.

Money is, in truth, a "formidable agent," as you say. *We* should say that it is a formidable foe. Nevertheless, it is a powerful agent. It is a means for innumerable ends, good and evil, great and small; but unfortunately some of us have more ends than means. It procures a pinch of snuff, a penny paper, and a polish on the boots, and it likewise procures broad domains, palaces and pictures, and splendid equipage. It procures misery and pains too; but then it finds the doctors to cure such ills. It purchases men and women, services, sometimes love, souls even. It brings pleasure, but with all its might it can't get happiness.

Gold and silver are generally supposed to be the true currency, the only real money, and when one can get them they are certainly not to be declined. Even paper money — those pretty pictures which men "make believe" *are* money — is not to be altogether disregarded. But there is another metal, which, though not absolutely "legal tender" (nor, in fact, *tender* in any way) is quite as current and quite as potent with those who have enough of it. *Brass* was a common and very useful coin, in olden time, and for many centuries it has been used more or less, but chiefly among the most enlightened nations.

At the present day, though it do not always bear the regal effigies or the national mint stamp, it never was more current or more potent. Some people style it a base metal. But if its value be measured or weighed by what it purchases or accomplishes, it is wonderfully precious.

Some of us, Trifle, have as little of this latter currency as we have of the former. It is a great misfortune, for he who has not gold and silver, ought surely to have brass. Else how can he get along in this world, where everybody progresses only by means of 'hese metals ?

Let us look around and see how the world, just about us, goes. Don't you see the force of brass ? Observe how H —— prospers in his business on that large capital of this same metal ; — how B —— rapidly mounts the political ladder by the liberal use of it ; — how L —— achieves matrimony and wealth at once by wearing a circlet of it under his "Hyperion curls." In short, see how in things great and small it is as formidable as gold — if in skilful hands. There is one inconvenience to some people about it; for however rich it makes its possessor, they who part with their goods under the temptation it offers, seldom find that they have an equivalent for that with which they parted. It makes him who buys with it rich, but impoverishes him on whom it is bestowed.

But after all, what are the effects of any of these metals, gold, silver, or brass, wherewith men get possessions, upon the heart and soul? Do they not weigh heavily there? — overshadowing and crushing out the affections, and the hopes and aspirations which but for this dull, solid weight, might have grown upward and borne good fruit, — might have secured possessions more lasting? From the world come silent answers in numberless examples.

Look up, then, ye unfortunate, who possess neither gold, nor silver, nor brass, but have that within you which can look up. Around your hearts shall not be reared the hard, cold walls over whose battlements you may not look forth upon God's works. No canopy of earthly ores shall shut out from you the sight of the heavens. No clanking chains, whether of gold or silver, shall fetter you to earth. Thus far have ye an advantage over some ye deem more fortunate. For the rest, be earnest, thoughtful, courageous, just and honest, and notwithstanding an occasional rebuff or defeat in your campaign with fortune, you will triumph in the end. Yes, all of you, — Trifle, Stubs, Umber.

Even Umber, though we begin to have some doubts about him, he has become so despondent, at times.

Ever since the return of Madame Hard and Bel, he has appeared dull, sometimes even stupid, as if he were in a dream. The shock of that sudden return which found him domesticated at the mansion seems to have had a bad effect.

A day or two since he came in, bringing a letter which he had received from Abel Hard. Handing it to us he asked us to read and "make a note" of it, and seizing a book he threw himself on the sofa with no more words, but a troubled expression on his face. We read the letter, which contained the following:

"Our worst fears are but too certain to be realized, and even now we begin to dread only the hour of that sad certainty, that Lily must die. Too surely, too plainly, she fails. Hemorrhage and a cough wear upon her weakened frame but too rapidly and too perceptibly. How has she changed since I first learned the rapture of our mutual love! Pale and thin she seems to have grown ethereal. Her soft eye has acquired an unusual brilliancy and an expression of deeper feeling — of more heavenly feeling, I think, as it turned upon me with a bright glance, but with unutterable tenderness.

"We have conversed much, and freely. I think I have listened to an angel as she spoke, she has uttered such words of truth, and cheering hope, and of deep religious faith. And while I stand, as it were, on the very verge of an overwhelming sorrow, she has borne me up across the chasm, and pointed me on to a happy future. She has, like the sun, gilded the clouds that hang about her departure, and opened through them visions of far reaching, infinite beauty. She leads me on — O God! that I may follow her! — by endless progress onward and upward towards the perfect.

"I marvel, myself, at the change which has come over me under Lily's influence. I came here in restless sorrow, tortured with the dread of losing the priceless treasure I had just found. In my grief my spirit was rebellious against the decrees of Heaven. But now, when I know more certainly that what I most feared must come, and watch the days go by which surely bring the end, I look upon it calmly, — I look beyond with an indefinable but a sustaining hope. Something of that heavenly resignation, which seems now to be the very essence of her being, is infused into my own nature by the force of its purity and strength, and the passionate spirit, chafing with a selfish sorrow, is subdued, and softened, and cheered.

"Lily's father, in his anxiety and affection for her, has forgotten his misanthropy and his misfortunes even. Her gentle — oh, more than gentle, her angelic spirit has wrought a change in him, too. But his heart is full of an unutterable grief. And for him, whom she will leave alone in his sorrow, is Lily's deepest regret.

"I wish that Bel were here. The icy garb which envelopes her warm, true heart, would be swept away forever. Commend to her care, when she returns, the boy, for the sake of Dawson, who nurses Lily with so much devotion."

When we had read this letter, of which we give you but a part, we turned to Umber. He was looking intently on the book which he held, but it was upside down. He started as we spoke.

"Abel tells a sad story, yet he is hardly more to be pitied than congratulated."

"He is much more to be congratulated than pitied. He has attained the true happiness of love in a return of his affection."

"But is he not to be pitied that death must divide them so soon?"

"Better be divided by death than folly. But even there he is not to be pitied; for under less affliction their affection would have been less pure and elevated, and would not have had the influence which it now has. It is because he loves, as it seems to him, an angel, and listens to words spoken almost from another world, that Lily has so broken through his second nature and lifted up his thoughts from selfish sorrow to pure hopes."

"It is a little strange that the change should have been so quickly effected."

"Not remarkable. Abel has, under the surface, a deep religious sentiment, which needed only a breaking of the crust and the gentle encouragement which such a spirit as Lily's affords him. It is a sentiment that may not tolerate creeds and the dogmas of theology, but accepts the great truths of religion which tower above all the mists raised by church and sect. When he was in Italy some of the better influences of the church might have made him a Roman Catholic, but that he was more repelled by dogmas and forms that offended his religious feeling. Now, that sentiment, aroused by impending affliction, is addressed in a manner more consonant with itself, and it follows the aspirations of the purer nature which has become his teacher without forms and creeds.

"Will this state of mind continue?"

"As it is founded on a sentiment really strong, and is sustained by affection, in which it has in part its origin, why should it not continue? But I did not mean to discuss Abel's sorrows or hopes. I came to ask a favor."

"What is it?"

"That you will take this letter to Bel Hard."

"Abel's?"

"Yes."

"Why do you not go yourself?"

"I cannot. Since her return, Bel has pointedly shunned me when I have called to see the sick boy, and once when I found her in the sick room, she hastily withdrew after a most cold and hurried salutation. I shall give her no further offence, and no opportunity to slight me."

"How can we interpret this?"

"Her nature is twofold, and the external, fashionable, hollow and insincere has triumphed over the real, true and lovely."

"The letter shall go."

While speaking of Bel, Umber's manner was unusually disturbed. All his tones clearly expressed a deep disappointment which could only be inferred from his words. We had no idea that he was so irretrievably lost in a hopeless attachment. Why, is he not poor and of no account in the world? He will, perhaps, some day achieve a name; but he will be gray then, and future fame, or greatness, or wealth, self-achieved, do not pass current in the present.

We went to the mansion and inquired for Bel. We

were shown into a parlor where she was, alone. We had anticipated that the Hon. Mr. Weed might be there, for he has arrived from Washington, we learn. For what purpose he has followed so closely on the returning steps of the Hards, we may guess. Bel was alone. As we entered she laid down a book — it was a volume of Tennyson — and rose to meet us.

Has female beauty any charm for you? We doubt if it has. Your idea is satisfied with the loveliness of Pat., or Pink, or some other friend, and you have no glance, even, for the beauty of a stranger or a less dear friend. *We* presume to be more sensible. Bel never appeared more beautiful than she did then, and she is certainly *belle*. She has been more brilliant and probably more attractive. But now there was a look of deep sadness — not discontent, as we have formerly seen — on her face, and her eye was soft rather than cold and languid. As she spoke, a faint smile softened, but did not dispel, the sad look, and lent a charm to her expression such as we had not before seen on her face. She was more like Umber's fancy portrait than we had seen her of late, only the happy expression was wanting.

Formalities being over — there must be some formalities at a mansion like the Hards', though Bel and Abel are not particular about them — we presented the letter which Abel had written to Umber, saying it was the request of the latter.

"And could *he* not come?"

She looked us full in the face with earnest eyes, and

we could see them fill with tears, as she uttered these words with a slight tremulousness.

We are afraid we stammered as we attempted some excuse for Umber, and doubtless made bad work of it, for the expression of bitterness, too familiar on that fair face, returned, and she turned coldly towards the table to read the letter.

"The contents of the letter are somewhat sad."

She seemed not to hear, for she opened it not. She rested her brow upon one hand, the other dropped at her side and the letter fell to the floor. There was a struggle going on in her mind, and we were compelled to be an unwilling witness of it. But we could not quite comprehend it all. After a few moments we ventured to pick up the letter, saying,

"Your brother writes sadly, but do not anticipate bad news."

"Thank you. And pardon me for my weakness."

The 'weakness' was not all gone, for the effort to speak calmly was not quite successful. She opened the letter, but we knew that those swimming eyes could scarcely decipher the touching words of Abel's letter. We intimated that we would not trespass upon her presence that she might read the letter more at ease. Shall we ever forget the look with which she replied? — the sweet, sad, grateful smile that opened to us the knowledge of a heart we had not dreamed was possessed by Bel Hard?

"Thank you."

Those were the only words, but the look and the tone expressed infinitely more.

And so we departed, pondering on the mysteries of life, and pitying Umber, who is to lose so much womanly tenderness and worth, — pitying Bel, who is to cast such pearls before — the Hon. Mr. Weed.

What think we of the world! Trifle. That there is much goodness in it which we have not yet discovered.

XXIX.

TRIFLETON HOUSE,
In February of '56.

HAVE you ever read Ovid's beautiful poem of the Four Ages? If you have, you will doubtless remember how he speaks of the inordinate pursuit of gain — *amor sceleratus habendi* — and that he describes it as one of the marked features of the Iron Age. Is not all he says as true now as it was in his day? I think so, notwithstanding all our rapid strides in civilization of which we boast so much.

But Ovid knew nothing, or, at least, tells us nothing of *failures*, as we call them. They are quite of our day, and incidental to our mercantile communities. We best illustrate the credit system. We all owe each other, and so far is it possible for us to live on mere credit, and nothing else, that, when a great merchant *fails*, nobody is astonished that for years he has been sustaining an establishment, equipage, and what not, on borrowed capital; and that he hasn't had sufficient moral courage to come out and tell the world, like a man, of his bankrupt condition. We are a "fast" and "stunning" people, and each one of us is eager to keep up with the times, and outstrip his neighbors in external display and glitter. We, therefore, spend money not only after, but before we have earned it, and, when we become embarrassed, we run large risks in hopes of large gains, and the result is, every year, a series of "failures."

In any point of view, it is a sad thing for a man to fail. A true man, indeed, never fails in the proper significance of that term; but I use it now in its mercantile and American sense. Many a man would rather die than fail. No matter what anybody else may think, he at least sees something in it to be ashamed of — something ignominious almost; and if his nature be proud and sensitive, he will be inclined to quite break up, or rather, to employ a cant phrase, "break down" under it, unless he is sustained and encouraged by those about him.

Have you ever been called upon to sympathize with a man in such circumstances, and to persuade him that he had still something worth living for? Have you ever met his creditors face to face, and stood in the gap between their indignation and his despondency — despair even, oftentimes? If you have not, I have. I have seen all sides of human nature, the worst and the best, and my belief is, that though men are selfish, they are still open to conviction: and however harshly creditors may bear upon a failing man in the first flush of their excitement, in the end they will generally deal with him justly, leniently, generously, if he prove himself to be an honest man.

In a world like this we ought certainly to make allowances for each other. None of us are infallible. All of us are liable to misfortune. When a man fails, then, however improvident and foolish he may have been in his manner of conducting his business, let us be at least charitable. Let us hear before we strike, and treat him as men and Christians should treat a fellow in his distress. We shall thus lose nothing, and we may gain what is invaluable.

I have been led into this train of thought by observing the actions of Stubs, since my last letter. Forgetful of his own misfortunes, he has undertaken the settlement of the affairs of Pink's father. He called a meeting of the Boston creditors, which I attended at his request, and I was much struck with his conduct and management.

Who reviles lawyers?

Let such an one see a real, Christian lawyer, and attempt to set a value upon the influence he is capable of exerting, and we shall hear no more contemptuous flings at the profession. It is indeed the noblest of professions, in worthy hands, and more good is accomplished, more differences healed, more acerbities soothed, and more bitterness subdued and softened by it than most people are aware of. A true, genuine lawyer is the most valuable man in any community. He can do more practical good than a minister, because, while he may be just as pure, charitable and religious, he knows men better, and can judge better how they should be treated for their own good. If the clergy would practise law a dozen years before attempting to preach, they would preach more efficient sermons, and their influence in our communities would be more commanding. I sometimes wish I were a lawyer myself.

It is not for me to furnish the reasons why — but Pink has never before shone with such a lustre as she has appeared in since her father's failure. She has no mother, and she is to her father, as he told me, at once daughter, friend, and wife. She is the bulwark of his strength and safety. She infuses a courage into him he thought himself incapable of. She shares his sorrows, and dissipates his anxieties. Like a true woman, in a good cause, she gives him her heart and her hand, and makes him hope, in spite of himself. Without the least embarrassment, so far as she can, in the nature of things, she co-operates with Stubs in the adjustment of his affairs, and Pat. tells me she is astonished at her energy and character.

She is a daughter indeed, and if the man with the corn-colored gloves gets her for his wife, he will get a true woman. She has never indicated herself before. Indeed, my theory is that no woman is fairly tested and discovered till she has suffered. Discipline makes a woman, as it does a man; but in real distress a woman surpasses a man. In prosperity, a woman will be, oftentimes, frivolous, weak, inert, and selfish. In adversity, she is superior to a man. Where a man will break, she will simply bend, and, with an admirable elasticity, rebound to her place. Without women, what weak fools we men should be! We call ourselves self-reliant, but how dependent are we upon their sympathy!

We call ourselves brave; but, in our extremities, how do we look to them for courage! We call ourselves energetic; but how little could we accomplish without their aid! They are, indeed, the "better half" of our life. When we despond, they comfort and sustain us; — when we break, and faint, and despair, they appeal to and evoke the hidden resources of our nature.

Stubs talks of Pink in the most enthusiastic manner. I begin to think he is still in love with her, notwithstanding all that has occurred. He says he has done her much injustice; and, in fact, from a variety of such remarks, and my own observation in general, I rather incline to the opinion that it would be much better for her to marry him, than to marry the man with the corn-colored gloves.

You may explain it, if you can, but never was her cheek ruddier, her eye brighter, and her lip fresher than it is now. From the ashes of her father's ruin, and her own despondency during Stubs' absence, she has come up with an extraordinary recuperativeness. Pat. says that she is very happy, in spite of all her unhappiness. What this means I cannot tell, but I never could understand women. They are full of contradictions and inconsistencies. Still I am very glad Pink is so bright and hopeful, just at this time, because, consider how wretched her poor father would be to see her depressed and down-hearted! He would break at once.

As for Stubs, he seems like anything but a man who has just lost most of his property in a lawsuit. He is calm, collected, and natural, and evidently quite forgets himself in —— Pink; that is, in her father's misfortunes, and in her as connected and identified with them. He is full of charity, and does what he can to console both father and —— daughter. Pink evidently regards him as an admirable lawyer, and defers unhesitatingly to his counsel and directions.

As he must now practise his profession for a living, I am glad he has such a case in his hands. The result of it may affect his whole career. Who knows? Slight circumstances make or mar one's fortunes.

Meantime, my Editor, the winter of '56 pushes on vigorously. I am told there has been nothing like it for thirty-two years. I tell Pat. we shall be ruined on the coal question. Trifleton House has been surrounded with snow and ice for more than six weeks. Inside, we manage to make our thermometers act respectably; but outside they lose all their courage, and are worse than nothing. They are weak to such a degree that they can seldom get above *zero*, if that interesting point may be considered as a degree. In fact, they show no character at all, and keep in such a dingy, low, disreputable state that I am becoming quite ashamed of them.

Pat. thinks she sees indications of a thaw — by and by. She has been seeing them for a month.

"Why, Trifle," says she, "our January thaw hasn't come yet!"

I'm afraid not, and do you think it ever will, my Editor?

I understand this is Leap Year, and I incline to the opinion that the January thaw aforesaid has skipped over our heads.

I gather from various valuable treatises that the month of February will be a good time in which to trim the Trifleton grape vines. But how can I do that while they are buried up in two feet of snow, or ice, rather, and what will become of *your* grapes? Will you please to inform me.

Prig keeps house all the time, and wishes to know daily when the Spring will come; for in the Spring the velocipede grandma has promised him will arrive, and he will play in the dirt and gravel once more.

Ah, my Editor, how many weary hearts are yearning for the Spring! Burdened, and chilled, and frozen by the winter of life, they hope to be happier in — the Spring. When the Spring comes, they will, perhaps, postpone their expectations of happiness till the Summer; when Summer comes, till the Autumn; and when Autumn comes, till the Winter. And so do they subsist on hope, and hope alone.

My theory is, that we should enjoy what we can *now*. We havn't long to live in this world, and we are too apt to grow old in searching for happiness such as we can never find. We are all too fond of living an ideal rather than a real life. The regular and actual details of duty well performed must, if anything can, constitute our happiness — *here*.

Item. — Last night about eleven o'clock, just as we were retiring, our door-bell rang violently, and a moment afterwards Goody Green rushed in, in a state of prodigious excitement. The cold had tipped her nose with the color of tomatoes, and if I had never seen her before, I should have regarded her as a somewhat suspicious looking visitor. She declared in voluble terms that she had called to see me upon a matter of the most urgent importance.

"The happiness of two feller beings," said she, "Mr. Trifle, depends on it."

With much solicitude, and no little anxiety, I begged her to communicate its nature, and promised to do what I could for her. "Promise me not to tell, sir, no, not nobody," she exclaimed, with earnestness. I promised.

Taking a letter from her pocket, she asked me for the address of the man with the corn-colored gloves. Happening to know it, by the merest accident in the world, I gave it to her immediately, and she wrote it down with her pencil in the most precipitate manner. She then read a letter she had been writing him.

It was in her own style and language, but was surpassingly eloquent, it was so full of noble feeling. She wrote that she *knew* that Pink's heart was in the keeping of Stubs, and had been for a long time, even before her engagement; that Stubs was the noblest of men, and idolized Pink, but was far too generous ever to tell her of it, and thus embarrass her and make her miserable; that it was right in the sight of God that they should marry; that, if she married any other man, she would sacrifice the happiness of her life simply on a point of delicacy or honor; and that *he* would perform an act of genuine manliness if he would come immediately on, and release her from an engagement entered into under the excitement of anger and hurt pride.

Poor Goody! The wedding day is fixed, and marriages have little to do with hearts. What think you of life, serenest and most excellent of editors?

XXX.

The Arm Chair,
In the time of the first thaw of '56.

It has come at last, that thaw which the weather-wise prophesied and the snow-sick hoped for in January. That hard old warrior, Winter, has got a repulse at last. He has been besieging us for six weeks, growing more and more bold and defiant, until we were almost desperate. But he is down now, and some people say his back is broken. The warm south wind took the spirit out of him, and the sun has shot arrows through and through his white and shining armor. The snow banks are turning into floods, and if Trifleton House shall not be carried away by a freshet, you may congratulate yourself and your household.

"Have you ever read Ovid's beautiful poem of the Four Ages?"

That is a proper question for a close student of the Ledger like you, O classic Trifle! But we do remember that, far back in the days of our boyhood, we scanned and translated those verses with no little pleasure, considering they were always a task. We think we have never opened those pages since. We are of opinion that if Ovid lived now, or were by some spiritual medium to express his views, he would find the present an age of mingled bronze and iron, and of gold and silver too, in one sense of the words — a mass of glitter and base metals which would confuse all his former ideas of the ages, — unless, indeed, he looked deeper than the surface, much deeper, into the crystal springs and among the gems that are hidden there, beneath the cold, hard exterior.

"Who reviles lawyers?" is another quaint question in your last letter. Who reviles lawyers? Not we, certainly, after your praises of a "real Christian lawyer." Doubtless there are good men who are lawyers (professionally), and good lawyers who are *men*. But what is a lawyer who is —— a lawyer and nothing else? You may have seen such, growing gray before their time, inhaling and inspiring Coke and Blackstone, pleadings and reports, until the real, warm blood of humanity is deprived of vitality, and becomes a cold, slow stream, that clears the brain but stupefies and chills the heart. They look ever on the dark side of human life, seeing only vile passions, dishonesty, or meanness, or poverty, which to them is both dishonesty and meanness. They are sceptics in honesty, and honor, and truthfulness; the affections are unknown to them; sufferings and despair touch them not. Sometimes with noiseless feet and oily tongues they spread their nets about the unsuspecting unfortunate, and sometimes drive a car of Juggernaut, an unyielding mass of forms and precedent, which they foolishly call "Justice," over weak and despondent victims.

And what are they socially? They are sharp enough intellectually, and correct enough, morally — perhaps. But socially they are cold, ungenial, barren; they contribute nothing to human happiness, and derive no happiness from others; they measure life and human beings by precedents and authorities, and imagination and hope, friendship and love, are always convicted felons at the bar of their opinion.

These are lawyers who are *lawyers*. Thank Heaven! there are, even in this age of iron and brass, lawyers who are *men*, who acknowledge the claims of humanity, who have hearts, who, in fine, do not leave their Christianity at the church door, but carry it into the office and the court room, and into social life. But what proportion of "the bar," think you, are these latter individuals?

But let us not discuss such ungenerous subjects when we have something of more interest to communicate.

A few days since we received our "Six Months in Italy," with a note of the following tenor: (is not that the way you clerks or the lawyers express it?)

"I trust my friend, Mr. ——, will excuse my long detention of these volumes, and will attribute the fault in some degree to the events of the last few months in our domestic affairs. I have many thanks to return for the pleasure which I have taken in reading them — a pleasure which will be the more fondly though sadly remembered, because it is the last which I can so enjoy. I am very grateful to you, also, for your kindness on other occasions. With much regard for yourself and M——, and a kiss for Rompy-Dompy, I shall hope ever to be counted your friend, BEL HARD."

'What means this note and the peculiar tone of its expression,' thought we, as we passed it over the table. Our doubts were soon settled, however, by the information, which women always have in such cases, that Bel was to be married in a day or two to the Hon. Mr.

Weed. The wedding was to be very private, — no company, no parade, no levee, no calls, — but a marriage at church and a departure on a long journey. And it was all to gratify Bel, who would not listen to her mother's wish for a "splendid wedding."

This was rather sudden, but it was agreed upon at Washington, hence Madame Hard had hurried home somewhat unexpectedly, and the Hon. Mr. Weed had followed to secure his prize. That is the information which feminine curiosity obtained, and are we not, therefore, bound to record it?

"Poor Umber! that is the end of your dream," thought we, and we fell into a reverie on the subject of the artist's love, his folly, his talents, his pictures of Bel, his genuine worth and manhood. We had not concluded whether to pity him or to wish him joy at this abrupt termination of his idle hopes, if he entertained such, before he was yet more deeply involved in the meshes. And we were in doubt what to think of Bel. We were approaching our conclusions, however, when a ring at the door disturbed us, and another note was placed in our hands. It read thus:

"Madame Hard requests the favor of Mr. ——'s company this evening, to attend to the execution of certain legal instruments. Madame H.'s solicitor informs her that the attendance of a magistrate is necessary, and Mr. ——'s presence would be most desirable. The bearer will await Mr. ——'s convenience."

We were a little disturbed. Dressing-gown and slippers, the easy chair and Macaulay's fourth volume promised a quiet and comfortable evening, to say nothing of the company so agreeable to our domestic habits. But Madame Hard's request appeared somewhat of the imperative sort. We looked out the door, and found Abel's span of bays, with a light sleigh, awaiting us, a clear night and a young moon; so we hesitated no longer, but made ready and departed. Abel's fleet bays made our journey a brief one.

In the parlor at the mansion, we found Madame Hard, who introduced us to the Hon. Mr. Weed and her solicitor, Mr. Fee. The Hon. Mr. Weed's manners were gentlemanly in form, but exhibited none of the genuine courtesy which comes from the heart. Have you ever marked the difference, Trifle? We observed his face more narrowly than ever before. The freshness of youth must long since have departed, and unsubdued passion assumed the place of manly vigor and high purpose, and we thought there was something sinister in the glance of the eye. But all this must have been imagined, for how could Bel Hard become the wife of such a man as we saw in the Hon. Mr. Weed?

Mr. Fee is a man of note in his profession, a man of shrewdness and probity. Past the middle age and gray haired, his face bore the marks of intellect, but no great degree of benevolence. Yet there was something kindly in his eye, and there was a geniality about him which showed him not of the class of *lawyers* of which we just now wrote. He had been their guardian during the minority of Bel and Abel, and he informed us that we were called upon to attend the execution of a marriage settlement between Bel and the Hon. Mr. Weed.

We expected it. Nevertheless the information wasn't pleasant. It was another step towards the end, — the end of our interest in Bel. We expressed a regret to Madame, that Abel was not present at this time.

"Abel is wayward, and pays no heed to our letters except to say that he cannot return."

A slight look of vexation passed over Madame's features as we spoke and she replied. It signified more than she uttered. We still wondered why the approaching nuptials had not called forth some expression from Abel, — a strong dissent, we had hoped. But Madame took up that fertile topic of conversation, the weather, and while she was speaking of 'deep snows' and 'extreme cold,' Bel Hard came into the room.

She was very pale, and we thought her eye wore the cold and languid expression of old. She greeted Mr. Fee cordially, and responded pleasantly to his short sentences, till he rallied her on the business of the evening, saying:

"So you could not give *me* the slip, Bel, as you do everybody else. You find me almost as important —"

He stopped suddenly, for Bel looked in his face with a look of sad and earnest entreaty, which manifestly made him forget what he would have said, or regret what he had said. The expression of his face changed to one of inquiry, and his eye seemed to read an answer in Bel's face, for he said nothing more, but uttered a half suppressed

"Ugh!"

We found that was a frequent expression with him on all occasions.

Bel next turned to us, and with a salutation which seemed something more than formal — almost affectionate. We then saw that what we had mistaken for a cold, languid expression of her eye, was in truth a deep sadness, that the signs of tears had not disappeared. She spoke to us in a somewhat low tone, and we saw the Hon. Mr. Weed watching her from the opposite side of the room, where he was seated with Madame.

"Have you heard from my brother?"

We replied that we had not since we had delivered to her one of his letters.

"Has *he* received a letter?"

"Umber?"

"Yes." It was a half stifled "yes."

"He has not mentioned it. Indeed he has scarcely been seen of late."

"He is not sick?"

"No — not physically."

Bel's pale cheek was slightly tinged as she saw we had noticed the tone of her question, and she felt the meaning of our reply, but she spoke quickly, —

"I wish Abel were here."

Evidently it was an earnest wish, it was so deeply uttered, as if from the heart.

"Have you written to him?"

"After reading the letter you brought, I wrote to him, telling him my — unhappiness. I have received no answer."

Tears filled her eyes and fell upon her pale cheek. She spoke in a low tone still, but there was a severe look in the Hon. Mr. Weed's eye as he watched her. Of course she had no right to speak confidentially and with feeling to another than himself.

It matters not how we expressed our sympathy with Bel. It is sufficient that we witnessed again that look of mingled sadness and gratitude which we had seen before, and which dwells in our memory ever. There was not time for many words, for Madame Hard arose and proposed that we should walk into the library to attend to the business of the evening. Bel took our arm and we followed the other three into that cheerful library, where the Cannel, flaming and hissing, shed its ruddy glow over the room.

Mr. Fee quietly unfolded his papers, and spreading one on the table, said :

"You know the contents, Bel. Here is the place for your signature."

Bel's agitation was palpable as she seated herself and took the proffered pen. She gazed at the paper intently, as if she were examining its contents with professional scrutiny. Some clause must have been unintelligible, judging from her long and fixed look at it, and the whole instrument was evidently wanting in clearness, so much time did she take in looking over it, although she had read it before. Madame and the Hon. Mr. Weed grew impatient, and after a jest or two between them on Bel's delay, Madame spoke to her.

"Come, Bel, we shall become fatigued standing here while you study the paper. Others desire their turn."

Bel started a little, and a tear fell upon the paper. That was a very improper seal for a marriage settlement. Mr. Fee and we saw it, (he uttered another suppressed "Ugh!") Madame and the Hon. didn't,—or noticed it not.

"Come, Bel, sign the paper."

"I cannot!" Then fell more seals upon the instrument.

"Cannot!"

Both Madame and the Hon. Mr. Weed spoke; but the tone of the latter, half angry and half scornful, alone was heeded by Bel. She rose suddenly, and turned towards the Hon. with a glance as scornful as his tone. It was the proud, spirited Bel Hard once more, and for a moment her eye flashed fire, even through tears.

"I *will not!*"

She threw the pen down. Madame and the Hon. Mr. Weed were startled — stupefied for a moment; and the one was vexed, and the other was flushed with anger.

"But to-morrow, Bel?"

"To-morrow!"

She uttered it with passionate grief, and sunk with hysterical sobs into a chair. Madame Hard spoke in a tone of severity.

"Bel! what folly is this!"

But Bel was insensible to her words, or the mutterings of the Hon. Mr. Weed, which sounded much like oaths. She had fainted, which being seen by Madame, maternal solicitude succeeded to anger. Restoratives were applied, and the usual confusion of such occasions followed. Domestics were called, and finally Bel was removed to her room, and the library was left to the Hon. Mr. Weed, the solicitor, and ourself.

The solicitor seated himself before the grate, and stirred the Cannel, saying to himself:

"Ugh! I am glad of it."

The Hon. Mr. Weed walked the room fiercely, and there was no doubt now that some of his mutterings were oaths. Once he approached us with a lowering look, and said:

"Perhaps *you* can explain this, sir?"

"Indeed, sir, the explanation would seem not very difficult."

"And what is it, since you are in the secret?"

"What is perfectly evident, that Miss Hard does not wish to be married to-morrow."

Mr. Fee looked up from the grate, and probably supported my assertion with a glance. The Hon. Mr. Weed glared at us a moment, then, sitting down at the table, hastily wrote a note, directed it to Madame Hard, rung the bell and ordered his carriage. It was all done with remarkable energy, even to the suppressed exclamation, as he went out:

"Fool!"

The sound of his sleigh-bells had hardly died away when Madame Hard again entered the room. She was surprised but manifestly relieved by not finding the Hon. gentleman there. Bel had revived, but was not herself. So said Madame. But we surmised that Bel *was* herself, and was no longer to be unresistingly led to her own misery. The letter was handed to Madame, and we departed.

"A better night's work than I anticipated," said Mr. Fee, as he drove away from the mansion.

Postscriptum. Did we mention a thaw? Did we anticipate freshets? Verily, with the mercury sinking below zero, the waters won't rise very high. Winter is conqueror again, and has quite got his spirits up. Shrimp has been running back through the long years of his experience, and he don't think there *ever was* anything quite equal to this winter, take it all in all. He is under serious apprehensions that the ponds and rivers may freeze quite solid, and destroy all the fish.

XXXI.

TRIFLETON HOUSE,
Still in the tough Winter of '56.

THE Winter's back is by no means broken. Ask Pat.!

"Well, Trifle," said she yesterday morning, "I never did see such weather (that's what she said — '*see*,') in my life. There's the cistern frozen up, and the girls can't wash. We havn't a drop of water. A pretty cistern, indeed! and as for that pump, which you have praised so much — almost as much as you have the cistern — it won't work at all. It's sucked, or something!"

When you consider that this cistern was built after serious consultation with the gentleman who undertook the repairs of Trifleton House for me, and the argument was advanced by him that a nice, new brick cistern, with pipes, and an iron pump, &c., though somewhat expensive, would be invaluable, (which said argument met the hearty concurrence of the mason he had with him while renovating the chimneys, fireplaces, and so on of Trifleton House,) — and that I have, as indicated by Pat.'s speech, been rather disposed to congratulate myself upon my superior sagacity in having it built according to his suggestions, you will not be surprised that I was a little indignant at its presuming to freeze. I addressed a note to the gentleman alluded to, requesting him to immediately look into the state of things, and added, with some tartness, that the pipes couldn't have been fixed properly in the beginning, or some equally sharp thing, which I intended as a "crusher." He came to Trifleton House with his men, and while Pat. looked on, they tore up the floor, and put salt in the pump, and tried in every way to melt this obdurate, cold-blooded, frigid cistern.

"To think of its assurance to freeze so!" said Pat.

The relentless cistern, in nowise discomfited at this remark, maintained the most imperturbable indifference. Through salt and through fire it refused to yield any water. The men were becoming wearied, and Pat. was, I think, getting a little out of patience (at least I should say so were she ever guilty of such a thing), when it occurred to some one that they would better go into the garden and lift off the cover of the cistern.

They did so, and *mirabile dictu*, the bricks looked very nice and clean, as if they had just been polished down by sand paper, but they had also an exceedingly dry and thirsty look. There wasn't a drop of water.

But then a cistern has no right to freeze, even if it has no water. That's the way I argued to Pat., and — *it's so.*

The affairs of Pink's father are brightening under the management of Stubs. He has nearly completed for him a composition with the creditors, who, it seems, are willing to accept fifty cents on the dollar as a full discharge of their claims. This will leave him in tolerably comfortable circumstances, and give him an opportunity to immediately resume his business.

He has received a rebuke, though, which he will not soon forget; and if it shall make him more circumspect, and teach him that the mere accumulation of wealth is a small part of the object and end of life, and shall purify and elevate his nature, at the same time that it humbles it, his failure will be of no great consequence, in my judgment.

There are three things of capital consequence in a man's career, the first and the most important of which is his moral education and development; next, his intellectual, which is, indeed, in some sense, identical or allied with his moral, and lastly, his pursuit of wealth, within reasonable limits.

If this order be not practically reversed in our day and generation, to a very considerable extent at least, then I am by no means a shrewd observer.

Hence, as Goody Green, or a person of large *faith* would argue, are reverses of fortune, which seem so inscrutable to most of us. They are the necessities of Providence to make men better, even against their will.

Pink's father, like the majority of his kind, in similar cases, labors under the idea that, while he himself can bear the change of his condition, she will repine and suffer under it. So little does he know women, with all their inconsistencies.

He has exhibited the usual quantity of weakness on her account, though something, confessedly, is to be set down to a father's anxiety.

He remarked to Stubs that he felt quite ashamed that she was about to carry no larger dowry to the man with the corn-colored gloves.

"To think of my daughter's going to live in the Fifth Avenue of York, and marry a man of wealth and standing in society, with no possibility of an ante-nuptial settlement such as he will undoubtedly expect. It's too ridiculous and mortifying!"

I have given you his exact words, as Stubs told it to me.

I replied, "Bah!" and I believe, even, "pshaw!" in which opinion Stubs concurred.

He added, also, very earnestly, and his voice trembled as he spoke:

"I do not think she cares to marry a rich man. She has tested the value of money, and its uses. She is evidently tired of ostentation. Glitter has lost its charms for her. She seems to like only what is real."

"She has passed through a severe ordeal," I observed.

"Yes, and with credit. She is a true woman, and I hope she will be happy in her marriage."

"*She will!*" said I, emphatically, lighting a cigar, and handing him one.

I generally light my own cigar first, and then hold the match or lighter for my friend; for I have discovered that otherwise I am apt to burn my fingers while he is dawdling and biting the end off his cigar, or sticking his knife through it, or some such thing. He can do that while I am lighting my own cigar, and I know just how long a match will burn. My skill in this particular is the result of careful calculation and experience. He sees the match getting most burnt out, and he stirs himself at once; whereas, give him his own time, and he will keep you waiting until you burn your fingers. Practice, and you will become an adept.

We puffed in silence for some time, when Stubs finally began to talk of his case at Washington, and the loss of his property under it.

It seems he is now worth, to use an absurd phrase, about five thousand dollars. All the rest of his property is gone forever.

"But," said he, "I never felt so rich before in my life. I have now something to work for, and I intend to work. I mean to take and make opportunities. I am resolved to make my mark."

All this is very well; but I have heard young men talk so before. However, I have strong hopes of Stubs. He has capacity enough, which is the main thing, and the sharp spur of necessity will goad him to effort, even though he should occasionally falter. We shall see.

Since this conversation, which occurred some evenings since, Stubs and Pink have had an interview of a very peculiar character. Pink told Pat. of it, under strict injunctions of secrecy. Pat., for that reason probably, told me of it, and under a similar injunction; and I now, therefore, tell you of it, in the same fashion. I think it likely you will have the assurance to publish it in your paper; for I have observed that people who are requested not to divulge a secret, generally do.

When you wish to have anything kept very privately, never say to those to whom you confide it, "you musn't tell!" When you say this, it becomes worth mentioning, you perceive. It becomes invested with a mystery, at once. What you don't wish to be told by others, refrain from telling yourself; or at least, when you tell it, impose no injunction of secrecy respecting it!

Stubs, it seems, was sitting in the library of Pink's father, jagged and wearied over certain papers he had been examining, when she happened to enter the room. She was struck with his pale face, and anxious cast of countenance at once, and asked him if he were not well.

"Ah, yes," said he, smiling; "I am only tired a a little, and my head aches."

"Have you these headaches so often as you had formerly?"

"No, only when I am excited."

"You are too assiduous in my father's affairs. I hope you will give yourself more rest. I cannot bear to see you so anxious. You will wear yourself out. You are too kind and devoted, and we can never be sufficiently grateful for all you have done and are doing."

A proud and generous man dislikes to be thanked; and, as a look of pain passed over his face, he remarked that he had done no more than any one would have done in the same circumstances, and added:

"I was examining into my own affairs at the moment, and not those of your father, dear Pink."

With a passionate burst of feeling, she could not restrain, she exclaimed:

"We have all the while selfishly occupied your time and interest in regard to ourselves, without once considering that you needed our most affectionate sympathy. Can you forgive me?" said she, extending her hand. "I have treated you very ungenerously."

She was in no fainting condition now, and he had not just met her upon his arrival home, after a protracted absence. Besides, he was in her father's house, in a mere professional capacity. He shuddered, and said, somewhat proudly and coldly, without taking her hand:

"You have doubtless a right to address me thus; but I am not aware that I have made any complaint of you. Still, I am quite ready to say that I forgive you, if you desire it; but I have nothing, really, to forgive."

"And is this all? Have I wholly forfeited your affection, then, which was once so truly mine? Am I so unworthy?"

Her eyes filled with tears as she spoke, and she turned her face away from him.

"Can it be possible that you are trifling with me *still*?" said he, as if deliberating upon the selection and meaning of his words. "Will there never be an end? Why speak to me of affection? Such language is unnecessary. Whatever may be, or may have been, once, my affection for you, I have no right to receive or demand your affection for myself, and you — pardon me for the remark, but you force me to it — have no right to grant it."

"You are mistaken. I have a right, but I have no need to avail myself of it now," said she, sobbing vehemently, and wholly losing her self-control. "I have always loved you; but my love is neither worth giving nor receiving. Alas! how I am punished! but bless him, Father!" she continued, lifting her arms to heaven, and gazing upwards with streaming eyes, "not for my wretched sake, but for his own!"

Then she buried her face in her hands and wept bitterly.

So she told it to Pat., and Pat. told it to me.

He stood and gazed at her, like one abstracted, and utterly confounded. Had she no self-respect? Was this real, or was it all a dream? Where was he? Could this be Pink? Was he himself? Did he hear aright, in tones of tenderest and most touching pathos, "I have always loved you."

An electric thought shot through him, burning him like fire, and he asked, like one whose whole existence hung upon the response,

"Are you not bound to *him*?"

"No."

"Have you not promised?"

"No."

Then the sweet voices of the past seemed to address his soul, and in his fancy, he wandered back to the days of his hope and his happiness. But this was mere weakness. Life was real, and as he recollected what he had suffered since those days, he thought how dangerous it would be to be too sanguine again, and he said, distrustfully:

"I do not understand you. I have been otherwise informed, and have acted upon my information."

"Read," said she, "and judge for yourself."

She handed him a letter. It was her answer to the offer of the man with the corn-colored gloves. It was as follows:

"I am obliged for the honor of your proposals. I will accept them — *conditionally*. My heart has always been, as I have supposed, another's. We have quarrelled. He is nothing to me now. I am not in the habit of disguises, and you may consider me bound to you, if you desire it, for the space of three months. I shall examine and test myself in the meantime, and if I discover that my affection for you is not sufficiently strong to warrant the risking my happiness, which is, like my honor, in my own keeping, and in regard to hazarding which I must be my own judge, I shall frankly tell you so, and ask, and expect to be released from my engagement. Upon these terms, and these only, I am willing to accept your proposals, for which I am much indebted. With respect, &c."

He read the letter through, as a condemned man would read his pardon.

"The time of the probation is past," he said, at length, "and —"

"I am wholly free once more."

And this strong man, Stubs, buried *his* face in *his* hands, and the large tears rolled from his eyes, as in the days of his boyhood. He was a child in the presence of the woman that he loved. She went and kneeled involuntarily before him, and took his hand in both her own, and kissed it, and asked him to forgive her.

He forgave her.

And they prayed together, (not in words,) and the holy spirit of God fell upon them, and blessed them, and they were both purified and humbled.

So Pink told it to Pat., and so Pat. told it to me.

And they twined their arms together, and their lips met, and she lay her head upon his breast, when ——

Pink's father entered the room.

He started, but Pink rushed into his arms, and cried,

"You know all, dear father. I love him — idolize

him — almost worship him, as I told you ; and (jubilantly) he loves me, too."

And she went back and nestled in his arms again, with all the eagerness and simplicity of a child. And Pink's father placed his hands upon the head of each of them, and, with the tears now in *his* eyes, said :

" The good God bless you, my children ! " ——

" Well, Pat.," said I, knocking my ashes off my cigar, " I don't see but what Pink really has a heart."

" I *guess* she *has*," said she, (it's exactly what she said — " guess,") rather indignantly, as it seemed to me, " and so has *he*. He wrote a very handsome letter to Pink, as soon as he got Goody Green's letter. This was before Pink wrote to him at all, and (with great volubility) he's coming on, and — as soon as Goody, and — before Pink had time — and —— hark ! —— *Patience !* there's that baby again. He always wants *me*. Kate can't —"

" I shouldn't suppose she could — naturally," said I, but she was off, and didn't hear me.

My opinion is that Pat. likes that baby. Everything has to yield to him. Yesterday he exhibited two teeth, which circumstance she thinks is extremely wonderful, and when she discovered them, she nearly choked him with caresses, and said she wanted to " eat him up," the cannibal !

It's true, for I heard her say it, and so did Prig.

XXXII.

THE ARM CHAIR,
In the last days of the Winter Months.

FEBRUARY is passing, Trifle, and notwithstanding Time has lent it an additional day, it will soon be gone. But winter seems loath to depart with it. A bright sun and softer winds for a few days have made large draughts upon his accumulated wealth, and there are some signs that it will, in time, be exhausted. But he clutches and guards it like all misers, and in spite of his age, he holds on bravely. He must be conquered, at last, however, and that, too, by gentleness and smiles. Even his hard nature will finally yield to these, which are, after all, the most potent weapons for a victory, and he will depart to prepare for another campaign in those regions where he reigns perpetual king. Let him go. He has taught us something; he has brought us some treasures. But we can look forward to a gentler reign with hopes of something better.

Verily, the winter has taught our friends something. Madame Hard and Bel, Umber and even the Hon. Mr. Weed, who has departed with his experiences for a more genial latitude. At least, it is supposed that he is gone, for he has not been at the mansion since the eventful evening which snatched from him his prize. Let him go, too. He was a darker winter to one heart than the natural winter has been to the earth. Even Madame is incensed against him, now, for the note which he left for her was insulting.

A few days after that evening we looked into Umber's studio. He was sitting in deep thought, and looked sad. After responding to our hail, he said, abruptly:

"I am going to Europe again."

"Why, you havn't been at home six months."

"I wish I had not come at all."

"But why go back, now?"

"I have several commissions to copy paintings in the Louvre and at Florence. Besides, I——"

He hesitated.

"You have not been fortunate here. The Hon. Mr. Weed, probably, did not *pay* for his picture before he left."

Umber looked at us doubtfully. He did not know what had transpired at the mansion, so we related faithfully what we had seen, heard and done there. He listened to us in silence, but he was deeply moved, and notwithstanding his usual control over his feelings, his face expressed both delight and sadness. He said nothing, even when we finished our recital, but, placing the portrait of Bel on the easel, he deliberately painted it over till Bel's fair face and cold look had disappeared, and there was nothing but a plain dark canvas to be seen. Then he spoke, as if to himself—

"If I could as easily undo the injustice of painting her thus!"

"Injustice! Why, did not her friends pronounce it a *perfect likeness!*"

"It was a picture of her sorrow and her anger, not of her real self. It was painted in pique, and for the purpose of wounding, if it possibly might convey a meaning to her. It was utterly unworthy of her and of myself. I know now that it must have added torture to an already troubled heart, and I feel guilty of a mean and ungenerous action."

"But you had no reason to suppose that it would wound her?"

"That is the only excuse I have, and that is a paltry one. A generous man should at least measure his actions by his own feelings, but I deliberately did what I knew must pain feelings no more sensitive than my own, — and that, too, towards a woman."

It was more his manner and tone than his language that indicated emotion. He might have spoken thus in relation to any other woman, but Bel called forth something more than words, something more than chivalrous feeling. But he had little time now to indulge in feelings, or contemplate going to Italy, before a knock at the door called his attention. The door being opened, Dicky Dawson entered and handed a note to Umber.

Dicky appeared quite the gentleman, in new clothes and with his bright, intelligent and healthful face. While Umber read the note — and it seemed to take him some time — we spoke to Dicky, inquiring after Bel.

"She's quite well, now, sir."

"Quite well! Has she been sick?"

"She has *looked* sick, sir, — and sad."

"And she's better now?"

"Yes, sir, — she's happier — but she *cries*, too, sometimes."

"Why do you think she's happier?"

"O, sir, she speaks to me more, and is kinder than ever, — and she seems as if she had got over a great trouble, she speaks and smiles so. She didn't smile before."

"But she cries, too, you say."

"Yes, sir, sometimes I see her wiping her eyes. When I wished I could see Mr. Umber, who read books to me when I was sick, she cried most. But then she gets over it quick, sir, and smiles again. I know she must be happier than she was."

"Observant boy," thought we, as Umber, who probably had not heard a word of this conversation, handed to us the note he had just received. It was as follows:

"The relations which might have entitled the Hon. Mr. Weed to my portrait being terminated, I desire that no one but myself should have the picture which you painted. Please retain it until my brother returns. I could wish, indeed, that it had never been painted, were it not for the few pleasant memories which are mingled with much pain and bitterness. The picture itself can only be suggestive of sorrow and regret, not the least of which will be for the unkind words that I may have uttered to you, and for which I ask your forgiveness. BEL HARD."

"She ask *my* forgiveness!"

He spoke with suppressed emotion, as we finished reading the note, and paced the narrow open space of the room rapidly. He was deeply moved, and though to our apprehension there was more reason for his rejoicing than sorrowing, there was a most unhappy look on his face. Suddenly he stopped before Dicky, who had watched him with wonder.

"How did you come, my boy?"

"In the carriage with Miss Bel."

"And she ——?"

"She is in the carriage, now, sir."

"Did she tell you to wait for an answer?"

"No, sir,—but she said *perhaps* you might wish to send one."

Ah, Bel! how much that "perhaps" revealed, mask though it was intended to be.

"I will." And Umber hurried to a writing desk.

Just then there was another knock at the door, which Dicky opened, and Bel Hard entered, saying,

"Why, Richard, I thought you were lost."

At the sound of that voice Umber started from his seat and rushed across the room. There was as sudden a motion on the other side and a double exclamation.

"Bel!"

"Paul!"

Umber's name is Paul. Bel had always called him so when they were children.

Bel put out both her hands, which were eagerly seized by Umber, and she looked up in his face with an earnest, tearful gaze, in which were expressed the struggling feelings of her heart, a tried, chastened, loving heart. He looked back into those eyes as he never before had looked, tenderly, lovingly, sadly.

"It is not for *me* to forgive," he said softly, but with deep feeling. "I ought rather to ask your forgiveness, a thousand times, for the cruelty with which I wounded you — when you were suffering, too."

Her head fell on his shoulder. She spoke not audibly, but there was that in her action and in her tears, which expressed all that words could. And thus these two, without declaration or acknowledgment, knew that each was beloved by the other. Our eyes were somewhat dimmed, Trifle, but we saw it all, and the boy looked on in wonder. But it was not courteous to suffer any further scene to occur while Bel was unconscious of our presence, so we emerged from our corner and spoke as she raised her head. Her self-possession had gone, but seeing who we were, she extended her hand, and we were better friends than ever. But she soon turned to Umber, asking,

"But where is the evil picture?"

He pointed at the canvas on the easel.

"If I could as easily obliterate the memory of the pain it has occasioned!"

"Obliterate it! O no! *now* I would remember it, for out of that suffering have grown purer hopes and feelings, and a truer happiness."

A few more words and Bel was gone. When Umber returned from the carriage, whither he had accompanied her, he threw himself in a chair, and covering his face he groaned aloud. A great struggle was going on in his mind, and for the first time we saw him entirely overcome, and he wept. But it was not for joy. Such an inconsistent, perverse thing is the human heart. Solitude is the best remedy for such illness, and we left him.

Umber has received another letter from Abel, in which he writes thus —

"It is all over now! I have seen the end — no, not the end, for the love of earth has passed on to love in heaven. Lily is dead — rather her spirit, that made her earthly form so beautiful, the spirit that has so charmed, purified and elevated my heart, has passed into another world, and carries with it my thoughts, and hopes, and love.

"It was Sunday evening. She had grown weaker and weaker through the day, and we felt that with the fading twilight she would depart. She had uttered a few words during the day, a touching farewell to her heart-broken father, and words of holiest love, sustaining comfort, and tender entreaty, to me. The sun went down beyond the snowy hills, and the shadows came stealing into that silent chamber — the shadows of night, the shadow of death. Her hand rested in mine, cold and motionless. Her breathing grew fainter as the light departed. Then, while we counted the too rapid moments, our agony calmed by silent prayer — prayers that went up to heaven with the forereaching of her spirit — there was a sudden, faint grasp of my hand, a scarce heard utterance, yet distinct to our startled minds, 'In Heaven!' — and there was no more breathing. The light of day had departed, and the light from those eyes forever. The shadows of night had come — and of death. O God! My beloved was dead!

. . . .

"We have laid her at rest now — near the little village church, in the frozen earth, under the deep snows. The summer will make it a beautiful spot, shaded by the noble elm in whose branches now the wind wails mournfully. The summer shall bring flowers and verdure over that grave, now so desolate. But the sorrow of laying that beautiful form down on such a couch is lightened, not by the promise of summer's flowers and foliage, so much as the assurance that the more beautiful spirit is with infinite beauty and light eternal.

"We have performed the last rites and returned to the desolate home — ah, how desolate, to the stricken father! O for the power to teach him to endure! The light of his home has departed, but there is a star in heaven to lead him thither."

. . . .

We were not requested to take this letter to Bel, for Umber performed that office himself. Touched by her brother's grief, Bel's heart was the more ready to seek sympathy and support from another, and could Umber deny it?

As we have this from good authority, Trifle, you are not to question the truth of our account, nor to ask us how we know what we tell. It is true that notwithstanding the irresistible feeling of love which attached him to Bel, and would seem to promise happiness, Umber was sad and silent. There was an expression of deep distress on his face as he sat in the parlor, after the reading of the letter and after the still firmer union in their hearts. Bel saw it, and resting her hands on his shoulder she looked anxiously into his face, saying,

"What troubles you?"

It was an exquisite tone of love, but it seemed to increase, rather than alleviate, his distress, and he answered nothing.

"Will you not tell me! Will you not let me have the privilege of friendship — of *love*, that if I cannot relieve your distress I may at least share it? Come, you have not learned the power of woman's sympathy, and it must be my privilege to teach you."

"Your words — your tone — your love, even, is a torture to me!"

Bel started back and turned pale. The suppressed anguish of his voice and his words alarmed her heart.

"Am I deceived then! — you love——"

"I love *you*, — passionately, — with all the strength of manhood, all the ardor of youth! I have loved you from boyhood; — in distant lands during years of absence, and here when I felt that in your beautiful womanhood my boyish love were worse than folly."

A look of joy, almost of triumph, passed over Bel's face as Umber spoke his first passionate words. It changed to one of tender reproach.

"And I, — do you doubt, any longer — my feelings?"

"O, no. Through the habit of a false education and of fashion I still saw your true nature, and knew that it struggled with the false. Under a severe trial and through much suffering the true has triumphed over the false. But——"

"But! — Do you still doubt?"

"I am poor. By my own toil I must earn my bread, and not always sure of successful toil even for moderate wants. You are wealthy, educated in luxury, accustomed to society, and fitted to be one of its brightest ornaments."

"And is that all?"

She spoke as if greatly relieved.

"It is enough to forbid our love. It places a barrier between us, and I should be false to my sense of right and false to you, if I attempted to overleap it."

"And should I be false to womanly delicacy if I removed the barrier? I have wealth, but I thank Heaven that it is a means of doing good and procuring true happiness, as well as ministering to heartless folly and selfishness. With my fortune I should not be a burden to you — and it is at my own disposal."

"And do you think me such a craven as to be dependent on you?"

"I think you everything that is generous and noble. I would not wound your self-respect or pride. I would not take away your motives for effort. You could still labor, but for that distinction and fame in your art which I know is dearer to you than wealth. May I not aid you in this honorable ambition?"

She looked earnestly into his eyes as if to enforce more than she dared to utter in words. He involuntarily threw his arms about her, and pressed her to his bosom.

"Noble woman! I should be utterly unworthy of your love were I to suffer you to do what your generous affection prompts. You have a position to cherish — the opinion of the world to respect — friends to be regarded. I should be base to suffer you to sacrifice these to a generous impulse."

"Her friends shall honor her, and approve her

choice," said a voice behind them. They started, and Bel threw herself into the arms of her brother, who, entering unperceived, came forward, and had heard the last of their conversation.

"And you are not married, then!" he exclaimed, "Thank heaven! you have escaped that, and have made a nobler choice."

He then explained that he had not received her letter until the messenger who carried his last letter to the post had brought it on his return. He lost no time in coming, dreading that he should find Bel's misery sealed by marriage vows. There was a new earnestness and decision in Abel's pale face, as he spoke, and its sadness gave a dignity and impressiveness to what he said. So it was that he calmed the doubts in Umber's mind, and pressing his hand warmly, said,

"You and Bel shall have a brother's blessing."

Again we ask *you*, Trifle, what think you of the world?

XXXIII.

TRIFLETON HOUSE,
As the Spring commences.

SPRING once more! Soon the buds will be out on the trees, the birds singing, and the fragrant lap of earth filled with flowers of every hue and name! The sweet blue violets will appear on the hills, and the dark, wintry frown pass from the sea. All nature will be wreathed in smiles again, and the long, dreamy days of sunshine and hope come back. All the inhabitants of Trifleton House rejoice in anticipation.

I have become much addicted to studying the "New England Farmer," of late. Pat. threatens to show me how flowers can be induced to flourish under her superintendence, and Prig seriously contemplates an accession of several rabbits to his existing stock of valuables, and he even has thrown out hints of a small dog, to accompany him in his excursions with his velocipede. We shall see.

But, my Editor, I wish to call your friendship to the test, and have a favor to ask, and you a duty to perform; an arduous one, I admit, but I see not how you can escape it. So courage, man, courage!

I understand the exuberant Miss of nineteen summers (twenty now), and your smart subscriber, too, have both been extremely interested in this correspondence. It is stated to me authoritatively, and I believe it to be as true as the veracious telegraphic despatches from Washington (which nobody ever yet doubted), that the actual experiences of life therein recorded, have, in some sense, come home to them.

"Why," said your smart subscriber, "if Pink's father has *failed*, why may not I, by possibility? Who can tell?" And the exuberant Miss has been heard to remark, "Why may not Bel Hard's case be mine, and am I not thinking and acting as Pink used to last summer? Wouldn't I better pause a little?" She also added, (so they say,) "As for that Pat., she's a darling!" — which, I must "own up," I esteem as quite a compliment to — myself.

Now, what I desire of you is this. My pens of every kind are quite worn out, and I, myself, am passing into desuetude. Hence, this correspondence must cease. I can write no more, and I wish you to announce that fact to your readers. You must break it to them as gently as possible.

You could do it in this wise. You might call on the exuberant Miss, and send up your card — "The Editor" — and after waiting an hour or two for her appearance (she changing her dress and "fixing" her hair meantime), you might, when she came in upon you, after the usual commonplaces, and a slight discussion respecting Lagrange and Didiée, casually remark, "Trifle is in a bad predicament. His pens are all used up, and he can't afford any more. No doubt you are tired of his platitudes, &c., &c." At which she will say something, and then you can say something more, (all the while collecting your courage,) and then she will interrupt you with great volubility, and while she is rushing on at railroad speed, you can prepare the announcement in fit terms, that Trifle is really about to say good-bye. It might be well to have a bottle of Cologne with you, in case she should see fit to faint.

Your smart subscriber must, I think, be managed somewhat differently.

It would be well, perhaps, to ask him about his clipper ships, and comment upon cotton, corn, and consols, and freights to California and Australia, and the amount of his loss by the last peculation from some Railroad Company, Insurance Company, or Bank, in which he is largely interested as a stockholder, — and then add that the paper (there is only one paper — "the Editor's" paper), henceforth, will be filled with something else than this *stuff* from Trifle. There's been quite a sufficiency of it. The thing must be managed very adroitly.

So, mind!

He will say that he's rather sorry on the whole (non-committal, you perceive, that is, business like), for he's been somewhat amused with the correspondence, occasionally; but that there have been a great many words wasted in it; that there hasn't been enough coming to the point, and that it's hardly worth while for "a business man" to spend his time reading too much of such sort of writing; and he supposed it was about drawing to a close; but, really, he would like to know how Pink's father was getting on, and whether he intended to let her marry that man, Stubs, who is a strange sort of a fellow, and *worth* nothing now, though lately, he must confess, he has " done the right thing," (elegant expression,) and that he appears to be " pretty smart," (another,) and if he were only a little more " wide awake," (another yet,) he could probably " get along," and " go ahead," (a couple of 'em,) well enough.

To all this, you can make such a reply as you think expedient, and then tell him that Trifle bids him an especial good-bye, and that he is much indebted to him for the interest he takes in his friends, and (privately) that he would be glad to see him at Trifleton House next summer; that Trifle invites him to dine, in a word; and that he will meet Pink's father, Stubs and his beautiful wife, (Stubs intends to marry somebody, in the early summer, — so Pat. says, and I presume she will, of course, be beautiful,) and, that he will, possibly, meet, too, the man with the corn-colored gloves. This gentleman has left us, and has promised Pink that he will come again next summer. Perhaps he will, but I consider it somewhat doubtful. He is much changed. He is more subdued than he was. His conversation, too, is of a different order.

Have you observed how circumstances often change, abruptly, the whole style, tone, and character of a man? Pink tells Pat. that we have never done the gentleman justice, and that he has been far more generous to her than she had any right to expect, and that she shall never cease to regard him as one of her best, truest, and most tried and disinterested friends. Queer! Isn't it? but, who pretends to explain women?

He called to see Goody Green, while he was here, "in answer to her fine letter," as he said, and she declares "he is a gentleman, every inch on him." Let us never, my Editor, accuse any human being of wanting a heart. Most people have hearts, in their way. The wretched conventional habits and requirements of our time make us suspicious of each other. Mere style and courtesy pass so current for feeling, that we become apt to question the existence of feeling. There are so many counterfeits, that we grow into the belief that there is nothing real and genuine. Fashion has put truth to the blush, and diplomacy is becoming to be regarded as a higher quality than sincerity.

In case the exuberant Miss should ask you whether Pink intends to marry, as well as Stubs, you may say that she would better inquire of Goody Green on that point. I can't keep the run of such things. Pat. is looking over my shoulder at this point, and if you consider her exclamation worth having, I will give it to you, she says:

"Why, Trifle — how you talk! You know the wedding day is fixed."

This is very true, and I presume Pink will not change her mind, for what woman was ever yet known to change her mind, from Eve down?

While I think of it, I'm rather inclined to the opinion that the exuberant Miss would better come to Trifleton House and make a slight visit. She, possibly, might be permitted to see the wedding dress, and be consulted upon the style of its cut, etc. Has she good taste?

And now, serenest of Editors, I bequeath to you my

farewell. There is always something sad to me in saying "good-bye." But meetings and partings are about the substance of this life. Friends come and go. Enjoyment is but for a season. Blessings are at best periodical, and happiness, if there be such a thing, has wings. There's nothing fixed this side of Eternity.

But let us hope on! Separation and absence, and non-intercommunication, even, are impotent in case of a real attachment; and, most excellent of friends, and most imperturbable of Editors, Trifle wears you in his heart, and will henceforth. When hope grows dim, and expectation dingy, please to reflect that down in humble Trifleton House are those that think of you most tenderly! Mrs. Editor, too, and the incipients, are remembered and talked of by Pat. Come! — by several means, if not by all means, come and see us! Be with us, and of us!

We are unfashionable, and little skilled in the ways of this world, and we know next to nothing of *society*. We are simple and unsophisticated. We dress poorly and talk plainly. We are of those who reflect that our Lord and Saviour, Jesus Christ, associated with humblest fishermen, while illustrating his earthly career, and we are disposed to guage people by their moral and intellectual worth. We are not ashamed to call Goody Green our friend.

Sufficiently stupid we are, doubtless, but we hold that pretence and affectation are inadmissible; we are quite willing to pass for what we are — commonest of folks. No grandest men or fashionablest women will come to Trifleton House; and therefore, it is, we thank

God. To all simplest and sincerest, and most natural people we say, 'come!'

The way to find the house is this. You get into the cars (without purchasing a ticket), and when the conductor comes along and says, "ticket, sir!" or "ticket, ma'am!" you reply simply, "Trifleton House;" at which he politely says it will be so and so, (when you are with Trifle there will be nothing to pay, for no friend shall ever visit his house, in his company, at a pecuniary expense,) and you travel on till you stop. You stop several times, indeed, before you get there. And when you arrive at the Station, and get out, you see — not much of anything, as I should say. There's a river, and a hill, and two shoe manufacturers' shops. You walk on a considerable distance, and then you turn, and then you walk on again; and then, after a slight advance, you turn once more, and then you go straight forward till you arrive at Trifleton House. You can't miss it.

After these explicit directions, we shall expect you to come, all of you, readers of "the Editor's paper."

We shall be glad to see you. So come! come!! come!!!

XXXIV.

THE ARM CHAIR,
As the end approaches.

It is quite true, most worthy Trifle, that all things earthly must have an end, and notwithstanding your letters are not altogether earthy, we have feared that they must sooner or later be subject to the immutable law. Nevertheless, your announcement is somewhat abrupt, and we were disposed, at first, to lament, both on our own account, and on account of the numerous readers to whom, after perusing them, we have passed over your letters. But upon reflection we are rather inclined to rejoice, for of what should we tell you in return?

We were at the Hard Mansion a day or two since, and discovered that we should have little more to say of its inmates. Bel's portrait was hanging in the library, — the beautiful picture in which Umber, looking deeper than the surface, had revealed Bel's real loveliness. Bel was there, too, with a radiant smile which made her more beautiful than the picture. It was a smile of happiness as she looked at the artist, who, with such rare skill, had revealed her heart and stamped its beauty alike on the original and the counterfeit. Umber was there, with no trace of trouble in his look, and the light of genius glowing in his face. Abel, with his pale face, half sorrowful, half happy, sat by, resolving, rather than dreaming, as of old. And Madame Hard was present, also, somewhat subdued, but looking well content, as if she heartily assented to the aphorism "whatever is, is right."

They were arranging plans for a tour in Europe and a sojourn in Italy, and are to take their departure ere many weeks have gone by. So, you perceive, Trifle, we shall have nothing to communicate to Mrs. Trifle — you are of secondary importance, you know — unless it should be an account of a wedding, and that's of no consequence to her or to us. The truth is, that these people, who have been playing some scenes in the drama of this life, as it were for our especial benefit, are about to make their exit. The curtain is to fall, and whether they shall appear again, or what strange plot shall be developed in the succeeding acts, it is not for us to know. The veil cannot be lifted.

Of what then should we write? Shrimp, having three times prepared his rods and lines, his hooks and flies, and all his piscatorial paraphernalia for the coming season, and having committed to memory the pages of old Izaak Walton, has turned his attention to mending the world and repairing the ravages of time. But he does it so practically and moderately that we can make no account of it. As for Rompy-Dompy, we shall say no more of her at present, but shall send her to Trifleton House to share in Prig's delight over the velocipede, the rabbits, and the small dog.

Therefore — have you read the premises? — we, on

the whole, have few regrets that this correspondence ends here and now, provided (that's the way the lawyers put it, is it not?) we retain the friendship of Trifle's household, and all other people who may be disappointed by so sudden a termination. Yet — these letters have grown upon us like some of those habits which you acquired in your city life, and being shaken off we shall probably feel at a loss how to get along at first, as you did. We believe in homœopathy, however, and habit, which produces the misery, will also cure it.

We pondered some time upon the request you preferred, and the arduous duty which you imposed upon us. Havn't we said, that we are not overburdened with brass? If we recollect aright, we said that *you* and *we* have as little of this as of the other metals wherewith men make their way in the world. We are disposed now to except you from that proposition, seeing the coolness with which you propose to put our friendship to the test. But *we* seem still to be wanting in brass, notwithstanding you impose such a quantity on us.

We reflected for a time — longer or shorter, we can't tell which — how we should manage to escape the duty assigned, and still retain the good will of Trifleton House. We to call on the "smart subscriber," and on the "exuberant Miss!" It was utterly out of the question. Why, every time we have met him in the street, or seen her riding in her carriage, since you presumed to address them so familiarly in one of your letters, we have trembled lest on our devoted head should fall the vengeance with which we feared they would visit such presumption. And to visit them — to offer ourself a voluntary victim! — it was not to be thought of, even to deprecate their anger, by the hesitating announcement that Trifle has ended — his — platitudes, and we — likewise. No, we couldn't do *that*. But after profound thought we hit on an expedient which proved the right one. "Ευρεκα" we shouted, and sat down to adopt it.

The letter being printed, we marked the passages which contained the important information, in two copies of the paper, and directed them, one to the "Exuberant Miss," and the other to our "Smart Subscriber." With them each we sent a note of the following import:

"We are requested respectfully to call your attention to the marked paragraphs in our paper. THE EDITOR."

And so we despatched them, feeling as Atlas might, relieved of the world. We pray you, Trifle, don't inflict such a task on us again. We congratulated ourself that it was well over. We said —

"Trifle thinks these people have read his platitudes — and ours, — and that they have been touched by the experiences which he has (and we have) recorded. He thinks that some things 'have come home to them,' (most people have things come home to them) — that they will profit by what they have read in his true history — and ours. And above all, he thinks they will regret that he can no longer write — and we reply. But here's the end of it. He'll find how much they have read and to what purpose — when they condescend to announce it. In the meantime he can 'flatter himself,' and 'wonder,' and 'suspect,' till the whole is forgotten, — till the 'smart subscriber' has become a millionaire or a bankrupt, and the 'exuberant Miss' a dignified matron, or — "

That's what we said to ourself. But even *we* can be mistaken, in private. Our domestic conjectures are not always reliable, though our opinions put forth to the public are not to be doubted. Why, Trifle, we actually received replies from the " smart subscriber " and the " exuberant Miss ! " And they wrote thus : — the smart subscriber as follows :

" Mr. Ed. : — Yours of this date is received and contents noted. Trifle is about to stop writing because his pens are worn out, and I suppose he isn't able to buy more. I shouldn't suppose that a man entertaining his views, and living as he seems to, would have much money, and it is pretty evident that his credit won't last long. He isn't right, and he isn't far wrong in the sentiments which he presumes to ascribe to me. I have read his correspondence, though there is a good deal in it that I don't understand. I find some good things, and I have been a little interested in some of the people mentioned, but I think that you and Trifle both put bad notions into young folk's heads ; making them undervalue the good things of this world, and encouraging our daughters to marry poor men. The example of these people ought not to have been made so public. However, the young men are rather promising, and I feel disposed to encourage them. I will, therefore, send to Stubs some law matters, and I should like to have a picture or two from Umber, for my new country house. He's a lucky dog to marry an heiress, as I suppose he will, unless he is fool enough to lose the opportunity.

"On the whole, I am rather sorry that these Trifleton Papers have come to an end. The greatest fault I have to find with them, is, that I have several times been reading them when I should have been calculating the chances for a speculation, and on several occasions they have set me *thinking*.

"I should like to accept Trifle's invitation, but really his direction to Trifleton House, like much else that he says, is not clear enough for a practical man like myself.

"Your obedt. servant, S. S."

"P. S. As Trifle is in want of pens, I send you, for him, a package of commercial pens, such as I use in the counting-room."

That's what our smart subscriber says, and on the whole we are rather proud of him. The exuberant Miss writes thus:

"My dear Mr. Editor:—I am quite shocked to learn that Trifle will write no more letters, and for *such* a reason, too. I have really been exceedingly charmed with the Trifleton Papers. To be sure I havn't read them all, but all those parts which tell about people,—Stubs, Pink, Pat., Bel, Umber,—I have delighted in, they were so much like a story. And then it was so romantic for Bel to break off her match with the Hon. Mr. —— I forget his name—and marry that fine fellow, Umber,—and for Pink, after breaking with Stubs in a pretty little pet, to be reconciled so beautifully with him when he had lost his fortune.

"And they are to be married! Why, it is just as good as a novel.

"I shall be delighted to come to Trifleton House and see the bride, that is to be, and to talk about the dress. But to think of that Goody Green writing to the York gentleman, telling him that Pink didn't love him, — how queer! I read some parts of the letters to Pa, and told him I would do just as Bel Hard did — and as Pink did; and that I never would marry a man made of money. He said it was all nonsense, and I must not let such foolish stories turn my brain. As if they were not true! But Pa is like all pas, — he'll have his eyes opened some day.

"And now, to think that we are to have no more letters, — it is really too bad. My dear Mr. Editor, I have a favor to ask. Pa gave me, a short time since, a beautiful gold pen to write with, from New York. Now I send it to you, and beg you to transmit it to Trifle, as his pens are worn out, so that he need not stop writing. But pray don't let him know that it comes from me. Perhaps, with a new gold pen he will continue to delights us. E. M."

That is what the exuberant Miss wrote. But as Trifle has fallen into desuetude, we have concluded to keep the pen ourself.

It is settled, then, Trifle, that here our correspondence closes. Be it so. Henceforth when we wish to communicate, it shall be at Trifleton House, and following implicitly your directions, we shall come to partake of the joys about your hearth-stone.

Glancing back over our letters, and the histories

therein recorded, we are under the impression that we have found hearts where we least suspected their existence — warm human feelings lying underneath the cold exteriors which fashion and fortune had formed. Trial and suffering tear away the masks which men and women too readily assume, and we can look upon their real natures and love them better. Alas for the folly that so covers the true with the false!

Spring! You talk of Spring, most sanguine Trifle. Verily, we envy you the fancy that can can see violets underneath the huge snow banks that still remain, and feel the warm winds, while the mercury squats at zero. But there is nothing like Hope and Faith. To them the Spring *will* come, with its sweet blossoms and its singing birds, with its genial sun and its soft airs. Let us also look onward to a better spring, — beyond the dark winter of death, into the fields of everlasting beauty.

And so, most genial and excellent of friends, master of a household whither our thoughts come often and where our love lingers, farewell, for of the Trifleton Papers this is

THE END.

www.ingramcontent.com/pod-product-compliance
Lightning Source LLC
LaVergne TN
LVHW020230110826
845151LV00003B/885
* 9 7 8 1 4 2 5 5 3 0 9 2 1 *